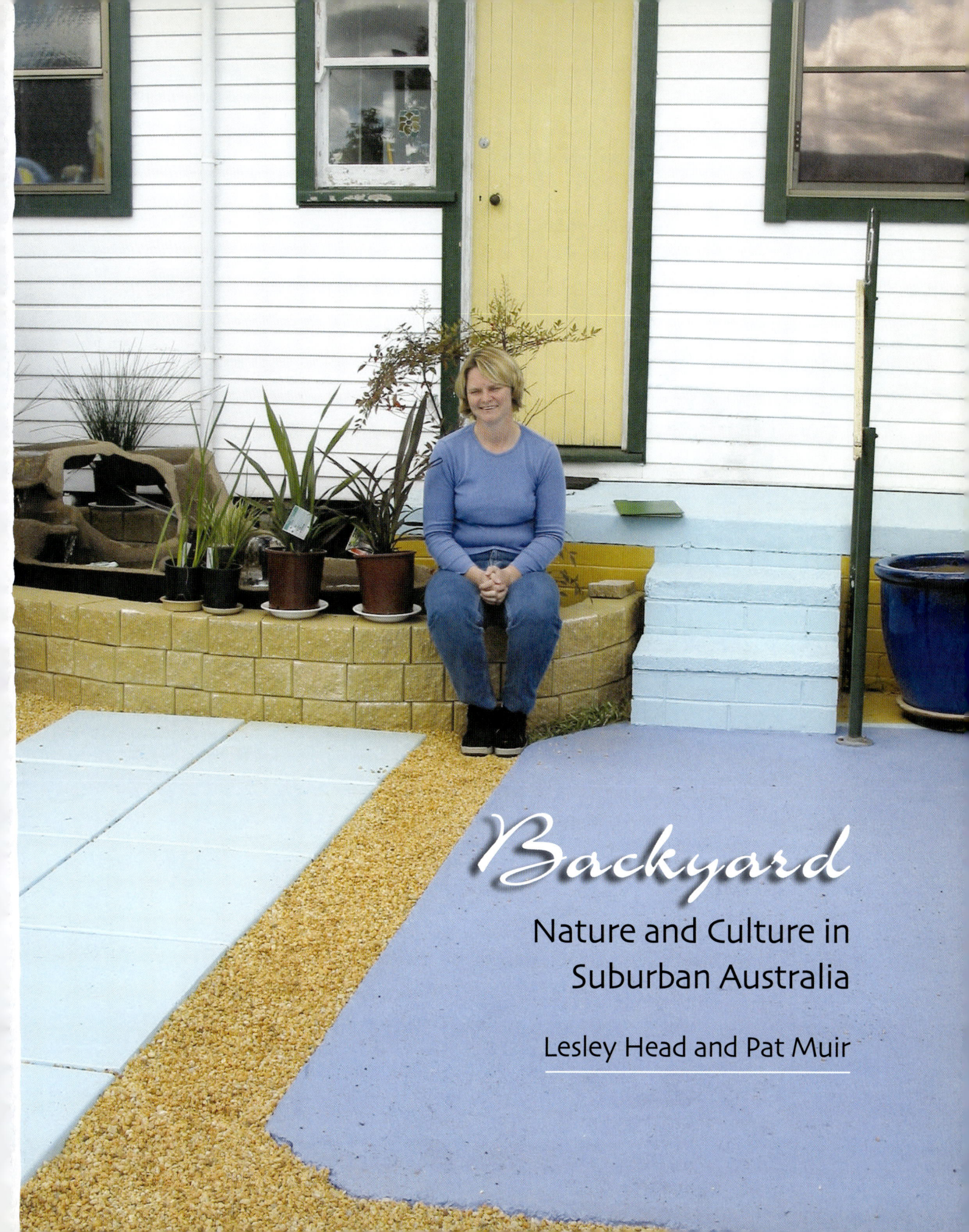

Backyard

Nature and Culture in Suburban Australia

Lesley Head and Pat Muir

DEDICATION

To Hugh and Hannah (LH)
To my parents, Bob and Mary Muir (PM)

ACKNOWLEDGEMENTS

The study was funded by the Australian Research Council (ID No: DP0211327), following a pilot study funded by the University of Wollongong. It was approved by the Human Research Ethics Committee of the University of Wollongong.

Our greatest debt is to the people who welcomed us into their backyards and gave so generously of their time and insights, and to a number of backyard professionals who also agreed to be interviewed.

The following people worked on the project at different times, and we thank them all; Eva Hampel for interviewing assistance, backyard diagrams and sketch diagrams, Lynette Jacona and Linda Phillips for transcription, Sue Fyfe for plant identifications, and Angela Hing for interviews with landscape suppliers. Laurel Waddell collated the magazine analysis as part of a Directed Studies project under LH's supervision. Richard Miller drew the maps.

We thank Mendo Trajcevski and Kim Hong for liaison with the Macedonian and Vietnamese communities respectively, and Verica Sajdovska and Tim Huynh for interpreting. Yasmine Musharbash assisted with liaison and contacts in Alice Springs.

Ruth Lane first alerted us to the National Museum of Australia collections. These were accessed by permission, and we thank Carol Cooper and Faye Maron for their assistance. We had useful discussions with Lynne McCarthy and Ian Coates at the NMA. For comments, discussion and assorted assistance we also thank Michael Adams, Jane Alexander, Chris Cleirigh, Shooshi Dreyfus, Richard Fullagar, Andrea Gaynor, Nick Gill, Jamie Kirkpatrick, Lesley Knapp, Katarina Saltzman, George Seddon, Marie Stenseke, Zoe Sofoulis, Elizabeth Thompson, Gordon Waitt and Diana Wood-Conroy. David Trigger provided valued support and critique. He and Jane Mulcock offered productive comparative discussions with their own work, and Jane generously commented on a draft of this manuscript.

Seminar and conference audiences in Australia, the USA and Sweden helped us hone our arguments. The final draft of the manuscript was completed while LH was King Carl XVI Gustaf Visiting Professor of Environmental Sciences at Kristianstad University, Sweden, and thanks are due to Joachim Regnell. Di Walton provided valuable editorial assistance. Paul Sharrad and Matthew Richardson helped bring the book to fruition.

The following images are reproduced by permission:
Figure 2.2 by permission National Museum of Australia
Figures 4.11 and 4.12 copyright, Burke's Backyard
Figure 7.2 by permission Cathy Wilcox and *The Sydney Morning Herald*

Contents

Figure 1.1: Eucalyptus maculata *with native and exotic herb layer, inner Wollongong*

CHAPTER ONE

The Conceptual Landscape

A STONE'S THROW from the Port Kembla steelworks, Lennie and Connie live adjacent to a small formal reserve that helps protect a remnant stand of spotted gum (*Eucalyptus maculata*) in the middle of the suburbs. Their backyard is dominated by an extensive and productive vegetable garden and chook shed that maintain traditions they brought from Italy more than forty years ago. Lennie has established some small vegetable beds out on the reserve, where he also grazes his rabbits in their mobile hutch. He is very careful to protect spotted gum seedlings, which he marks with stakes and tape, and is in active discussions with Wollongong City Council officers about these activities.

In talking about his garden, Lennie does not talk about endangered species. He talks about productivity and his family and being involved with

Figure 1.2: Connie, Lesley Head and Lennie in the Eucalyptus maculata *reserve adjoining the house, inner Wollongong*

Figure 1.3: Mira looking out onto her backyard, inner Wollongong

the soil (Figure 1.2). However, the outcome is ongoing stewardship of a locally endangered species. For Lennie, if the spotted gums go, the reserve status of the adjoining blocks goes, and they will be sold off. People building a new house on such prime real estate are unlikely to be happy about a large chook shed and rich compost pits right on their boundary. For the moment, protecting *E. maculata* gives him a buffer to pursue his intensive production without upsetting any neighbours.

On the other side of the hill lives Kris, an environmental scientist. The remnant stand of *E. maculata* and other eucalypts was the reason she bought her block, which contains a number of very large spotted gums (Figure 1.1). She has been actively trying to restore the native vegetation, including spotted gum seedlings and associated understorey vegetation, since she moved in.

> *It was just lawn and trees and azaleas and geraniums . . . and a whole lot of other pests, so I have been trying to reintroduce the native vegetation . . . There's some pittosporum coming up which is really nice seeing that my neighbour's cut down most of hers.*

In her goal of 'merging of the Australian natural environment and our living environment', Kris has strong views about which parts of 'our living environment' should be tolerated. She is in varying levels of conflict with the neighbours on her three boundaries, each of whom has a different attitude to trees in general and natives in particular.

Further down the hill, in Mira's backyard, the strongest impression for the visitor is of order and tidiness. Mira describes this area as being like a 'small house', which it is necessary to look after, clean and decorate (Figure 1.3). Under current water restrictions she cannot keep it as clean as she would like, but when restrictions are lifted, she plans to 'clean it up like a vacuum cleaner' with the hose. When Mira mows her lawn or feeds her roses she is loving and nurturing a backyard which is 'everything in my heart'. Despite, or perhaps because of, her demanding full time job, her morning routine begins with half an hour in the garden, looking at every plant, checking its needs and watering when necessary. She describes this as a time that 'makes me relaxed', when she notes the cycles of plants and their flowering, and plans what she needs to do for them in the next few weeks.

According to current theories about 'settler Australian environmental relations', Mira is alienated from nature through taming and domesticating it, and Lennie is projecting a European ethic onto it, rather than coming to terms with the essence of Australian nature. Kris's backyard work would be seen as representing the appropriate conservationist response, but because it is done in an industrial city it would be deemed far less important than her professional work in nature protection outside the city. All three backyards would be deemed peripheral to the urgent work of protecting the 'real' nature in remote areas.

Such perspectives contain two central rifts; between an immigrant Australian nation and its environment, and between nature and the city. For more than two hundred years in Australia, the distinction between the city and the bush has roughly paralleled that between culture and nature. In debates, writing and painting, the focus has been on the bush, the outback, the desert, the wilderness and the beach. When we

preserve nature, we preserve it 'out there'. The city is seen as the place of culture, for better or worse, but totally separated. It can represent both the highest forms of human civilisation, in which people ascend far above the state of nature, and also a fatally flawed place that is basically 'anti-nature'.

In this book we aim to cut across those divides and provide fresh perspectives on Australian relations to nature. Our evidence comes from the suburbs, what Robin Boyd called the 'half-world between city and country' (Boyd 1952: 14)—or the middle ground, where most Australians live. We use suburban backyards and gardens as a lens through which to take a fresh look at the ways Australians interact with the environment. That these three backyards, and the many others in the book, have lively, interesting and different mixtures of culture and nature will not surprise readers who have looked out their own back doors or over a neighbour's fence. Lennie, Kris and Mira all engage with the nonhuman world through their bodily labour using all their senses. They are not alienated, but embedded in it. Their 'environmental cultures' provide a means to identify shared understandings and differences in a diverse society.

It is often said in Australia that we need cultural change to be able to achieve environmental sustainability. But how well do we understand our 'environmental cultures', which have received only a fraction of the research attention that has been invested so productively in the scientific dimensions of sustainability? In this book, we aim to illustrate the benefits of cultural research for understanding environmental values and practices, and how they are likely to stand up or change over time.

The dualistic thinking that separates nature and culture has been under challenge in recent years. We now admit that environments 'out there' are full of culture. Places that White Australia has called wilderness have experienced thousands of years of human interaction. (Most Aboriginal

Figure 1.4: New houses under construction in Kellyville, Sydney

people do not insist that only native plants and animals belong. Aboriginal responses indicate intellectual flexibility in dealing with changing ecological and socio-economic conditions—rather than a simplistic separation of nature.)

When we attempt to corral nature into bounded places known as national parks, or transmit images of it into the global tourism market, we are subjecting it to cultural processes. By the same token, as Lennie, Kris and Mira illustrate, cities are teeming with diverse combinations of plant and animal life shaping and shaped by human activity. Nor are the city and the bush separate, but linked by complex networks for the production and distribution of food and other resources.

We use the metaphor of the network to understand these complex connections between all sorts of human and nonhuman entities. The network that currently protects spotted gums in Wollongong includes not only the legal instrument of formal reserve status, but also intensive vegetable production on private land, rabbit grazing on public land, and restoration of native understorey vegetation on private land. It connects to production of vegetables for Kris and land outside the city, and the historical circumstances that brought hundreds of thousands of immigrants like Lennie and Connie to Australia after World War II. The network is held in place by personal passions and a sometimes fraught configuration of neighbourly relations.

Backyards are hybrid places—part of the betweenness of suburbia itself; between city and country, culture and nature, inside and outside, public and private.[1] Backyards are an important part of the domestic environment of 'middle Australia', defined by sociologist Michael Pusey, in *The Experience of Middle Australia*, as

> the broad urban middle class, and indeed just about all of us who live between the rich and the poor. Yes, 'between' . . . Middle Australia is as much an outlook as a demographic category. (p3)

Why Nature? (and What is it?)

Nature is a word for a slippery set of concepts. In the first instance we are using it to mean the nonhuman world, a use that is often interchangeable with environment. What started this project was the need to understand better the attitudes and practices that are driving people to transform their environment, often in profound and destructive ways.

But that concept of nature separates and excludes people. Some readers will argue that it is better to think in terms of the set of relationships in which humans and nonhumans co-exist. We agree. Part of our purpose is to go beyond the separation of people and the environment into discrete entities. However to explore human relations to nature, first we need to examine what people

Figure 1.5: Tao composting take-away cutlery made from cornstarch, Campbelltown, Sydney

mean by nature and how they construct boundaries, borderlands and relationships between themselves and the world around them. What is in, what is out, and where do they put themselves, the dog, the weeds, the weather? Thus this is also a book about boundaries, both physical and conceptual. According to the geographer, Noel Castree,

nature is simply a name that is 'attached' to all sorts of different real-world phenomena. Those phenomena are not *nature as such* but, rather, *what we collectively choose to call 'nature'*. (Castree 2005: 35, citing Urban and Rhoads 2003, emphasis in Castree).

Boundaries are made and crossed not just by words but by physical structures, and by practices of inclusion and exclusion. Lennie crosses a line between his private space and what is called public space, but no one seems to mind. The fences between Kris and her neighbours mark not just four different blocks and owners, but four different attitudes to spotted gums. Mira includes the rubber ducks she has floated on the pond and angels she has hung in the tree as important parts of the life of her garden. We wanted to find out about the experience of nature as lived by people, and how people understand their own influential participation in nature.

According to how we think of nature, we might want to put a fence around it, create a bureaucracy to look after it, kill it, eat it, plant it, or remove it. This is not one way traffic, either. Nature has a life of its own and can act back, or in any other direction.

Why Urban Australia?

Most Australians belong to the broad urban middle class, concentrated on the coast. Middle Australia. They have an influence on the environment. Their votes change governments, their food comes from lands vulnerable to salinity, their water usage affects ecosystems at the other end of the pipes, and they are managers of urban land.

We need to understand their thinking and behaviour, and what environmental influences affect them. So our main method is semi-structured interviewing and field observation in the ethnographic tradition; what academics now often call 'the anthropology of us'. We focus on their personal lives, but in the context of power, media and fashion, social and household change, technology and ecological systems. The research methods enable us to discuss contradictions and complexity in individuals and households.

In 2001, 76% of Australia's population occupied 0.33% of its land area, and 84% lived within 50 km of the coast (Hugo, 2003). However, that population absorbs resources from a much more extensive area. The people of middle Australia have a lot of things in common, a lot of diversity; it was important that our research captured both. It includes a few people on waterfront Sydney real estate, and a few public housing tenants, but many more in between these socio-economic extremes. To analyse their relations to nature and their 'environmental cultures', it is necessary to consider the social and economic processes in which they are involved.

Why the Backyard?

Urban Australians interact with nature in many contexts; parks, supermarkets, beaches, television programs and kitchen benchtops, to name a few. When they turn on a tap, eat rice or drive the kids to school, they are affecting ecosystems both close by and a long way away. The backyard is just one site worth knowing about. It is urban, suburban, private, outdoors and part of daily life. Or is it? Look closer and the clear delineations between urban, suburban and rural are becoming more blurred. As places for hospitality, backyards are increasingly sites of public display. Outdoor rooms and houses that 'bring the outdoors in' challenge the clear distinction between inside and outside. And our daily lives are connected to distant lives and places in ways that we often prefer not to think about.

Backyards are both fascinating worlds unto themselves and lenses onto a broader range of connections between people and their environment. This makes them interesting spaces in which to examine the complex interpenetrations of nature and culture. Most Australian children begin to experience 'the environment' in their backyards. In mundane domestic experiences in the backyard, Australians of all ages live out their attitudes to nature beyond the fence as well as within it. They mulch, recycle, compost, grow food and experience pleasure and displeasure in their encounters with birds, insects, frogs, possums, cats and dogs.

In our backyards, we are also connected to distant environments. When we water our plants, we are linked to catchments hundreds of kilometres away. When we create a 'natural' haven with African slate, white Cowra pebbles, South American palms and a timber garden seat from Bali, we are remaking nature not only in an Australian suburb, but in Africa, Cowra, South America and Bali. The creation of new backyards contributes to land clearing, increased runoff and quarrying for garden materials, and provides places for animals that in other contexts would be considered feral (Figure 1.6).

Backyards contribute to the direct negative impacts of suburban expansion—land clearing, quarrying, spread of pavement, increased car travel, and expanded habitats for feral animals. On the other hand, backyards provide opportunities for restoration of native vegetation, connection of habitats to remnant bushland,

Figure 1.6: Karen with free range pet rabbit, North Shore, Sydney

Figure 1.7: Participants in their entertaining area, with cubby house and pool behind, Campbelltown, Sydney

Figure 1.8: Bob in front of his shed, inner northern suburbs, Wollongong

Figure 1.9: Paling fence, Penrith, Sydney

recycling, water collection, subsistence agriculture and environmental education and experiences, particularly for children (Figures 1.10, 1.11). They reflect adaptations to local environments such as coasts with salt laden winds, deserts, and nutrient poor soils.

It is not surprising then that the backyard has been a focus of debates over whether urban consolidation is better than urban expansion. Critics of urban sprawl point to the savings in energy and infrastructure spending offered by denser occupation of a smaller area. Champions of the suburbs, on the other hand, point to the environmental practices that are possible with a separate house on its own block of land.

The backyard has acquired iconic status and carries a broad symbolism. It is the archetypal middle class space. TV characters Kath and Kim sit and chat in the backyard to end their show as the credits roll. When private individualism demands exclusions it is put down to the NIMBY – not in my backyard – phenomenon. The backyard in that term stands for the places to which we have local connections. These connections can be affectionate. For example beaches are often referred to as 'Sydney's backyard', and ABC Radio calls the internet gateway to its local stations 'The Backyard'.

Backyards can also be used to exclude others, or at least to signify anxiety and threat. In the fraught debates over the implications of Native Title in the 1990s, Aboriginal land rights were often positioned as a threat to the land held sacred by mainstream Australia, the Backyard. Frequently asked questions about Native Title included, 'Is my backyard safe from an Aboriginal land claim?'

In fact of course the High Court had said very clearly that native title had been extinguished on freehold land and the vast majority of leasehold land.

By 'backyard', we mean domestic outdoor space, often but not always enclosed. We say 'garden' when we discuss the area where people relate to plants and soil. A place cannot be thought of as the back except in opposition to the front. The domestic outdoor space which is most private, and over which people feel they have most control, is not always the physical 'back'. Even when it is, it must be considered in relation to the surrounding space – the house, the front and side yards if they exist, the street and neighbourhood. We are using the backyard then not as a fixed entity, but as a somewhat arbitrary membrane around a set of social and ecological relationships that are in constant flux. It is a way to examine both the conceptual and material dimensions of Australian engagements with environment.

Dualisms and Hybrids

Beyond the false dichotomy of nature and culture, backyards can teach us about people and their environment precisely because of their betweenness (see Appendix 3). That doesn't mean there are purely natural or purely cultural

Figure 1.10: Kids on the trampoline, Alice Springs

spaces somewhere else. Wilderness areas and New York City are hybrids, just as backyards are, though perhaps not so obviously (Gandy, 2002). Yet recent writers on the theme of the interpenetrations of nature and culture try to go beyond these categories and the notion of pure spaces. Given their more flexible understanding, an important question is why, in the backyard where notions of hybridity and networks would make much more obvious sense, does thinking which separates nature from culture have great resilience and vernacular appeal?

It is not easy to dismantle the dualisms and boundaries that pervade Western thought and practice. People aspire to order and purity and work at a whole range of ordering and purifying practices. We encounter Kris who gets rid of lawn, Lennie who removes weeds from his vegetables, Mira who tidies up and marks out different parts of the backyard with physical structures. In showing that boundary making and purification are widespread and variable, we argue that the conditions under which that separation of nature from culture is reinforced and maintained need much more detailed attention from geographers and other observers of our way of life.

The conditions under which that separation breaks down are also variable, but they have in common that they occur through close engagements between people and the nonhuman world. It is these, we will argue, that provide as yet hazy visions of alternative futures.

What understandings of human belonging do we find among those Australians who insist on native plants for their backyards? Do plants and animals occupy parallel spaces of belonging? Could we expect those who oppose further human immigration to have similar antipathy towards introduced flora and fauna? Such themes pervade the book but are the particular focus of Chapter eight.

The betweenness of the backyard is a source of challenge, hope and alternative possibility.

Figure 1.12: Thelma embracing a tree she planted many years ago, inner northern suburbs, Wollongong

Writing and Reading this Book

We aim to give voice with empathy to people who have let us into their lives, and to express their lived experience of nature in its own terms. We have made many selections in the process of sampling, analysing and writing, pressing individual and group experiences into the service of bigger questions. Pseudonyms are used for some participants.

The first group of chapters establishes the background and overview. Chapter Two provides a historical context. Some readers may prefer to go straight to Chapter Three, an overview of the backyards in our sample.

The next group of chapters explores themes arising from the study in greater depth. Chapter Four looks at gardens and gardeners, analysing people's relationships with plants and soil. Chapter Five focuses on 'my place', the theme of the backyard as a haven. We discuss the various ways people engage with this environment. Chapter Six links the theme of food production with that of the reproduction of tradition and practice in the migrant experience. Chapter Seven explores attitudes and practices especially in relation to water. Chapter Eight returns more explicitly to questions of boundaries and belonging.

Chapter Nine draws the threads together and makes some suggestions about potential applications of this work. It summarises the way environmental dualisms are being both reinforced and broken down. We look among the ideas and behaviour of study participants for a basis for further action, and at areas of difference and potential conflict.

Figure 1.13: Neil propagating plants in his potting shed, inner northern suburbs, Wollongong

Figure 1.14: Nhan's daughter with topiary deer, Fairfield, Sydney

Figure 2.1: Arboriaphobiaville'.
(Source: Boyd 1963: Plate D)

CHAPTER TWO

The Sewer Pipe and Other Moments in *Backyard History*

Australian suburbs were established as the antithesis of the urban slum, allowing people to live the dream of the country life in the city. The high value placed today on the private space of the backyard has historical connections to the independent yeoman ideal of owning a small farm. There is a long standing debate over whether suburbs are environmentally evil or good—a debate largely removed from the experience of those who live there.

hen a young Malda Groth stood among sewerage pipes about to be installed in her Maryborough, Queensland, backyard in 1939 (Figure 2.2), the occasion was momentous because she would no longer have to brave the backyard dunny at night. But she was also standing in the middle of a key shift in suburban infrastructure, in which people's engagement with cycles of production, consumption and disposal would be radically transformed. One aspect of the networks by which suburban life was sustained was about to become less visible, literally going under ground.

This chapter traces historical continuities and changes in backyards since the time of white settlement. Over that time we have seen a shift from the backyard as a place of production to one of consumption, although there are various challenges to this interpretation. A recurring feature is the persistence of the yeoman ideal. The key feature of yeomanry, the ownership of a small farm, has clear links to contemporary suburban assertions of independence, individuality and privacy. This chapter also shows how these historical changes have long been entwined with a sustained critique of suburbia and suburban life. Much of the critique is about whether the suburbs have culture, not nature. As scholars have commented, the critique is often from outside, and at odds with the lived experience of suburban lives. The third section, using historical materials from the National Museum of Australia collections, provides a better understanding of how people like Malda Groth and her family experienced some of those changes.

Historical perspective is also important because it has become commonplace thinking that the Australian backyard is changing irrevocably. It is a subject often raised in the context of media panic about diverse issues that include urban consolidation, architectural ugliness, childhood obesity, 'McMansions', population growth and the heritage of suburbia. These debates often evoke an idealised past where backyards provided the basis of a good childhood—spaces to play cricket and football, and the requirement that kids make their own fun.

There is an echo in this of the search for the ideal rural past in England. Malor (1996) identified 'the first death notice' in a *Sydney Morning Herald* feature article on 'our shrinking backyards' in 1989. There have been similar obituaries throughout the life of our project. New suburbs such as Kellyville in northwest Sydney are just the latest to provide a lightning rod for these debates. Robin Boyd for example, in *The Australian Ugliness*, christened early 1960s versions of such suburbs 'Arboriaphobiaville'. (Figure 2.1).

Figure 2.2: Malda Groth (later Bertram) in the backyard of her home at 186 Fort Street, Maryborough, Qld, 1939. (Source: National Museum of Australia 2006: www.nma.gov.au)

Figure 2.3: The (new) Great Australian Dream. (Source: Good Weekend, Sydney Morning Herald Magazine: August 2003: front cover)

The experience of people living in the suburbs is often quite at odds with the perspective of the critics. On 17 June 2003 when *Sydney Morning Herald* architecture critic Elizabeth Farrelly decried the 'ostentation and unashamed obesity of Kellyville's serried exurban megafauna', two local residents, who later became participants in our study, were stung to respond in letters to the editor appearing a couple of days later (19/6/03). Joe took it as a sign of class snobbery from the inner city: 'Sneer through the steaming haze of your decaf soyaccino if you wish'. (In fact Farrelly was criticising neither suburbs nor project homes, but rather the sheer size of most of the latter currently on offer: 'size brings ostentation, and ostentation is ugliness by another name'.) Both Joe and Anne referred to the importance of suburbs such as Kellyville in providing affordable housing options for families, but they took slightly different perspectives. Anne defended

the modesty of her home and the diversity of her backyard: 'you're welcome to pop over . . . and admire the gums, wattles and callistemons in the backyard next to our thriving vegie garden.' She admitted there are problems in Kellyville, but argued they were 'mainly caused by greedy developers and governments who renege on public transport decisions'. Joe's letter, on the other hand, defends the conformity of the suburb in terms of the community values it fostered: 'I can get social, cultural and aesthetic diversity any time I like elsewhere in this city, so I make no apologies for choosing to build our home amongst people (now friends) who share similar values, aspirations and even spiritual beliefs.'

Historical Changes in Australian Backyards

It shows too much hindsight to credit Australia's first colonial governor with the invention of that popular Australian institution, the quarter-acre suburban block; but it is significant that, from the outset, Australia's founders anticipated a sprawl of homes and gardens rather than a clumping of terraces and alleys. (Davison 1994, p. 100)

In his historical perspective on the Australian suburb, Graeme Davison argued that, as conceptualised by Governor Arthur Phillip in the earliest days of the colony, the suburb was to be the antithesis of the slum. Phillip's regulations included block sizes of 60 feet × 150 feet (18.3 m × 45.7 m), with a single dwelling permitted. This reflected aspirations to 'decency, good order, health and domestic privacy'. The determination to 'avoid reproducing the evils of Old World cities' (p: 102) drove state promotion of the suburbs during the early colonial period.

Davison identified four ideologies influential in the development of the Australian suburb.

Evangelicalism promoted the idea of separate spheres for men and women, with the wife as the 'Angel of the Home' and the husband as the worker away from the home.

In his leisure time he could spend time in the garden, reflecting the influence of **Romanticism**; 'the ideal suburb enabled the care-worn city man to repair his battered spirit through communion with the beauties of nature' (p. 101).

Sanitarianism saw the suburbs as separate and distant from the deadly pollution of cities, reflected for example in Govenor Phillip's concern to promote 'free circulation of air'. Fourth, there was **capitalism**, and its particularly Australian expression. Suburbs developed in many parts of the world in the nineteenth century. In the original British context, the suburb was exclusively bourgeois, but the Australian development was more egalitarian. The strong appeal of the suburbs to waves of immigrants, mostly from urban Britain, combined with relatively high nineteenth century wages, low unemployment, cheap land and government infrastructure provision such as extensive public transport, to ensure the early success of Australian suburbs (Davison 1994).

Most Australian gardens are both product and expression of immigrant experience. While there are numerous records of indigenous Aboriginal gardening practices, a different scale and intensity of landscape transformation was wrought by the gardens of the European colonisers. To analyse gardens is to increase our understanding of the immigrants' complex and ongoing project of 'coming to terms' with the Australian environment. Much discussion of these issues has focused on gardens and the associated horticultural industries as conduits for the introduction and exchange of many thousands of plant species between Australia and other parts of the colonial world (Fox 2004).

Complexity in the contemporary scene reminds us to be vigilant with regard to the historical record, in particular with the idea that early gardens were a simple transplantation of English plants and attitudes onto the colony. Tim Bonyhady in *The Colonial Earth* (2000) challenges the 'commonplace that the invaders were not simply untroubled by their destructiveness but

rejoiced in it, so great was their alienation from their new surroundings and their eagerness to turn the land to new uses.' (p. 3)

He documents examples of indigenous plants, including gum trees and treeferns, being fostered in Colonial gardens. Australian trees such as Moreton Bay Fig (*Ficus macrophylla*), Bunya Pine (*Araucaria bidwillii*) and Hoop Pine (*Araucaria cunninghamii*) were on sale in Sydney nurseries in the 1860s (Gelding 1983). Victor Crittenden (1983) argues that the nostalgic Englishness of early gardens has been overstated, as many English plants did not survive in hot, dry conditions. Jacarandas from South America and Peppercorns from the Americas did thrive, and were highly valued for their shade.

Further, the idea that the early Australian suburb was to be differentiated from the city rather than the bush had implications for the kinds of gardens that were created.

> As a modern ideal extending back over two hundred years, [the suburban ideal] reveals itself as a bourgeois search for residential separation from the industrial city, which is inspired not by a desire for country living itself but rather by the redefinition of the urban residential landscape through the images and symbols of nature and rurality. In the garden suburb and its derivatives . . . we can recognise the symbolic confusion of city and country. (Bunce 1994, pp. 153–54)

Commenting on a 1909 debate between two leading landscape architects, Louise Johnson argues that

> the cottage garden was seen as the alternative not to primeval nature but to urbanized, industrial society— a merging of suburban ideology with that of the cottage garden makers . . . In this the suburban garden was firmly demarcated from the inner city yard. (Johnson 1999: 101)

The desire of many contemporary gardeners to reconnect with the bush represents a change from these earlier intentions.

The differentiation between front gardens as public showpieces and back gardens as utilitarian work spaces was a widely identified feature—

evident in the front view of the War Service home plan shown in Figure 2.4. Particularly in the early decades of the twentieth century and the interwar years, gardens were seen as turning houses into homes. As Katie Holmes (2000) points out, gardens reflected stability, a submission to duty, pride of home and country.

The functional roles of the backyard are summarised by George Seddon, writing of the decades around the 1930s:

> The backyard, equally in the town and the country, was complementary to the house in providing resources for living; storage, water, fuel, washing facilities, food input, and food output (by way of the dunny and the compost heap). (1997:155)

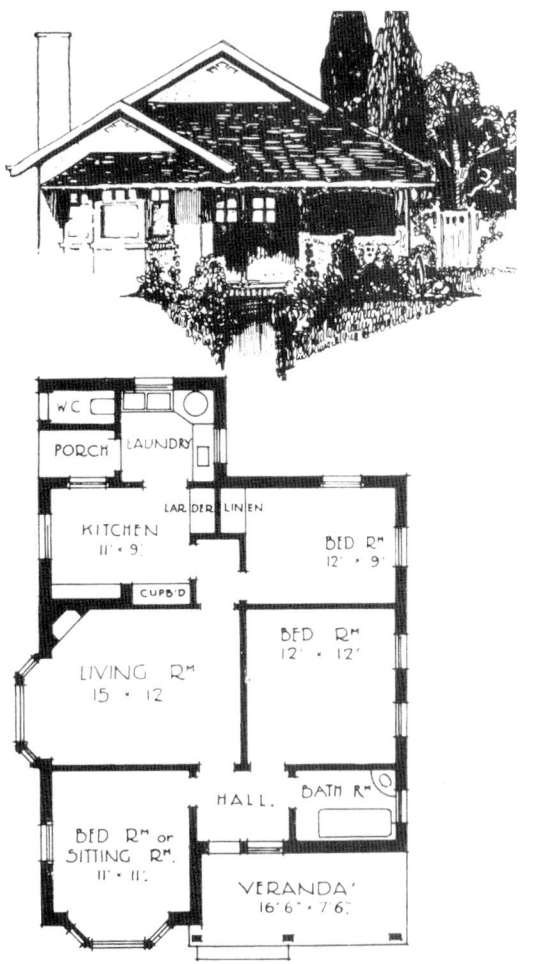

Figure 2.4: Plan and elevation for a War Service Home offered in NSW in 1920. (Source: Cuffley 1989)

Seddon identifies changes in the infrastructure associated with water, particularly the coming of sewerage, as being largely responsible for the changing role of the backyard.

The functional backyard was often a place of great productivity, especially of food. Valerie Allen talking about her father's beautiful garden in 1920s Concord, a suburb of Sydney, remembers

> **the back was full of fruit trees—every fruit tree you could imagine—and he grew every vegetable we ate [and] we had chooks . . . we ate very, very well. (Karskens 1987, p.136)**

The idea that many pre-World War II suburban households were undertaking a version of subsistence agriculture contributed to the development of the so-called 'urban peasant thesis'. Drawing on studies of suburban Brisbane, Mullins and Kynaston (2000) argue that a highly developed domestic economy was based on single family housing, and involved intensive mostly female labour. A key component of urban community life, it began to disappear with the rise of consumer capitalism after 1945. Andrea Gaynor (1999, 2001) challenges this thesis, contending that home food production was more prevalent among the middle class than the working class. In her study of suburban food production in Perth and Melbourne she argues that high levels of domestic food production did not usually arise from necessity, since it was sometimes more expensive to grow one's own fruit and vegetables than to buy them (Gaynor 2001: Chapter 7). Rather,

> The focus on agrarianism in Australia saw the ideology of independence attached to the figure of the yeoman, and the production of food in suburban backyards thus came to represent a symbolic link with the myth of the independent rural yeoman . . . (p. 25)

What was being produced, according to Gaynor, was not 'food' but 'home-grown food', a distinctive category of produce of particular value to middle class views about status, health and the body.

Yeoman mythology had been important in closer settlement schemes throughout Australia in the second half of the nineteenth century. Joe Powell links the Land Selection acts passed in each of the Australian colonies between 1860 and the mid-1880s to the mythical figure of 'the independent freeholder, who lived with his family on a small, intensively cultivated farm, which he carefully tended until it was duly inherited by his equally stable and industrious offspring.' (1976: 82)

The ideal is traced into the middle decades of the twentieth century by Judith Brett in her analysis of Robert Menzies' 'forgotten people' speech of 1942. 'Landless men smell the vapours of the street corner. Landed men smell the brown earth and plant their feet upon it and know that it is good' (1992: 51). Brett argues that Menzies was trying to locate the home as 'the seat of the individual's sense of dignity and worth', in contrast to the anonymous and over-regulated world of work. By inviting people 'to identify their political interests with their private and domestic rather than their economic roles', Menzies distanced himself politically from Labor, and appealed both to workers from a range of occupations and, importantly, to women (Brett 1992: 46).

> In opposition to the negative images of modernity associated with the labour movement, Menzies associates the middle class and the home with a simpler, pre-modern life . . . Most of the people Menzies was addressing were city dwellers, but this would not have prevented them from recognising the opposition he was evoking between the virtues of the simple, family-centred country life and the corrupt modern city. The dream of an independent yeoman farmer underlay many an Australian suburban home. (p. 51)

Ian Halkett did the most systematic analysis of post-World War II garden usage in the suburbs of Adelaide in the 1970s. He mapped and recorded the contents of a sample of front and back gardens, and developed a typology (Figure 2.5). Relying on a quantitative survey of usage patterns, Halkett argued that 57% of adults and 51% of children spent at least half their outdoor recreation time in gardens, and that the 'back garden was used

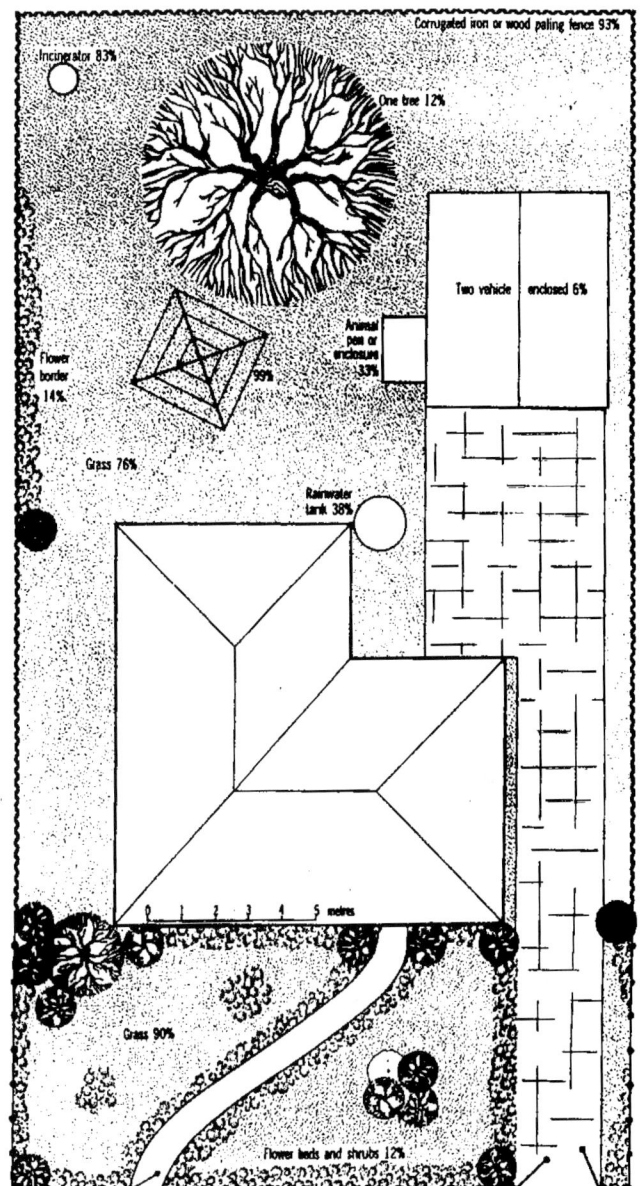

Figure 2.5: Plan of a garden with an elaborate front and plain back showing percent of sampled gardens with each design element. (Source: Halkett 1976)

for more recreation activities by more households than any other single venue' (p. 126). His 1976 findings on the importance of the backyard were invoked in many urban planning debates.

In 1994, Kim Dovey compared project home plans from the period 1968–71 with those of 1985–89. Important changes occurred over this period in the relationships between house and backyard. In the earlier period there was a single exit to the backyard, commonly via the laundry. By the late

1980s small informal meals areas had expanded into a huge informal zone now 'formalised' as the heart of the house. The backyard was segmented into hidden service areas for garbage, washing and storage, and formal display areas for barbecue, patio, pool and garden, 'closely connected visually and functionally with the informal heart of the house' (p. 136). 'At the same time the backyard has been transformed from a place of production to one of consumption' (p. 137). The areas for formal living-dining remained constant at about 28 m^2 over the study period, but areas devoted to informal living (excluding the kitchen) inside the house rose from an average of about 8 m^2 to 32 m^2. It was often also associated with the idea of 'bringing the outside in' through extensive windows and glass doors between the informal zone and the formal backyard area which had also 'become a primary place of social performance' (p. 134). Another internal change over the study period was the enlargement and separation of the parents' realm.

The main trends Dovey identified—separation of service and display areas in the backyard, expansion of informal living zones in the house, more integration between inside and outside space —can be widely seen in early twenty-first century house design and renovations. Thirty-two square metres of informal living space would seem paltry in many project homes today. The Australian Bureau of Statistics reports that, while average block sizes have been declining, the average floor size of new houses built in capital cities between 1993–94 and 2002–03 increased from 196 m^2 to 235 m^2 (Australian Bureau of Statistics, 2005). The integration of indoor and outdoor living spaces has intensified, not only with bringing the outside in, but with the common media reference to outdoor 'rooms' as a way to conceptualise and delineate garden spaces.

The transition from the backyard as a site of production to one of consumption around 1950 is real. However, as we have seen, Gaynor cautions that the distinction is not as straightforward as it first appears. She argues that the trend has been over-generalised through an emphasis on the written record at the expense of oral history. As we will demonstrate, backyards as places of production are rich in meaning and lived experience. As places of consumption they can also produce things, albeit less tangible things such as the sociality of family and friends, and the development of children.

The Suburban Critique

Antipathy towards the suburbs has been traced back at least to the 1920s. McAuliffe argues that there were then two threads to this antipathy; first, the suburbs were a threat to the bushman legend so influential in national mythology, and second, the Left was wary of succumbing to the creature comforts of capitalism. Writers and artists, such as D.H. Lawrence in *Kangaroo*, 'were quick to develop metaphors of uniformity, oppression, conformism and anonymity' (McAuliffe 1996: 53). Within this critique, the question was not whether there was any nature in the suburbs, but whether there was any culture. For writer Nettie Palmer in 1945, the 'suburban' was the antithesis of the 'cosmopolitan' (Rowse 1978).

In 1978 in 'Heaven and a Hills Hoist', Tim Rowse traced the history of criticism of suburbia, and found tendencies to homogenise Australian society, which ignored important ethnic and class differences, and to emphasise individual householders, 'ignoring the less visible but more important relationships which connect individuals' and give suburbia its history and politics (p 4). Others including Davison (1994: 109–10); Johnson (1997) and Malor (1996), have pointed out that the critique ignores the lived experience of people in suburbs.

Rowse notes that after World War II there was an ironic acceptance of the suburban fate of Australia; 'suburbia was coming to be seen not so much as an aberration of the Australian spirit, but as its abiding manifestation.' (1978: 8). For the critics, this was its problem. The most famous of the post-war critics was architect Robin Boyd (1963). Whereas earlier critics such as Vance Palmer had seen the suburbs ('villadom') as the antithesis of a pioneering bush nationalism (Rowse 1978), Boyd saw them as part of the same pioneering mentality. In dubbing it 'arboriaphobiaville', he described post-war suburban expansion as 'the second period of pioneering' (p. 91). 'The object of the pioneer cult, in short, is to clear all decks for action, to reduce everything to the same comprehensible level so that something new can be put on it' (Boyd 1963: 92). Rowse identifies the satirist Barry Humphries as an important indication of the shift to ironic acceptance, and notes that the negative image of suburbia was often equally a negative image of women.

A contemporary manifestation of these debates can be seen in the TV series, 'Kath and Kim'. Critics are divided on whether this satire is an affectionate celebration or scathing critique of suburbia, or both, and whether its creators Jane Turner and Gina Riley are reappropriating or reinforcing the relations between the sexes in suburban Australia. The popularity of the series would seem to lie in some considerable recognition of their lived experience on the part of the viewing public. Although neither Kath nor Kim is a gardener, the backyard is portrayed as an important site of relaxation and interaction at the end of each episode.

So after a while even critics of suburbia seemed—with a certain irony—to be accepting the backyard. After that, a strand of thought celebrating the backyard emerged once again. 'Environmentalists should stop thinking of cities and suburbs as enemies of the countryside or as worse land uses than farming,' wrote Hugh Stretton in 1976:

> Generous private houses and gardens can degrade the environment if people fill the houses with machinery and drench the gardens with chemicals. But the same relaxed housing forms also allow the best scope for good environmental behaviour. It is in private houses with storage space and some land around them that it is easiest to use more human energy in satisfying ways and to manage with less powered chemical services . . . Environmental policies will always be determined by people's values; and urban houses and gardens are the nursery of most of the best environmental values. People who live in town but grow some foliage of their own, and keep a cat to deter mice are the mainstay of all the movements which work to protect larger landscapes and ecosystems. Private residential land is both an environmental good which ought to be fairly shared, and a vital educator: a classroom for work-skills, play-skills, nature study and environmental values which an environmentally careful society would be mad to deny any of its people.
>
> (*Capitalism, Socialism and the Environment*, pp. 191–92)

In *Ideas for Australian Cities* (2001), he defends the detached suburban house—for enabling child, family and adult life to have 'overlapping territories' without being on top of each other, and for flexibility. 'The house-in-garden is the most freely and cheaply flexible of all housing forms. Tents are its only competitors' he writes. 'Each owner has considerable freedom to choose his own degree of privacy, publicity or neighbourliness. This freedom to alter his house without changing his address is an underrated one' [pp. 15–16]. He adds that people like gardens and the time they spend gardening. (See also Troy 1996, 2000.)

Vehement disagreement—between those who admire suburban life and those who scorn it—polarises arguments about urban planning, from the highest levels of government to the letters pages and talk back radio.[2] The planners, of course, are concerned with the big picture of infrastructure and service provision, and economic and environmental cost. They and other decision makers are more likely than householders to take an 'aerial view' of the suburban landscape; one that emphasises monotony and uniformity. On their flat template of 'the environment' human beings impose impacts, many of which are detrimental. The intertwining pathways which lead people through the landscape from day to day aren't always visible to planners.

The Backyard and the Workplace

In 1992 Wendy Hucker began working as a consultant for the National Museum of Australia, then being established in Canberra. Her job was to build a backyards collection. People around Australia responded to television and radio requests for material, and she got a rich collection of letters as well as valuable artifacts. She would often write back to people who sent letters and get them to enlarge on interesting points. Most of the initial correspondence is hesitant, from people wondering whether their backyards will be too ordinary to be of interest. But after several letters to and fro there is a rich and detailed record of backyard contents and activities, stretching from about the 1930s through to the 1990s. Most respondents were women, but in their descriptions, men, women, and children of both sexes are recorded as using backyards for a variety of activities. If the backyard for children was 'a place to let your imagination run wild', for adults there is a definite emphasis on work—domestic labour that often seems arduous by today's standards.

The Burkes' Backyard

Members of the Burke family remember their backyard in a New South Wales country town in different ways, depending on each one's role in the family. Maureen, mother of three children under five, wrote

> I was sitting having a quiet cup of coffee while my three children were away in the loungeroom watching **Playschool**. The radio was on the ABC (which I had only just taken to listening to), when I heard Wendy Hucker being interviewed on her research into backyards. Some of the backyards sounded just like my parents' at Oaklands. So I thought about it for a while wondering if our backyard would be of any interest, and finally contacted Wendy and here we are.

Somehow Maureen found time to almost fill an exercise book with memories of her childhood backyard—detailed childhood memories, sometimes refracted through the context of her own parenting role. Wendy Hucker encouraged Maureen's mother Evelyn and brother Phillip to write also, albeit more briefly. Evelyn's description of her marital home is seen through the lens of her own domestic labour, as the accounts of washday (below) show. Phillip's memories are full of detail about machinery in the shed, guns, and the hut where he and his brother slept.

In this and other examples, the washing areas are described as being in the closest part of the backyard to the house. This is partly because that was where the water was, whether tank or mains. It was also presumably to facilitate ease of movement between women's inside and outside work zones. Thus Evelyn Burke describes her backyard in the 1950s:

> It really began at the back door, there was no intervening area that separated the two. Right at the back door was the two rainwater tanks that the water from the roof ran into when it rained. This was used for everything, washing, bathing, cooking, cleaning . . .
>
> Next to the tanks was the concrete wash troughs where the washing was done and the copper in which the clothes were boiled. After boiling the clothes and sheets, tablecloths and towels were rinsed by hand in the wash trough, then rinsed again in water in which the Ricketts [sic] Blue had been left for a while to make the water blue, this blue water was supposed to make the whites whiter . . . Not a drop of washing water was wasted, it was all taken by bucket to the vegie garden and flower garden.
>
> When water was laid on to the town from Wagga in 1956, washday improved greatly. There was a shed in the yard that was improved and a concrete floor laid and one end became the 'wash house' with the wash

troughs at one end with water taps over them; and a washing machine!! But still I had to heat the water up in the copper and put it in the washing machine; and the water was still put on the garden after washing. (Burke 1992)

In daughter Maureen's description of the same backyard, the section furthest from the house, which included several sheds, was seen as 'Dad's domain'. The sheds were important work places for a variety of handyman and building activities. They were also important storage sites for fuel, equipment and materials.

Dad never threw anything out—you never knew when you might need something or 'something might just come in handy' . . . Dad didn't like spending money if he could do it himself. So everything was saved; any nuts or bolts found on the road, while walking, were pocketed and stored away. Even old thongs were saved for the rubber.

If it was a male domain it was one where kids of both sexes were clearly welcome. The shed, says Maureen,

was where we would find Dad most afternoons if he wasn't in the vegie garden . . . It was wonderful to be with dad in the shed. The doors would be flung open to let in the light and you could hear the hammer going or the saw. We all learnt to hammer a nail and saw a piece of timber. If we wanted to make something, dad was always on hand.

In front of the chook yard was the vegie garden—Dad's pride and joy. It took up most of the backyard after the sheds. He didn't just plant a couple of everything but dozens of everything. I'm sure he supplied half of the neighbourhood as well. There were cabbages, cauliflowers, beans; beans of all sorts, lettuce, tomatoes, radishes, corn, rhubarb, spinach, onions, shallots, garlic, potatoes, beetroot, strawberries, pumpkin, cucumbers and even peanuts at one stage. Plus the herb garden.

You could munch your way through the garden. My sister even used to eat green tomatoes when she was little. You'd go out to talk to dad while he watered, have a few beans, try a few peas, dig up a radish or two and finish off with a few strawberries and a drink from the tap. (Maureen Everitt, 1992)

In this household the transition between male and female spaces was perhaps at the woodheap. Maureen described her father's activities as including chopping the wood and building the woodheap. From these large blocks her mother 'had to chop her own wood for the fire'.

Clean, Dirty and Transformed Water

The central place of washday in women's lives also surfaces in backyard descriptions from larger towns and the inner city. Maria Kaika (2005) has a theory, discussed in Chapter 7, that natural elements are selectively allowed to enter the modern house, but

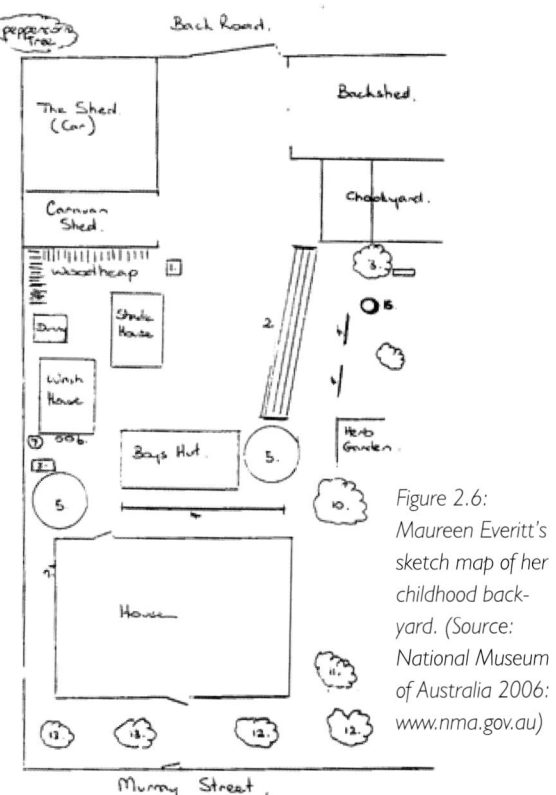

Figure 2.6: Maureen Everitt's sketch map of her childhood back-yard. (Source: National Museum of Australia 2006: www.nma.gov.au)

must remain invisible in order for it to be a space of comfort and familiarity. Transformations in the infrastructure of mains water and sewerage are important in creating this invisibility, contrasting markedly with the detailed knowledge that Evelyn Burke had about where her water came from and where it went. The following accounts show how these experiences were shared by women living in very different contexts.

Malda Bertram described her childhood backyard in Maryborough, Queensland during the 1930s and 40s:

> *Mum had a bench under the house and used to wash her clothes in big tin wash-tubs. The dirty clothes were soaked on Sunday afternoon. She would get up at 5 a.m. Monday and light the copper with chips and paper and then boil the whites, towels and tea-towels in water in which Sunlight soap had been cut up, and some washing soda. The washing trolley stood over a tin tub [which caught the soap suds] and she would lift the whites out with a clothes prop and put more clothes in. The fire was kept up all the time. She would wash the very dirty clothes on a [wooden] wash-board. She usually finished the wash for 2 adults and four children about 3.30 p.m. on Monday. She would throw the washing water left, over the dirt under the house 'to lay the dust'. She had lines propped up by wooden clothes props and used wooden dolly pegs—yes, she had a bag apron and bag peg-bag.*

Similar issues, but on a different spatial scale, applied in inner city areas. Val Brigden wrote that her childhood home in Woolloomooloo

> *had a larger than usual backyard, would have been 12 feet by 24 feet with a lavatory in the furthest corner and two wooden tubs on the diagonally opposite corner near the house. We littlies played in our own yard mostly and had lovely splashes in the tubs to cool off . . . the laundry/bathroom [was] on the end of the verandah.*

For Maureen Everitt, memories of the back-yard dunny involve all her senses, as well as her childhood imagination:

> *I always had to have someone come with me at night as it was dark way down there, used to have to take a torch. And if you had to go during the night you'd run down there, be very quick with your business and run back again— there were so many noises in the dark and if you ran into a spider's web that was the horror of horrors . . . Mum grew flowers in front of the dunny to disguise the smell . . . we could sit there and make out patterns and shapes in the grain of the weatherboards and make up stories about them. Clouds, ducks and faces were some of the memories.*

Maureen knew exactly where the cycle led; 'The seat lifted up so the bucket could be emptied in the vegie garden.' As in Malda Groth's family, the transformation from this cycle to its replacement was a more than welcome event for Maureen:

> *It was wonderful when we went septic. Watching the hole being dug and the tank lowered into the ground, and the lovely white bowl and black seat. And the luxury of real toilet paper— but it was never the nice soft stuff.*

The coming of sewerage, whether mains or septic, and relocation of the toilet into the house were perhaps the single most important change in making the backyard a more pleasant place to be. But as Malda's description from decades later shows, the transformation of the backyard to a place of adult leisure did not come straight away.

> *Backyards weren't used to eat in. Our parents were so glad to have a nice house, they didn't want to go back pioneering. They would have thought a barbecue (with flies etc.) silly when you had a nice table and chairs to use upstairs. So the kids and cats and dogs used the backyard at our house.*

For many readers the most obvious contrast between these accounts and their own lives will be in household labour. This is seen most clearly in the demise of washday, with increasing automation of the washing process. Ninety-five percent of households connected to mains water in New South Wales are now stated to have a washing machine by the Australian Bureau of Statistics (2002). Few would want to return to the tubs out the back, even though the withdrawal of clothes washing into the house has not meant much reduction in the total labour associated with it. The available evidence suggests that clothes washing has become a more or less continuous activity throughout the week. In New South Wales in 2002, 37.1% of households did three to five loads of washing per week, and 33% did more than five (Australian Bureau of Statistics 2002). Changes in the technology associated with cleanliness have led to increases in water consumption, partly because standards of cleanliness have increased.

We conclude this section however with two less obvious contrasts. First, these reminiscences of long ago demonstrate a more detailed engagement with the resource networks that sustained the household—food production, water supply, waste disposal—than most suburban inhabitants experience now.

Second, the storage habits of Maureen's dad, the frugal reuse of water after washday and the recycling of human waste exemplify a strong vein of feeling and practice identified in both the National Museum materials and among our older backyard interviewees. This applies to a wide range of materials that are re-used or recycled in various ways, and that require storage in case and until they are needed, and is a concern of both sexes. Maureen's mother Evelyn moves from her description of water and washday into a general account of household frugality that included making door mats out of the twine from around bales of hay.

I have beautiful patchwork bedspreads made from scraps of material cut up from old dresses and the remnants of my sewing; friends and neighbours would give me scraps of material. As I look at my bedspreads I can see so and so's dress, curtains or apron, they hold lots of memories.

For people raised in less affluent times or circumstances there is both virtue in thrift and disdain for waste. They emphasise the importance of hard work, self reliance, community support and thrift, and contrast this with the twenty-first century lifestyles of their children and grandchildren. Frugality and thrift constituted important resources for environmental sustainability, not that the term sustainability would have been used. To the extent that the networks have become invisible and we have lost the ethic of frugality in contemporary suburban life, we will need to find replacements.

Summary

Backyards and gardens have been important motifs in debates about the future shape of cities and suburbs, and—whether suburbia itself is a place of nature or culture—environmental good or environmental evil. Changes in backyards represent broader changes in the environmental relations of suburban infrastructure, exemplified by the expansion of sewerage systems in the middle decades of the twentieth century. This chapter has also identified differences between 'elite' and 'mass' opinion, and between theory and lived experience, that bear closer examination. From threads through time the next chapter goes to threads and variability across space.

CHAPTER THREE

Backyards

Studied

Stages in the human life cycle play a key role.
The view that backyards are desirable for children is
widespread. Most people value connections to plants,
birds and animals more highly than they do the
structural elements of their backyard.

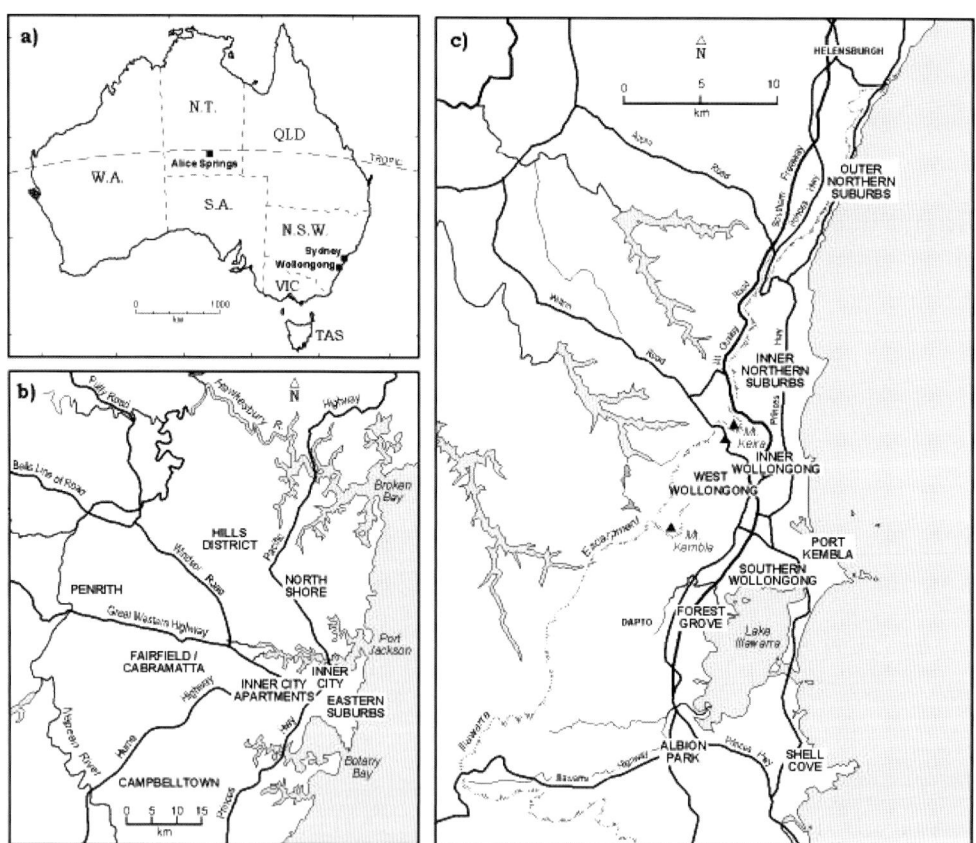

Figure 3.1: Maps of the study areas

Suburb	No. of backyards	Suburb	No. of backyards
Inner Sydney	20	Inner northern suburbs, Wollongong	23
North Shore	18	Outer northern suburbs, Wollongong	17
Campbelltown	16	Inner Wollongong	14
Hills District	13	Wollongong West	14
Fairfield Cabramatta	16	Port Kembla	15
Penrith	16	Forest Grove	11
Eastern suburbs	10	Southern Wollongong	10
Apartments	10	Albion Park	8
Other Sydney	3	Shell Cove	7
Total Sydney	**122**	**Total Wollongong**	**119**
		Alice Springs	**24**

Table 3.1 Number of backyards in the study by suburb. Total = 265

The Sample and the Participants

We visited 122 backyards in Sydney and 119 in Wollongong—located in regions that span the social, demographic and ecological variability of the metropolitan areas (Figure 3.1) (Table 3.1). In Sydney, low income households are primarily concentrated in the west and outer west, between the Parramatta and Georges Rivers. High income households are concentrated on the waterways, and in the broad sweep of suburbs north of the harbour and west to Rouse Hill.

With just over 26,000 people, Alice Springs (24 backyards) has a much smaller population than the Sydney and Wollongong regions, and as a study site provides a strong ecological contrast. Many of our Alice Springs participants have moved there from elsewhere in Australia, and have a perspective of their own on the experience of migration.

Obviously an outback town like Alice Springs is close to arid land ecosystems. Although it is less obvious, it is important to understand how larger cities such as Sydney and Wollongong are also still threaded through with animals, plants and landforms that long pre-date the establishment of the city.

In fact, as a result of its diverse geology, topography and climate, the Sydney Basin bio-region, which includes Wollongong, is one of the most species diverse bioregions[3] in Australia. It is a system in which humans and their domestic spaces are very closely embedded. According to Chen's 2005 figures, 9.6% of homes in the Greater Sydney region are located within 130 m of bushland. There could hardly be a better example of the challenges facing conservation management in 'an already fragmented system that we need to make the most of' (Saunders, Hobbs, and Margules 1991: 18).

The characteristics of a neighbourhood cannot necessarily be gleaned from summary statistics of the wider suburb. The *Social Atlas of Sydney* (2002) shows that there are pockets of high income households in otherwise less well off areas, for example Macquarie Links, a prestige subdivision in the outer southwest, near Campbelltown. Shell Cove, an upmarket residential subdivision in Shellharbour, south of Wollongong, provides a similar example in our study.

Two hundred interviews were with a single participant and sixty-five were with two, mostly couples, but sometimes parents and teenage children. Thus the total number of backyards and households was 265, and the total number of people interviewed was 330. Variables such as household structure, gender, age, ethnicity and socio-economic status all play a role in influencing the attitudes and behaviours discussed in the book. None of them are dominant, and they all interact with each other, but it is important to outline these characteristics as they apply to the sample as a whole.

Household Structure

Nearly half the participants (47%) were families with children. Thirty-five per cent were nuclear families; the other 12% were sole parent or extended families, or families comprising adult children living with parents. Of the households with children, 54% had two children, with 20% having one child and 19% three children. Children were not interviewed, and we depend on what their parents say about them for knowledge of their engagement with the backyard. Research directly with children would be productive. Most households owned or were buying their home (Appendix 2.2), with much smaller numbers of renters and housing commission tenants.

Age, Sex and Ethnicity

Two thirds of the participants were female. In most of the family households we interviewed the mother, in many cases the parent who is more likely to be home based. Nevertheless many of the female participants are very busy people, juggling jobs, family and other responsibilities.

The age structure of the study sample is summarised in Appendix 2.4. Forty-seven per cent of participants were aged between 36 and 55, reflecting the importance of family households in the sample. The couples were concentrated in the over-45 age group. Most of participants in the study were born in Australia (224, or 68%) (Appendix

2.5), with twenty-three other countries of birth represented. There were thirty-seven British born participants (11%), sixteen Vietnamese (5%) and fourteen Macedonians (4%). Our proportion of overseas born participants (32%) is higher than in the total Australian population, recorded in the 2001 Census at 21.9% born overseas, but consistent with figures for Sydney (33% born overseas 2001). The U.K. being the main country of overseas birth is consistent with the Australia-wide pattern. We deliberately focused on the Macedonian and Vietnamese groups to study the influence of migration in depth.

Socio-economic and Educational Status

We grouped the sample into broad 'class' divisions that combined occupation (as classified by the Australian Bureau of Statistics) and education (where the dividing line between high and low was a post-secondary qualification) (Table 3.2). We did not collect income data for our participants, but these groupings provide a generalised proxy of relative affluence. As the *Social Atlas of Sydney* shows in its analysis of the distribution of high and low income households, areas with high household incomes also have high percentages of people with university qualifications, white-collar workers and home ownership. Conversely

Socio-economic status	Education/ skills	Number of backyards	Percentage of backyards	Example occupations in backyard sample
upper	high	4	1	Paediatrician, barrister, broker
	low	0	0	
upper middle	high	21	8	Architect, planner, industrial chemist
	low	0	0	
middle	high	118	44	Social worker, aged care coordinator, accounts manager, programmer
	low	58	22	Miner, teacher's aide, administration assistant
lower middle	high	13	5	Bush regenerator, community arts coordinator, video editor
	low	34	13	Concreter, lab technician, fast food cook, lawn contractor
low	high	3	1	Unemployed computer technician, tertiary student, retired insurance office manager
	low	14	6	Storeperson, labourer, unemployed
Total		265	100	

Table 3.2 Backyards by class. Socio-economic status of householder derived from ABS occupation classifications. High education/skills = post-secondary qualification. Percentage data rounded to nearest whole per cent.

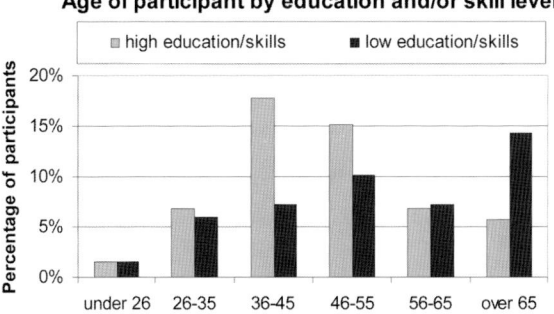

Age of participant by education and/or skill level

- high education/skills
- low education/skills

Figure 3.2: Age of participant by education and/or skill level

there is a correlation between high percentages of low income households and unemployed people, one-parent families with dependent children and, to some extent, people aged sixty-five years or older.

The analysis of socio-economic status should be treated with caution, as there is considerable blurring of boundaries. We have generalised for each household, although occasionally two partners have quite different status from one another. Nevertheless, the broad trends are robust. There is a clear concentration within our sample in the middle-class category, reflected across all household types (Appendix 2.6). None of our upper and upper middle class households have low education/skills, but a number of lower middle and lower class households have high education/skills.

Participants in the age range 36–55 have markedly higher education and skills than the two older cohorts, particularly those aged over 65 (Figure 3.2).

In 2003, the sociologist Michael Pusey published findings on how middle Australians responded to the upheavals of recent decades linked to economic reform and globalisation. Pusey put families into four broad groups by social class and whether or not they were reconciled to economic reform (Table 3.3).

The first group he labelled as 'survivors'—mainly of the manufacturing industry shakeout of the last few decades: those 'who have weathered the storm, and still hold secure jobs in what is left of those same industries, and even those who have taken voluntary redundancies from them' (p. 59). They often have an attitude that if you hold tight, you can still get through. In labelling the second group Pusey adopted a traditional Sydney stereotype, 'North Shore', long used to identify a human type as well as a geographical concept. 'Globalised North Shore people' are those doing relatively well out of reform, who have been able to take advantage of its opportunities. Prominent in this group are IT specialists, human resource personnel, financial services professionals and accountants.

Two other groups are not at all reconciled to the massive economic changes. 'Battlers and Hansonites'[4] emerge in Pusey's research in outer western Sydney and similar areas. Many are employed, if at all, as sub-contractors, and are reeling from permanent insecurity.

> Over and over we find these workers self-employed in their own business, for example, as courier operators, truck drivers, handyman repairers or car cleaners; they are doing virtually the same work as before, but as sub-contracted providers for often large companies. (p. 59)

Their lives are plagued by stress, irregular and long hours, and in their working lives they live by the mobile phone.

The 'improvers', teachers, a nurse, a geologist, a housewife, administrators,

> are up in arms about mortgage costs and the mounting pressures of flexible, rationalised, and demanding workplaces, and about managers who either don't care or cannot do anything to relieve the strain. One taproot for the discussion goes down to what they see as the wanton destruction of the public sector . . . (p. 60).

Attitude to reform	'Working-class'	'Middle-class'
Reconciled	1. Survivors	2. Globalised North Shore People
Unreconciled (and angry!)	3. Battlers and Hansonites	4. Improvers

Table 3.3 Attitudes to reform, by 'class'. Source: Pusey 2003: 58.

The workplaces of this group are typified by the comment that when people leave they never get replaced. We spoke to people similar to each of Pusey's four types about their backyards.

It is not surprising that Michael Pusey writes '*pressure* and *performance* are words that our middle Australians use to describe what is for them a changed experience of time' (p. 105). The same trend was documented by work researcher Barbara Pocock, also in 2003. She summarises The Work/Life Collision as 'a moving vehicle of change in work patterns and in family structures, meeting a solid wall of relatively unchanging labour market institutions, culture and practice' (p. 2). She particularly shows how women experience the collision.

Trends such as two income families, redundancies, working from home and changing patterns of leisure influence relations to nature as expressed in the backyard. Some people want to minimise time in the backyard and, for example, pave it over with low maintenance hard surfaces; others value it as an area of refuge and respite, and as a place where they can engage with plants and animals. For many, particularly Pusey's Globalised North Shore People, the experience of economic reform is an experience of increasing affluence and consumption. Pocock comments that

> the drive for 'more and better stuff' and the need to 'buy instead of make' especially when time is short, combine to enlarge the reach of the market into household time, and, in turn, the reach of paid work into life . . . (p. 45)

That applies to the backyard as much as the house itself.

It all means that looking beyond simple socio-economic status at the separate elements within it is important when it comes to knowing what people think about backyards. Often when we analyse people and behaviours by their broad socio-economic status (upper, upper middle, middle, lower middle, lower), there is no clear pattern—no influence of anything we could call 'class'. This is partly because our sample clusters very much towards the middle. However, by distinguishing between education levels and occupations, it is more possible to see patterns. The division between people with high levels of education or skills and those with low education and skill levels is more significant for backyards than the occupations people have.

Summary

Our sample is much broader than in any comparable study, and allows particular themes as we go through the book to be examined in terms of the above variables. As with any research method that involves participants in an in depth examination of issues, it is skewed towards those with the time and inclination to join in. On the face of things, the preponderance of women and significant proportion of retirees (albeit many younger than sixty-five) reflects home-based people with available time. Yet it is notable that many of the women were doing the 'double shift'; working part time or full time and assuming the bulk of domestic responsibilities. We were also able to interview shift workers and people who are only available on weekends. The self selection process means that we have many more backyard enthusiasts than people who never use their backyard or are uninterested for other reasons, although there are some.

Backyard Features—the Structure of Outdoor Living

Kim Dovey examining the configurations of Australian houses and gardens in 1994 found two broad trends underway. The first is people are dividing backyard spaces into zones to separate utilitarian functions (e.g. clothes drying and rubbish bins) from recreational ones (such as outdoor eating and entertaining areas, and swimming pools). Recreational areas are often now depicted and delineated as 'outdoor rooms'. The second trend is to greater integration between informal living areas at the back of the house and the outdoors. 'Bringing the outside in' is accomplished both physically (for example by large sliding doors) and visually (by extensive use of glass) (Figure 3.5). Blurring of boundaries between the inside and outside of the house is a very consistent trend among the people we spoke to. Two thirds of the backyards we looked at have an outdoor dining setting (how elaborate these were varied considerably) and 87% have a defined recreation or entertaining area adjacent to or attached to the back of the house (Table 3.4). Most participants have created some type of transition zone to connect their living space to the outdoors, but beyond that the processes of boundary making are much more variable.

Division of the backyard into zones is evident in both small (Figure 3.3) and large (Figure 3.4)

backyards. Beverley's small new backyard shows a typical pattern of separated recreation, work and display areas. There is a strong connection between the house and the recreation area and closed external boundaries to enhance the privacy of her actively used backyard. In the front garden, which is much less actively used, there is no fence, and a more open boundary to the street. Shooshi's and Mark's much larger and older backyard (Figure 3.4) also has strong internal boundaries, with an intensively used and fenced family living and play area closest to the house. Towards the back of the block the boundaries become more porous as there is a gradual blending with the forest to the rear. The open boundary in the northeast corner reflects not only the lack of a fence, but

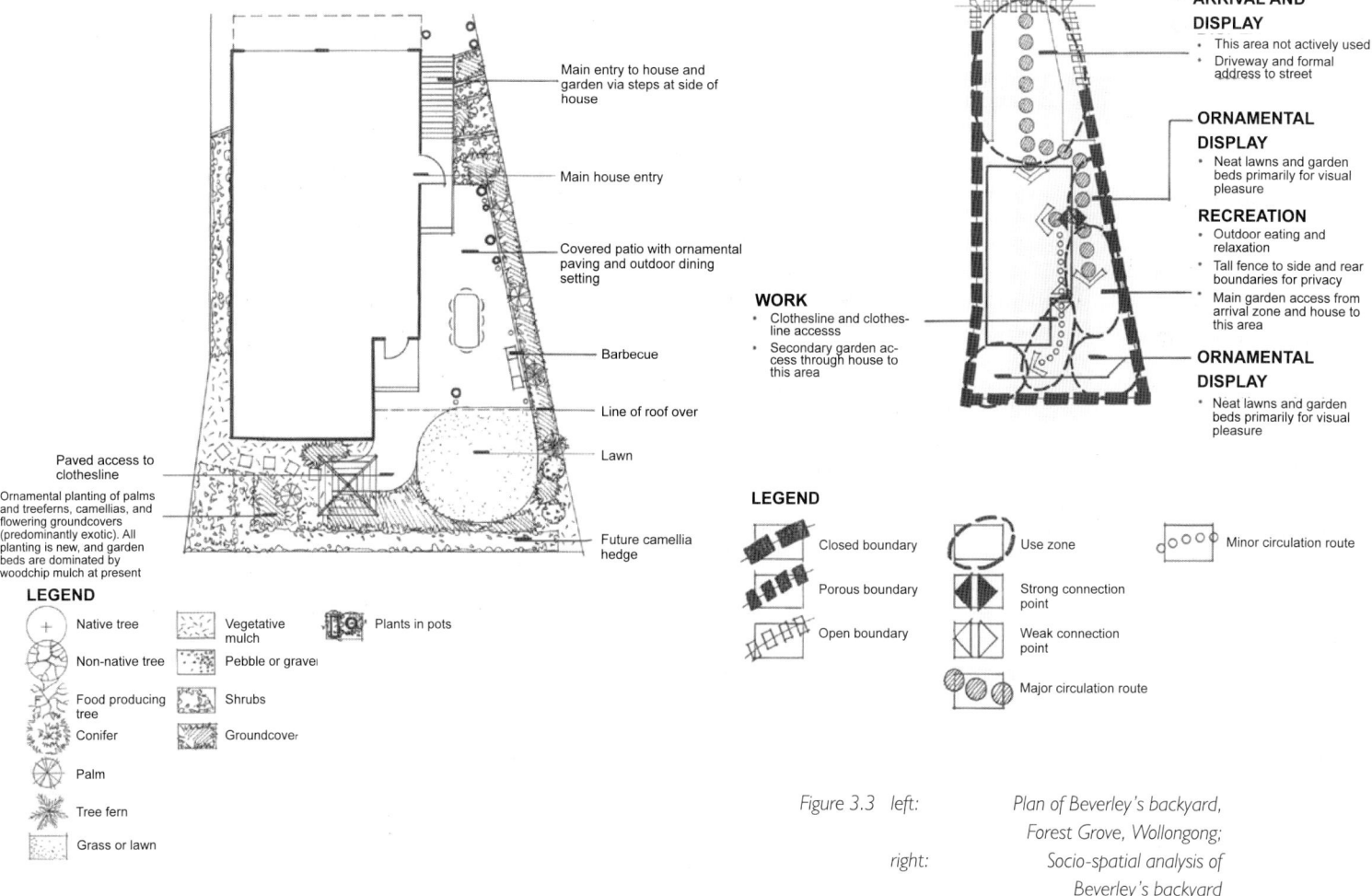

Main entry to house and garden via steps at side of house

Main house entry

Covered patio with ornamental paving and outdoor dining setting

Barbecue

Line of roof over

Lawn

Future camellia hedge

Paved access to clothesline

Ornamental planting of palms and treeferns, camellias, and flowering groundcovers (predominantly exotic). All planting is new, and garden beds are dominated by woodchip mulch at present

LEGEND

Native tree	Vegetative mulch
Non-native tree	Pebble or gravel
Food producing tree	Shrubs
Conifer	Groundcover
Palm	
Tree fern	
Grass or lawn	

ARRIVAL AND DISPLAY
- This area not actively used
- Driveway and formal address to street

ORNAMENTAL DISPLAY
- Neat lawns and garden beds primarily for visual pleasure

RECREATION
- Outdoor eating and relaxation
- Tall fence to side and rear boundaries for privacy
- Main garden access from arrival zone and house to this area

ORNAMENTAL DISPLAY
- Neat lawns and garden beds primarily for visual pleasure

WORK
- Clothesline and clothesline access
- Secondary garden access through house to this area

LEGEND

Closed boundary	Use zone	Minor circulation route
Porous boundary	Strong connection point	
Open boundary	Weak connection point	
	Major circulation route	

Figure 3.3 left: Plan of Beverley's backyard, Forest Grove, Wollongong;

right: Socio-spatial analysis of Beverley's backyard

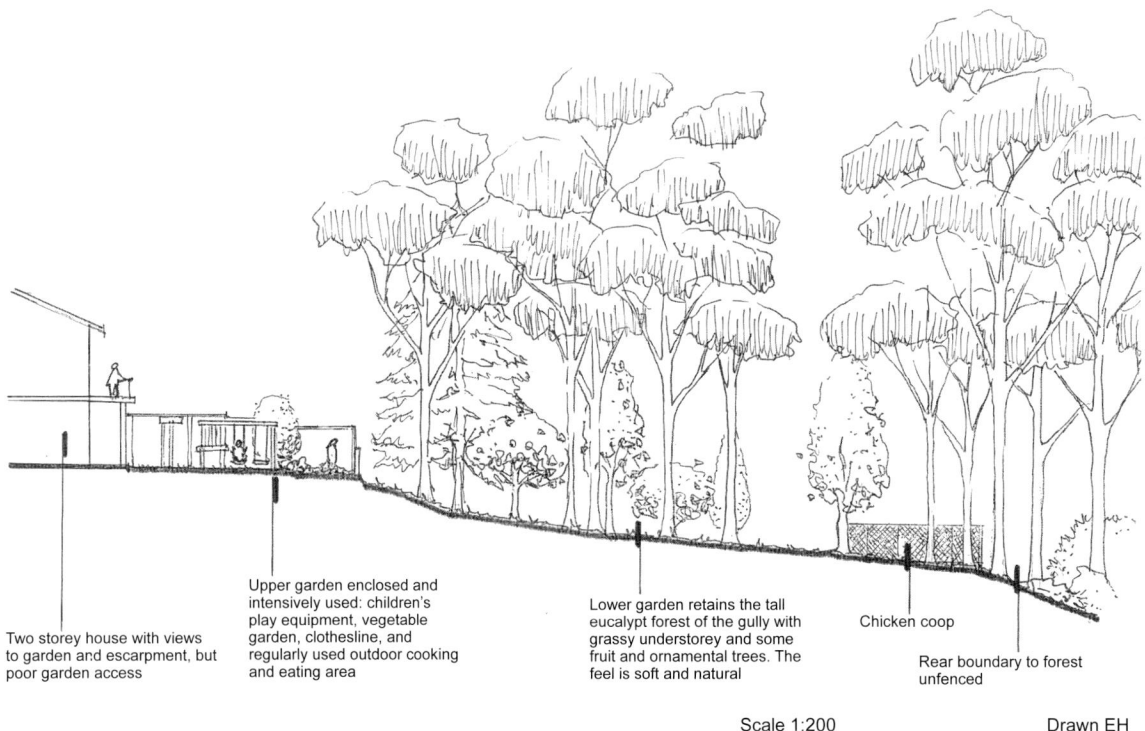

Upper garden enclosed and intensively used: children's play equipment, vegetable garden, clothesline, and regularly used outdoor cooking and eating area

Two storey house with views to garden and escarpment, but poor garden access

Lower garden retains the tall eucalypt forest of the gully with grassy understorey and some fruit and ornamental trees. The feel is soft and natural

Chicken coop

Rear boundary to forest unfenced

Scale 1:200   Drawn EH

Figure 3.4a: Cross-section of Shooshi's and Mark's backyard, outer northern suburbs, Wollongong

strong positive interactions with neighbours on that side.

Outdoor recreation/entertaining areas include covered and uncovered areas, such as decks, pergolas and verandas. Forty-seven per cent of

Feature	% of backyards
Clothesline	94
Defined recreation/entertaining area	87
Outdoor furniture	87
Barbecue	66
Outdoor dining setting	65
One or more sheds	39
Children's play equipment	29
Trampoline	26
Compost bin or heap	20
Birdbath	20
Pond	17
Swimming pool	13
Water feature (including water pots, fountains)	9
Water tank	4

Table 3.4 Common features as percentages of all backyards in the sample

areas we saw are covered and, in conjunction with the high proportion of backyards containing furniture (87%) and barbecues (66%), this indicates that eating and entertaining outdoors are a strong focus. The most common covered outdoor areas had concrete flooring (33%), then paving, indicating a relatively simple approach to outdoor eating areas. Seventy-one per cent of the barbecues are portable and the remainder built in, usually of brick, with varying degrees of technical refinement.

Clotheslines are a feature of most backyards. Fifty-three per cent have rotary hoists, such as the Hills Hoist or its more modern equivalents. Rotary hoists predominate most amongst middle and lower middle class families, and are predominant amongst couples and single participants. Retractable clotheslines account for 23%. There are still twenty-five post and line style washing lines, 11% of all clotheslines.

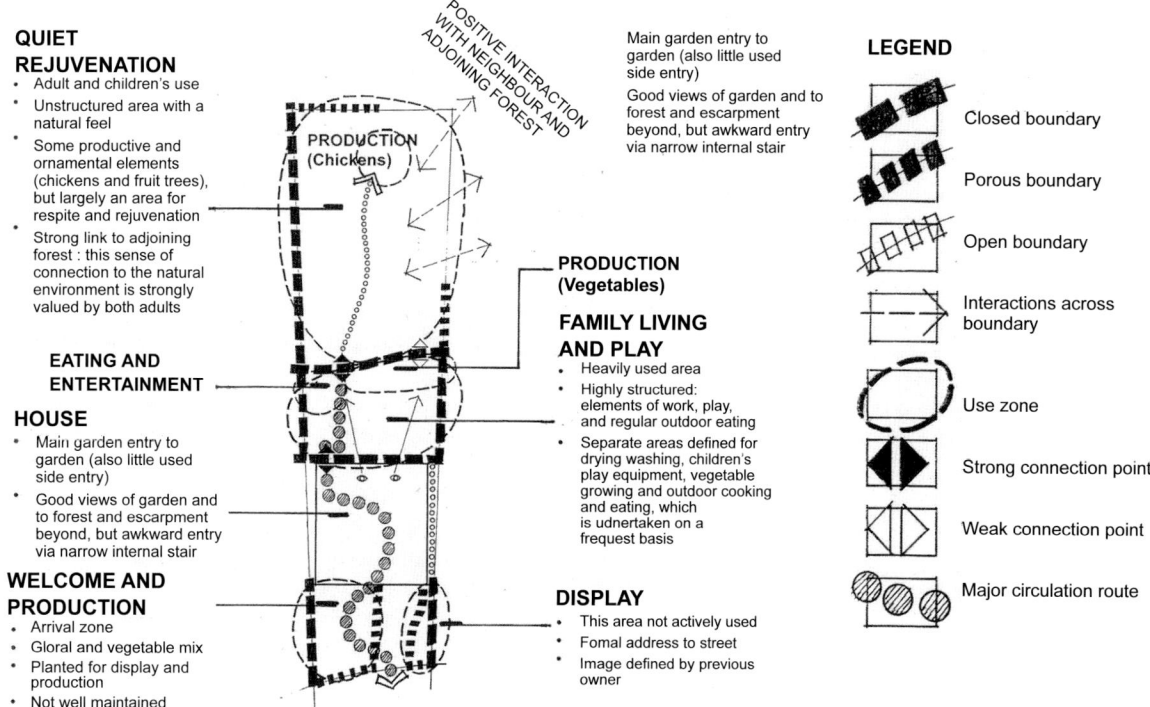

QUIET
REJUVENATION
- Adult and children's use
- Unstructured area with a natural feel
- Some productive and ornamental elements (chickens and fruit trees), but largely an area for respite and rejuvenation
- Strong link to adjoining forest : this sense of connection to the natural environment is strongly valued by both adults

PRODUCTION
(Chickens)

POSITIVE INTERACTION WITH NEIGHBOUR AND ADJOINING FOREST

EATING AND
ENTERTAINMENT

HOUSE
- Main garden entry to garden (also little used side entry)
- Good views of garden and to forest and escarpment beyond, but awkward entry via narrow internal stair

WELCOME AND
PRODUCTION
- Arrival zone
- Gloral and vegetable mix
- Planted for display and production
- Not well maintained

Main garden entry to
garden (also little used
side entry)
Good views of garden and to
forest and escarpment
beyond, but awkward entry
via narrow internal stair

PRODUCTION
(Vegetables)

FAMILY LIVING
AND PLAY
- Heavily used area
- Highly structured: elements of work, play, and regular outdoor eating
- Separate areas defined for drying washing, children's play equipment, vegetable growing and outdoor cooking and eating, which is udnertaken on a frequest basis

DISPLAY
- This area not actively used
- Fomal address to street
- Image defined by previous owner

LEGEND

Closed boundary

Porous boundary

Open boundary

Interactions across boundary

Use zone

Strong connection point

Weak connection point

Major circulation route

Figure 3.4b: Socio-spatial analysis of Shooshi's and Mark's backyard, outer northern suburbs, Wollongong

Thirty-nine per cent of the backyards have at least one shed, typically a kit construction manufactured from colourbond or zincalume (71%). Wood or hardiplank structures, improvised construction (corrugated iron, recycled materials, fibro) and brick are other materials used. Eighty-nine per cent of participants with a shed use it for storage; others are used as workshops, woodsheds or laundries, for accommodation or as studios. Families, followed by couples, are most likely to have a shed.

There is children's play equipment in 60% of the family backyards (but only 29% of the backyards overall). Families with toddlers and children younger than high school age have the highest proportion of children's play equipment. Play equipment is also present in grandparents' backyards. The five most popular items are swing sets, cubby houses, trampolines, sandpits and basketball rings, but there are variations and improvisations, particularly with regard to swing types and climbing equipment. More than half of all cubbyhouses are improvised, followed by kit style and modular plastic houses. There are also slides, plastic clam shells, pools and toddler's pools, but in small numbers.

The most common water-related feature is birdbaths (in 20% of backyards), followed by ponds and swimming pools. Almost half the ponds are home to frogs, tadpoles, turtles or fish. Only thirteen per cent have swimming pools, in-ground pools accounting for 7%, above ground pools 3% and other pools (including spas and larger inflatable style pools) 3%. (Smaller toddler pools are recorded as part of children's play equipment. Accurate figures for these latter types of pool are not feasible given the seasonal nature of their presence in the backyard.) Only 4% of the backyards have water tanks, although, like water features, they are talked about as something people would like to have. Participants frequently refer to water features as an object of desire in responses about what their ideal backyard would look like. This reflects a media trend promoting these items, and their availability and affordability in nurseries and hardware stores. Water tanks are also desired but from a socially responsible environmental

Figure 3.5, above: Outdoor
entertaining area accessed
through sliding doors,
Shell Cove, Wollongong

Figure 3.6. left: Back deck
and fibro extension on
a 1940s cottage,
inner Wollongong

perspective, reflecting rising awareness of water conservation, with water restrictions first voluntary and then mandatory during the 18 months of interviewing. As we discuss in chapter seven, these objects of desire have contrasting implications for water conservation.

Compost bins or heaps are found in 20% of the backyards. Couples are most likely to compost with 27% of all couples composting, followed by 19% of all families. Commercial plastic bins are more prevalent than heaps or improvised structures.

Space and Satisfaction

Size is the most obvious variable of backyards, and a lightning rod in current debates over urban expansion and consolidation. However, it is only one influence on people's level of satisfaction with their living spaces. Below we compare how people feel about backyard space in three contrasting areas. These case studies are examples in the trend to decreasing size.

Backyards are generally larger in older, more established suburbs than the newer housing developments of the last ten years.[5] The exception is old inner suburbs such as Erskineville and Newtown in Sydney which have small backyards. The older North Shore suburbs of Wahroonga and Turramurra in Sydney have the largest backyards in our comparison. In Sydney we found scatterings of large backyards also in the south as at Bexley, at Sans Souci in the south east and on the outskirts, in older areas of Campbelltown. Similarly, older suburbs of Wollongong such as the northern suburbs of Corrimal and Austinmer have the largest backyards. Alice Springs backyards are also large, generally over 300 m^2.[6] Houses built between the 1960s and the 1980s often have large backyards if they are located in outer suburbs such as around Fairfield in Sydney, or in what were then the fringes, such as Baulkham Hills, Campbelltown and Penrith. Backyards established in those times typically measure around 250 m^2.

The 'Leafy North Shore'

In the North Shore suburbs of Sydney, we studied eighteen backyards. Participants are most likely to cite the leafiness, tree cover and proximity to the bush as the reason for moving to these suburbs, followed by convenience either to local shopping areas or the city, with good transport infrastructure. Most backyards we visited here are bounded by other house blocks, but a few have bushland, an easement or a reserve close by. Angus is a long time resident, an enthusiast for the nature strip adjoining his garden, where he has been regenerating native vegetation. In this area he has replanted local tree species, mulched heavily, and laid a woodchip path where the footpath might otherwise be. He says that native herbs and understorey species have colonised the area spontaneously and that it 'provides a real connection to the natural environment'.

His connection to the natural environment is echoed by two others, who are both active in weed eradication in the adjoining bush. Coralie walks often in the National Park at the end of her street. She actively pulls out weeds there with her friends and she lobbies the council about adverse growth on disturbed ground in the park. Don describes his motivation to be active in the bush:

> *Just living so close and learning about the different plants that are growing around there; because I took a walk from the end of my street maybe five kilometres down into the Lane Cove River and I enjoyed it so much that I thought I'll belong to it and a leaflet was sent to me by National Parks and Wildlife . . . I sort of look after the end of my street which is part of the Thornleigh bush park area. It covers a number of streets including Pennant Hills and I do that once a month for about three hours. That involves weeding and identifying the plants and getting a lot of things done; trying to get the natives back to what it was before.*

In conjunction with an appreciation for the surrounding bushland, many express concern

Figure 3.7: Backyard in the leafy north shore suburb of Turramurra, Sydney

that urban consolidation would have a negative impact on their suburb. Two elderly male participants comment on the new developments of Kellyville and along West Pennant Hills Road, bemoaning the 'cookie cutter' nature of these suburbs. Two other men, both in their fifties, actively oppose what they perceive as the over-development of property space. Angus links this issue with an increasing pressure to remove trees and a subsequent loss of more exposed, individual trees to disease. He has been working on the committee of Friends of Kuringai Environment to draw attention to such issues. Theo is particularly scathing about the state government's actions:

Well, the state government for the last decade or so has been embarking on a policy of increasing population density within the urban areas and people don't like that so they have been forcibly doing it whether the communities like it or not. And I suppose I have an instinctive feel that increasing population density does reduce one's quality of life. I don't think that people should be divorced from nature and made to live in little boxes and be divorced from human scale and ornamentation. I think these are sort of qualities that people are attracted to naturally and I don't think it's good to deprive of these things.

Our North Shore participants are passionate advocates of the backyard. For some, this research project was an opportunity to express that, and they also belong to community groups opposing urban consolidation policies. The terrain in this part of Sydney means that patches and corridors of bushland are common throughout the area, a connection that is clearly valued.

Kellyville—a Choice for Families

Further west we looked at thirteen backyards in the Hills District. There is a contrast between the older suburbs of Baulkham Hills and Cherry-brook, and the newer subdivisions of Kellyville and Glenwood (Figure 3.8). Kellyville does not have the same green corridors and parkland as Shell Cove (discussed below), and many of the participants have a sense that the infrastructure of the suburb has lagged behind the rapid residential development. Regardless of this, many of the families with young children talk about not needing large amounts of space in the backyard when they have, or will have, access to recreational areas close by. For Joe and Kristine, parents of three children under the age of four, proximity to bushland with walking tracks was a major incentive to buy a particular block of land. Linda, mother of two young children and resident of less than a year, is hopeful for the future development of the suburb.

We read local papers and we read what's coming up and there are meant to be what they call 'open spaces'. It's not necessarily a park as what we remember as kids as parks, with swings and slippery dips and things like that, but 'open spaces' they call them. So I think they have bike tracks and things on them.

Linda's low maintenance backyard (Figure 3.8) consists of a back paved area and a side grassed area, a common arrangement of space in Kellyville, where there is often only a few metres between the back of the double storey house and the fence line. Linda explains that a small, low maintenance backyard of pavement and lawn is ideal in her view.

I don't want to be a slave to my backyard like my parents were and my husband's parents, like a couple of hours to mow some grass down the side is enough but not to spend a whole weekend doing lawns . . . I like to go on picnics and see friends and spend time, family time.

Focus on family is important for people we spoke to in the Hills district, mostly parents of primary school age and younger children. The newer suburbs of Kellyville and Glenwood, where families with young children are choosing to live,

Figure 3.9: Linda's no maintenance paved backyard with feature pot containing strelitzia, Kellyville, Sydney

are attractive in terms of their price, people and future infrastructure.

> We can't think of anywhere better as a place to raise a family in this phase of life. We've moved into an area where we've got people in exactly the same situation as us. Next door they've got two kids, we've got three; over there they've got four next to us. Across the road they've got five . . . And we are all people who are wanting to do the best that we can for our families. And that's important to us to live in a place where you can have that sense of community and the kids can play together and share each other's backyards and front yards too. (Joe)

Five of the eight new residents of Kellyville spoke about affordability and the investment value of the suburb. Brian, who recently completed his house, explains—'Well in all honesty, it's a question of finance and economics.' Mary, who had also moved into her new house in the previous year, talks about the availability of land to build a new house in this suburb.

Participants are very conscious of the rawness of Kellyville, with several people commenting on their memories of the suburb as past farming land or small acreage, and about the developer's practice of levelling the block of all vegetation. Brian talked about the family's anguish at the displacement of the local rabbits and his sense of shock at the clearing.

> When we came here we knew yes there is going to be land clearing. We know there's going to be house[s] but it is still a shock to the system. It is still a shock to the system because on this block of land next to us, rabbits run. They come from the creek and they run across.

While Brian did acknowledge the feral nature of the rabbits, he made no reference to native animals that would have suffered the same displacement. He mentioned being excited to see a butterfly recently, which he had missed with all the building process. He also has a sense of the land as a blank slate—

> I'm going to introduce worms in there. I've done that before because this is virgin land, so I'm going to bring worms in here into my garden. If I don't have worms then it's not going to work.

Another person comments about the destruction of the local native tree layer, with a sense of resignation that such practices are unfortunate but unavoidable for the end purpose of creating residential houses.

> So the original vegetation hasn't completely disappeared, it's just that we are not in the midst of it here where these houses are. They did raze the land when they were building these houses which I thought was unfortunate, but there was quite an impressive tree actually right in the middle of where our kitchen is at the moment.

Figure 3.9: Newly created backyard with feature pot, retaining walls and bark chipped garden beds, Kellyville, Sydney

Joe's and Kristine's decision to nurture the two 'weedy' angophora saplings left on the block is the only recognition of any local native vegetation in these new suburban backyards.

Anne, with a large backyard, is passionate about native trees and her backyard has extensive plantings of acacias, eucalypts, hakeas and melaleucas. Her priorities are space and privacy.

> *Space, I mean the reason we bought the house is because it's a battle axe block and we actually have a backyard, and we've got space for our vegie garden, and we've got our little pool, and we've got space for the kids to run around and have their play equipment. And we have space for some big trees. I like having the shade and the look of the larger trees . . . we needed a bit of privacy and we wanted the shade.*

If affordability is a major constraint in the choice of Kellyville, these residents nevertheless show high levels of satisfaction with that choice, provided the promised infrastructure of the suburb is delivered. Most have made a conscious choice to get more house and space for their money, trading off closeness to the city.

Shell Cove—'your home by the sea'

Shell Cove is a relatively upmarket residential subdivision reached by a single access road from a major arterial road, linking Shellharbour with Kiama south of Wollongong. Explicit boundary marking is a feature of this subdivision, with high external fencing enclosing it. This, in conjunction with the single access point, effectively segregates those who live here from surrounding developments which sprawl across the neighbouring hills. Such explicit strategies distance Shell Cove from its surroundings, creating physical seclusion and social distinction. Our seven participants here had made what are commonly called 'lifestyle' choices, moving to the area because of a desire for a smaller space, and a low maintenance, less demanding backyard. Shell Cove has views of the beach and the Illawarra escarpment, and comments about the location itself are in the foreground in these interviews to a greater extent than in the other two areas.

Advertising placards lining the main road, 'Cove Boulevard', use iconic images of young children playing by the sandy foreshore (which is some distance from Shell Cove), smiling young couples and active retirees walking. Advertising slogans such as 'your home by the sea' evoke a holiday lifestyle and, along with an avenue of Norfolk Island pines, the landscaped open space and a golf course, designate Shell Cove as an upmarket residential community. When other nearby developments in the late 1990s were reproducing a federation style of house facade, Shell Cove sought to distinguish itself with a 'seaside' style. Social distinction was created architecturally, with cash rebates for those who continued in later stages with the initial seaside theme of rendering and bagged finishes and, to a lesser extent, nautical curved roofs or gables. Homogeneity and distinction are thus often at odds in this suburb, with people wanting to increase the value of their property while maintaining conformity. One way to achieve distinction is through landscaping and gardening choices.

One of the Shell Cove residents we spoke to has a double income family with older children, and commutes daily to the southern suburbs of Sydney. For Jim, the lifestyle, natural beauty and managed outdoor space of Shell Cove are worth the daily drive.

I work in Sydney so I get a Sydney sort of wage and a South Coast lifestyle, which to me is the best of both worlds . . . and I suppose in Sydney it's a good example, it's built out, you know, there's a few little gardens and bits of grass and trees but there's nothing, whereas down here you can stand on the golf course and you look back and you can see the escarpment and it's brilliant, the space and all . . . But what I find over here is that because you are in the middle of like a big garden, there's no need to sort of create your own lawn.

For all the Shell Cove participants, having access to managed communal spaces is a major attraction, along with the beachside location. Four houses have open space across from or behind them and the other three are not far from generous green corridors, structured parks and walkways, which participants use regularly.

We use more of the natural environment, you know, using the bike, the cycle ways, . . . the beach, even simple things like sitting on the boat ramp at the beach and just putting a hand line in. (Emma, with two primary school children)

We noticed down here compared with the place where we lived in Sydney . . . they seem to have allowed much, much greater areas, like the park behind us . . . and over across the main road there, the whole centre of the estate is a big stormwater drainage system but it's done as a park as well. So it really makes the place look good. (John and Beverley, retired couple)

Evan and Sonia, a couple in their early thirties with a three month old baby, talk about what they like in Shell Cove and the sense of community they experience.

Figure 3.10: Backyards in the new subdivision Shell Cove, Wollongong

The ocean views . . . it's a young area therefore you don't get a lot of groups, clique groups, you know like if you moved into an already established area people have known each other for a long time. We've found that it's a mixture of older retired couples as well as like younger couples that are coming to the area like ourselves . . . Yeah definitely, it's very friendly, all the neighbours around seem to walk, you just start walking out the front and people just say hello and stop and talk and ask what you're doing and really take an interest. Because like I said I think everybody has got the common interest here where they're all starting from a bare piece of dirt and going for it and everybody has got their own ideas.

Most of the participants who had purchased in Shell Cove were happy with the size of their backyards, having decided to scale down and reduce the time and effort needed to maintain a larger yard. This is particularly true of participants with older children or couples whose children had left home prior to the move to the suburb. Marilyn, in her forties and a resident of less than one year, says 'the main thing, the block wasn't too big because now that we haven't got kids we don't really need a big backyard'. Norma and Eric, a retired couple, moved from their higher maintenance backyard in a neighbouring suburb so that they would 'have more time to dance and do other things'. The small backyards are compensated by the shared spaces of the subdivision, and the amenity of the surrounding environment. These are highly valued, as is the fact that maintenance is someone else's responsibility.

Courtyards and Balconies

Twenty-eight of the people we surveyed do not have backyards in the conventional sense. Four live in above ground flats or apartments with balconies and six are long term residents of a Department of Housing complex in the inner Sydney suburb of Erskineville, corralling off communal space to create their own gardens. The remaining eighteen live in detached or semi-detached houses, or villas, with small outdoor spaces, often referred to as courtyards as they are paved. Only one of this eighteen has a lawn. While most people with backyards have some lawn area and consider it an important element, particularly when they have children, people with courtyards eschew grassed areas. Primarily this is related to the difficulty of growing grass in a small enclosed space while still having room for garden beds and entertaining areas. The other major absence of this group, which could relate to the lack of lawn, is children.

These people have diverse household structures. They include empty nesters, young marrieds, singles and childless couples including four gay couples. There are three families with children still living at home who have courtyards, but the children are grown up. The emphasis for the courtyard people is on getting outside, eating and entertaining, with barbecues and gatherings mentioned far more frequently than any gardening activities except watering. But people who do not have backyards often value a visit to those who do, as Marietta—who lives in the inner suburbs but does have a backyard—reports:

> *a lot of our friends too are from Balmain and a lot of them don't have backyards or they are in units or whatever. Yeah they haven't had to travel ages to come here for lunch or whatever and it's like a different world in a sense. Last time we had a barbecue with my sister and friends of ours and they got in and started to separate the mondo grass and this kind of thing.*

Marietta's experience illustrates a strong theme running through all the smaller space participants who express a need to be outside. While some are explicit about this need, others articulate the need to get outside after a day indoors, in terms of having a refuge or retreat from the rest of the world. As one Vietnamese man puts it, 'One [reason], is for my health, because I sit here, can relax. Take a rest and considering everything in here'. For Danny in inner Sydney, outdoor space represents sanity.

> *I couldn't survive without an outdoor space. I lived in an apartment once that didn't have a balcony and I almost went mad. I lived in an apartment that had a balcony the size of this table and I was fine. Once I was able to get outside I was fine. But no balcony at all and I hated being at home. So without an outdoor space I couldn't be happy.*

The size of these courtyard spaces varies, from under twenty square metres to fifty square metres. The small courtyard size is not really an issue to this group, as it represents a trade off for the benefits of living in the inner city, such as the village atmosphere. Community feeling is strong for people living in Erskineville, a suburb only two train stops from the city centre. Erskineville is referred to as a village by several of the participants, a place where people say hello and know one another by name. At the time of interviewing, community feeling had been running high over recent State government efforts to relocate Housing Commission residents and to redevelop the Housing Commission site and the local primary school into dense residential housing. Hence the strong community articulation can be attributed to people's involvement in protest against the proposed changes. Events that threaten the 'taken for grantedness' of a suburb such as Erskineville become a focal point for people to reflect on what they value and are willing to try and protect.

The four people with balcony spaces also value their sense of space and being able to step outside.

Fig. 3.11: Ruby on the play equipment, Alice Springs

These spaces are very small, with room for a couple of chairs facing outward and a small table. Potted plants, such as bromeliads, cacti and succulents, are reasonably static. Engagement with the visual senses is strong, with descriptions of changing cloud patterns and spectacular flowerings. A sense of excitement is apparent in Mandy's and Bernadette's responses, talking about their inner Sydney balconies:

> And like that big huge bromeliad there . . . there were nineteen spikes and it was just so spectacular it was just amazing and I mean I didn't really do anything amazing to make that happen really except water it and pull the dead bits off, you know. But it sort of like threw all that out for me (laughs) and it was a really amazing show . . . But when they first come up that's really exciting going out every day and watching them get purpler and purpler, you know and then it's like they are at their peak and aren't they beautiful. So it's like a sense of reward. (Mandy)

> And this one with the leaves growing the hippeastrum . . . it comes out with this beautiful big red flower just once a year. So I took it visiting the first time it happened, I was so excited, I took it in the car. I couldn't believe it because I didn't know what was going to come out. (Bernadette, owner of a first floor unit)

These examples suggest that the intensity of engagement that people develop with a whole garden can be focused on one or two plants. People's desire for outdoor connections can be met in diverse ways. Size matters, but not in the same way to everyone.

Children and the Moral Power of the Backyard

The life cycle plays a key role in needs for different types of backyard. The strongest influence here is the widespread view that backyards are desirable for children. The purchase of many houses appears to be driven by this criterion above all others. Parents with young children cite having enough space for children to play safely as an important criterion in the initial purchase of their house.

> Yeah a little bit of it is designed, because we were very aware when we bought the place that we wanted the kids to use the backyard. And we wanted it to be a place where hopefully they would bring their friends where we could have a lot of room and be able to keep an eye on them so that they weren't wandering around the streets.
> (Julie, Hills District)

The backyard design and provision of play equipment are important, with some backyards having designated play areas with specific equipment, while others have less formalised play areas.

Space to play safely is talked about frequently in the context of very young children. Most parents with young children reiterate the theme of 'being able to get outside'. This is to engage in physical activity and imaginative play. Safety is not always mentioned as a specific concern but is implied by words such as 'watching' and 'knowing where they are'. An exception is Alan, an artist whose fascinating backyard in Alice Springs, filled with sculptures, adventurous play options and junk, would contravene many occupational health and safety guidelines.

> I'm not big on the amount of television and computer games that we seem to allow our children to watch in contemporary society. But you need strong competition to get them away from it otherwise they annoy the shit out you. So I try and provide them with activities and alternatives. I also believe in the dignity of risk for kids, and risk taking and physicality and learning your own limitations. It's a big part of my personal philosophy on rearing kids I guess.

A symbol of this tension between safety, surveillance, risk and space is the popularity of the trampoline, that allows children to extend themselves physically but within constraints. Children's engagements with other backyard activities such as harvesting produce, playing with or tending domestic animals, and observing other creatures, are mentioned less frequently. Very few parents talked specifically to us about children and nature. The moral power of the backyard lies more in its connection to open space and safe physical activity.

Imaginative play is mentioned in relation to both boys and girls. In most of these descriptions girls interact with imaginary beings, and boys re-enact particular imaginary scenarios.

> *I mean it's just a play that you can't define, I'll just call it imaginative play and it can be with anything that's available. I mean we have spare bricks left over and tiles and you'll find them building jumps for their bikes, things like that . . . But yeah, bits of wood, rope, just anything, they just make things. It just depends what the flavour of the week is . . . whether they have seen something on the TV and they'll make these sort of spy kids, where there's cubby house rope and things go up on the trees. So it's just imaginative play.*
> *(Glenys, Hills District)*

Figure 3.12: Kit style cubby house, Campbelltown, Sydney

Parents talk in quite different ways about their teenagers' use of the backyard. Teenagers tend either not to use the backyard, or to use it in ways quite different to when they were younger. So for example the trampoline becomes a place to sunbake or sleep rather than something to jump on. Indeed, several parents comment wryly that they are unsure whether their teenagers are aware there is a backyard outside. As Jacqui says, 'we joke because when she's outside we go ooohh she's seeing daylight!' Bonnie from Penrith describes a similar situation with her teenage daughter.

Jessie is a girl, she prefers girl things, she prefers being either locked in her room or glued to her TV, or if it was up to her out shopping somewhere. (Bonnie, Penrith)

Many parents with teenagers accept this shift in focus from the backyard as a place of activity to a more passive use. They talk of teenage friends coming over and using the outdoor space to gain more privacy from family, and about teenagers beginning to take responsibility for hanging out washing and lawn mowing as they get older, usually because they are made to rather than because they choose to. There is only one story of a father and son competing over who gets to mow the lawn, but several about teenagers mowing or 'grumbling their way around the mower' as one sole parent puts it.

Although many parents are happy to downsize when their children leave home, a surprising number of grandparents still structure aspects of their backyards around the needs of grandchildren. In a number of older people's backyards structural elements like swings and cubby houses are kept, or established anew, for the visits of grandchildren. Interactions with grandchildren are a valued aspect of backyard activities.

I come out with the kids, grandchildren a lot. Benjamin loves playing with the frogs and catching lizards, which I help him catch and then he lets them go, and just potterin around the yard (Joyce, Port Kembla)

The Value of Things and Things that are Valued

How important to people are structures and material objects in the backyards? We had an opportunity to explore this question further while working with the National Museum of Australia to consider the potential for museum collections and exhibitions based on our research. In May 2004 we wrote back to all our participants, asking them to list three objects that best represent their relationship to the backyard. We knew that many people would not perceive their relationship in such concrete terms, or would think their objects too ordinary to go in a museum so, as a prompt, we suggested these could be something of sentimental value, an everyday object or a structural object. Ample space was left for them to make comments and we asked if they would be interested in any of the objects becoming part of the Museum's permanent collection. Eighty-three people completed and returned the survey —31% of the original sample.

The most common responses relate not to objects but to plants, birds and animals. Results indicate that participants' relationships with their backyard are shaped primarily by the plants and trees growing in the backyard, and then by birds and animals. The most common type of response indicates that people value the shrubs and trees because of the wild birds they attract. Other responses indicate that specific plants and trees are valued for the memories attached to people, places and achievements.

People express pleasure not in a relationship to any kind of object but rather in connection with their sense of wellbeing. One quarter of them wrote about something that could not be represented by an object. They wrote about the experience of having a backyard, such as watching things grow, sitting in the sun or enjoying the peace and tranquility. Others were anxious to clarify that their relationship with their backyard is not fully or even well expressed through lists of objects per se, but through observation and engagement with living things.

There are no specific objects that typify our relationship with our backyard. Our relationship is represented by greenery, a relaxing and tranquil setting together with outdoor living in our fly screened enclosed patio. (List section left empty)

I don't really have any OBJECTS that I care about. It's the birds I am most endeared to. Perhaps then the bird feeder and bird bath would come into it, but they are not the things I care for. The bird feeder and bird bath are so 'amateur' no one would be interested in them—except the birds!

For me, my backyard is about the wildlife— both birds and mammals/reptiles that visit it and the plants and vegetables I grow in it. A portable BBQ and table and chairs are the only objects that enhance my own enjoyment of it plus the odd bird ornament—not really museum items!

Well, I could get you a chair just like it—it's pretty generic. I could collect more shells etc for you. If your exhibition has an audio/visual element I could capture the changing sky, the moon, city etc on video; the thrilling sound of a passing bat's wings.

These engagements, and the living parts of the backyard, are considered in the following chapters.

Marketing the Backyard

While we were doing our research there was a very high level of marketing and media activity related to the home and garden. Television programs such as *Burke's Backyard*, *Gardening Australia*, *Ground Force*, *Backyard Blitz* and *Better Homes and Gardens* all rated strongly at various times, and a number of these have associated magazines. The garden market is estimated to have been worth $5.71 billion for the year ended 30 June 2003, and the industry sees the lifestyle media as the driving force in trends such as garden makeovers.[7] While we were doing our fieldwork, Laurel Waddell analysed four magazines, to examine some of the messages about nature being portrayed in the media (Appendix 2.8). *Better Homes and Gardens* and *House and Garden* examine gardens as an adjunct to the home, whereas *Burke's Backyard* and *Gardening Australia* focus on outdoor spaces. An interesting trend in *Burke's Backyard* is increasing attention to the house, and related issues such as cooking. This exemplifies the blurring of the boundaries between outside and inside, and absorption of the backyard into the stylistic and lifestyle issues of the domestic setting as a whole. Laurel examined the twelve monthly issues of each of the four magazines covering July 2002 to June 2003. She categorised 547 feature articles on gardens and backyards according to subject matter, and analysed selected themes textually and visually in more detail. Advertisements were also analysed.

We are not suggesting that our participants are passive victims of such marketing. It is part of the contextual mix in which decisions are made. When asked about influences on their decisions in the backyard (but not asked directly about specific programs or publications), 31% of our sample mention television programs, and 19% magazines and books. Other important influences are nurseries (26%), close contacts (20%) and cuttings or seeds provided by friends, relatives or neighbours (18%) (participants could name more than one influence). It is interesting that the influence of the media is not necessarily a positive one. Several people comment, for example, that the last thing they would want is a backyard makeover in the mode of *Backyard Blitz*. It is noted as a direct contradiction to their idea that the backyard evolves over time.

Before

Before. More like natural bushland than a backyard. And with a rock wall that presented a number of design challenges.

Right. Instead of hiding it, the rock wall was turned into a garden feature. Now it's the prefect backdrop for a gentle waterfall.

Below. Water is an important element in a resort-style garden. The gentle sound of trickling water soothes the soul.

Figure 3.13: Water feature
(Source: Better Homes and Gardens, April 2004: page 100)

Gardens of stone

Choosing pebbles

■ When choosing pebbles for a garden like this, make sure they're no bigger than 20mm, otherwise they're too difficult to walk on. You'll also need a depth of about 50-60mm to create an attractive effect.

■ You can buy pebbles in bags from landscape suppliers and large nurseries. Take along the dimensions of the garden area and ask for advice on what quantities you'll need as this varies according to the size of the pebbles themselves.

These pebbles are from the Eco Concepts range. See Shopping Information page for details.

Billabong

Pilbara

Ebony

Bracken

Himalaya

Carpet your garden with the natural tones and textures of pebbles

Figure 3.14: Decorative pebbles
(Source: Better Homes and Gardens, June 2002: page 23)

Constructing and Consuming Nature

All the magazines and television programs are in the business of encouraging their audience to do things in their backyards and gardens, to undertake transformative activities by expending time and money. The picture of nature thus presented is one constructed at least partially by human activity.

> The aim of every gardener is to take hold of Nature . . . and then improve on her efforts just a little. (*Better Homes and Gardens*, April 2003: 94)

The categories 'model gardens', 'designer/ style' and 'landscaping' (together 18% of all articles) position the backyard as a blank slate on which nature can be improved and shaped. Manipulation of nature can be through specific plant assemblages, where plants create 'magic', or through the makeover of the space: 'Transform your garden in a single day' (*Better Homes and Gardens*, September 2002: 36–37).

Planting and design in these categories frequently draw on the concept of the exotic, in the senses both of being drawn from outside Australia, and being romantic and exciting. This is seen in titles such as 'Moroccan mood', 'Bali comes to the city', 'Asian fusion' and 'Viva Italiano'. The 'model gardens' category included articles that display immaculate and complete backyards, which are posed as completely achievable by the average backyard owner.

> The serene air of an Asian temple is captured in a compact Brisbane garden. *Created* to embrace a fusion of design, this is a space to delight all the senses. [emphasis added] (*House and Garden*, October 2002: 248)

Almost without exception, these created and designed spaces include a water feature, often with reference to the sensual and relaxing qualities of water, but rarely with reference to the supply of water. Creation of this ideal environment usually requires considerable consumption of materials

Figure 3.15: Garden rooms
(Source: House and Garden, *December 2002: page 175)*

from outside the backyard, for example pebbles, timber, sand, steel, paving and bricks as well as plants and water. Although such materials are often visually presented in a way that draws on their 'natural look' (Figure 3.14), their sourcing and the sustainability of that source are rarely discussed in terms other than price and ease of availability. An article on pebbles claims:

> They come in all sorts of colours and grades, are relatively cheap and, perhaps best of all, they're easy and quick to lay. (*Better Homes and Gardens* Christmas 2002: 154)

The emphasis on transformation and speed, combined with the need of the media to sell things, has normalised excessive use of materials to create instant landscaped backyards. Where the reuse of old materials is highlighted, it is often as a quirky craft idea, for example painting of old watering cans.

It goes without saying that the advertising content of the magazines exacerbates the consumptive drive, as that is the raison d'etre of the advertisements and, less directly, of the magazines themselves. Advertisements in the three magazines other than *Gardening Australia* overwhelmingly target women, indicating a predominantly female readership. Beauty products, homewares, food, cleaning products and family care, all dominated by highly gendered imagery, accounted for 64% of advertisements. Those that could be directed at men and women constituted 31% and only a small proportion was targetted directly at men.

Where nature is allowed inside the house it is a highly controlled nature, representing peace and serenity. Thus for example, the reader is exhorted to 'coax the sights and sounds of the outdoors into your slumber zone' (*House and Garden*, New Year 2003: 160). And an advertisement for an airconditioner encourages the family to 'stay inside and get some fresh air'.

Keeping the World at Bay

If the dominant message is about the creative power of the backyarder inside the fence, the emphasis on the backyard as a haven and place of private retreat often comes with a sense of disconnecting from the outside world, and engaging with a small patch of relaxing nature. The magazines both reflect and reinforce the trend for the backyard to be considered as an important leisure space, and as a site of transition between indoor and outdoor spaces. It is both private, in the sense of being enclosed from neighbours, and public, a space of display for the entertainment of friends and family.

These trends are illustrated in the themes of 'creating a sanctuary' and 'outdoor rooms'. Outdoor rooms are a physical manifestation of taking the indoors out, a complement to the housing theme of bringing the outdoors in, discussed in chapter two. The two themes together comprised a small proportion (4%) of total magazine gardening articles, but higher proportions in the two most popular magazines, those with a combined home and garden focus (17% in *House and Garden*, 9% in *Better Homes and Gardens*). The garden is presented as an extension of the living area:

> With plants for walls, grass for carpet, and the sky as your ceiling, almost any green space can make you feel at home (*House and Garden*, Christmas 2002: 175)

Privacy is significant in the creation of outdoor living space, with the magazines emphasising the value of the backyard as a retreat, away from distractions and possible work inside the home, and the world outside backyard borders. This is connected to the idea of a 'low-maintenance backyard'. These spaces are not ones where you work, but rather 'outdoor retreats where you can simply take some time out to relax' (*Better Homes and Gardens*, November 2002: 51). Associated visual imagery is of seats, day beds, glasses of wine, pots of coffee and water features, hiding the labour and materials that must go into the production of any of these. This view of the backyard chimes with the experience of those who talk of the project engagement (elaborated in chapter five), and the hope of seeing things 'finished'. It is at odds with the greater number who describe enjoyment in the rhythms of labour and engagement, and are reluctant to name material structures as the most valued aspects of the backyard.

The text and imagery of retreat, leisure and relaxation are often quite sensual, but with a strong bias towards the visual rather than other senses. Display is important for both the backyard owner and guests to enjoy, as exemplified in the current trend towards 'impact plants'. Colour is also associated with style, and may be as carefully crafted in the backyard context as in the choice of interior paint colours: 'Shades of Blue: Create a Winning Display with Cool Blues in All their Varieties' (*Better Homes and Gardens* February 2003: 50-55).

Ten per cent of the articles relate to the production of food, indicating that this activity is considered important to a significant minority of the readers. This theme is strongly concentrated in the two gardening magazines, *Burke's Backyard* and *Gardening Australia*, comprising together 80% of food production articles in the four magazines.

Sustainability

Of all the magazine articles, 9% relate explicitly to environmental issues and sustainability, with over half of these coming from *Gardening Australia*, and nearly a third from *Burke's Backyard*. Overt environmental messages are strong in both publications. Ideas canvassed include reduction of water, chemical and energy use, reuse of material (cardboard, fabric, food scraps) and control of weeds.

Many of these articles included statements suggesting that backyard owners do not have to compromise their garden space or comfort to be environmentally friendly.

> The words 'environmentally friendly' may conjure up thoughts of a shack in the back of beyond and mung beans for dinner, but, Clare Caldwell says, you can be urbane and an 'eco-warrior' too. (*House and Garden*, April 2003: 153)

This statement reassures the readers that their quality of life need not be interrupted, that habits and practices need barely change, for environmentally good outcomes to occur. It is a light green message for readers who would not think of themselves as 'greenies'. In contrast, *Gardening Australia* is more inclined to position environmentally aware practices as 'normal' for its readership. The presenter of the 'Gardening Australia' TV program, Peter Cundall, is well known for his passion for compost, and has recently adopted a more activist environmental position outside the TV series.

Multiple Messages and How they are Received

A striking but easily overlooked point is that a single issue of any magazine contains a diversity of articles presenting different messages. For example an article on water saving might be juxtaposed with one on how to have a perfect lawn. A feature on native plants might precede a profile of a garden dominated by twenty varieties of rose. Central to the attractiveness of each magazine is having in each issue 'something for everyone' within the target readership. In this respect the nature presented in all these magazines is very much hybrid; shifting, multiple and constantly reworked.

In the next chapter we go on to look more closely at these multiple engagements with plants.

CHAPTER FOUR

Gardens
and Gardeners

Committed native gardeners are a small group with strong attitudes, focused on locally indigenous plants. *General native gardeners* plant natives as well as exotics, for such pragmatic reasons as attracting birds and saving water. *Non-native gardeners*, the numerically largest group, either dislike natives for their 'straggliness', or love exotic flowers. *Non-gardeners* may be just as interested in their backyards for other purposes such as family and entertaining space. The market classes gardeners in different ways according to their purchasing behaviour. Lawn arouses great passions.

This chapter focuses on backyards as gardens: on people's intentional relationships with plants and soil. Not all backyards are gardens, but even non-gardeners have many living things in their backyards. The relationship between the gardener and the garden is not one way, and the gardener is not the one with all the power. Even in the most planned and controlled garden, birds, insects, plants and the thousands of unnoticed inhabitants of the soil interact in ways that have little to do with the intention of the gardener. Sometimes gardeners fight this process, as when plants are designated as weeds, or insects as pests, but at other times they are happy to observe and 'let nature do its own thing' (Figure 4.1).

In the diagram, the vertical axis indicates the dominant plantings in backyard gardens from predominantly native to predominantly exotic.

The horizontal axis represents a continuum from non-gardeners to passionate gardeners. The gardeners of each quadrant have a set of moral positions which define their gardening identity, summarised in the labels. Those people plotted at the tips of the diagram articulate the strongest moral positions on different topics.

Overall our research bears out studies which show that the most popular types of garden include exotic plant species, alone or in combination with natives (NPWS 2002; Zagorski et al. 2004, Trigger and Mulcock 2005). It is an attitude also evident in the gardening magazines.

Gardener Groupings

The people we spoke to fell into four groups, based mainly on the attitudes they express, and supported by evidence of what they plant. They are not intended as fixed categories though; indeed

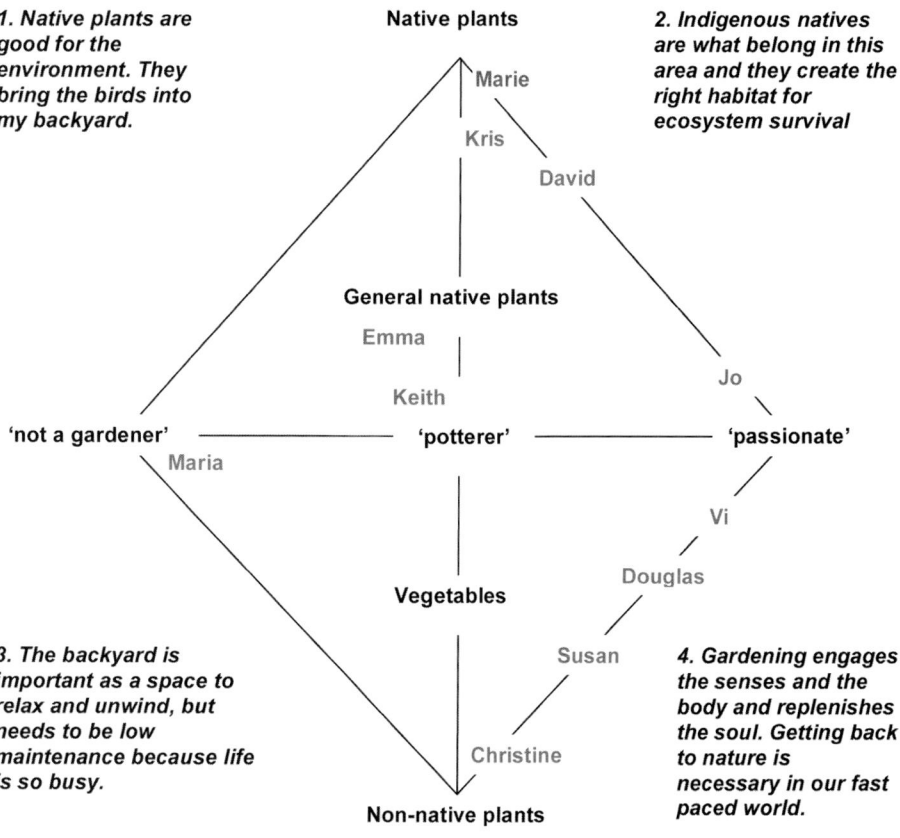

1. Native plants are good for the environment. They bring the birds into my backyard.

2. Indigenous natives are what belong in this area and they create the right habitat for ecosystem survival

Native plants

Marie

Kris

David

General native plants

Emma

Keith

Jo

'not a gardener' ——— 'potterer' ——— 'passionate'

Maria

Vi

Douglas

Vegetables

Susan

Christine

Non-native plants

3. The backyard is important as a space to relax and unwind, but needs to be low maintenance because life is so busy.

4. Gardening engages the senses and the body and replenishes the soul. Getting back to nature is necessary in our fast paced world.

Figure 4.1: Gardener types along axes of nativeness and gardening passion

Figure 4.2: Backyard with predominantly local native plants in an inner suburb

the ambiguities, contradictions and anxieties within and between groups are quite interesting. There are broad consistencies between what they say and what they do, but also incongruities.

One woman talked to us particularly about the 'healing' space of her garden, but her backyard was mostly concrete, with few plants in the vegetable garden and garden beds, and many weeds.

You might expect that members of a garden club would strongly identify as gardeners, and have spectacular gardens.

While this is certainly true for some, others simply enjoy the social interaction of the club and while happy to swap the odd cutting, are no more passionate about gardening than many non-members.

Figure 4.3: Native garden with native tree layer and a mixed herb layer

	Committed native gardeners	**General native gardeners**	**Non-native gardeners**
	34 gardeners	62 gardeners	136 gardeners
	13 %	23 %	55 %
Most frequent proportion of natives in backyard shrub and tree layer	81-100%	41-60%	Less than 20%
Planting preference	Local natives	General natives, e.g. hybrid cultivars like Grevillea	Non-native
Three main reasons for planting or not planting native*	1 Belonging 2 Aesthetics 3 Time	1 Aesthetics 2 Birds 3 Climate	1 Aesthetics 2 Birds 3 (equal) Climate and Time
Most common type of boundaries to adjacent bushland[+]	Unfenced or fence and gate	Unfenced or fence and gate	Fenced with or without gate
Dominant approach to relationship between backyard and adjacent bushland[+]	Bringing nature into backyard	Separation of domestic and natural spaces	Extension of domestic space

12 % of participants, not shown, were non-gardeners

*Based on a sample group   [+]For 38 gardeners (14%) with a bushland boundary.

Table 4.1 Attitude and practice of gardener groupings

Committed Native Gardeners—the Purists

We designated thirty-four of our participants as committed native gardeners (CNGs). As 13% of our sample they are over-represented relative to their presence in the general population, because they are one of several special interest groups we targeted. Fifty-three per cent of CNGs have 80% or more of their shrub and tree layer under native plants, which are also likely to include a higher proportion of plants indigenous to the local area (Figure 4.2). This group is also more likely to have natives in the herb layer, indicating their preference for planting deliberately rather than retaining the plants of previous owners. While the other groupings of gardeners are socio-economically diverse, the CNGs are collectively higher in education and skills, if not affluence (Table 4.2). They are usually ecologically well informed and a number work as environmental professionals or are involved in voluntary activities such as bushcare groups.

Education/skill levels	CNG	GNG	NNG	NG
High	88	68	51	52
Low	12	32	49	48

Table 4.2 Gardener groupings by education/skill levels, as percentage of each group. (High education/skills = post-secondary qualification)

The CNGs are almost by definition to be found close to the tip of Figure 1, where they are exemplified by Kris, whom we met at the beginning of the book, and Marie, because of their strongly expressed attitudes and practices. These people are not accidental gardeners. They are more likely to propagate their own plants from local seed, seek out specialist suppliers and facilitate the process of self seeding of local plants. They tend to express disparaging attitudes towards 'exotic' or 'foreign' plants, and the neighbours who enjoy them. This is reinforced when we compare participants'

reasons for planting or choosing not to plant natives (Table 4.1). For them, the importance of natives as 'belonging' is paramount.

For some in this group the notion of gardening, with its connotations of planting and humanly assisted productivity, is inaccurate. Rather they see themselves as restorers of native bushland, or eradicators of weeds that prevent native bushland restoring itself. Brendan and Claire of Alice Springs are a good example. Asked whether they think of their space (which is actually a number of courtyards and small areas around a split level house) as a garden, Brendan replies,

> Only in the context of being able to talk to somebody about it and having something that they can relate to. I mean we just see it as an extension of the bush and our house sits in that.

Claire has been on a mission for many years to remove the introduced buffel grass from their block.

> My object is to eradicate all the buffel[8] and noxious grasses out and let the natural regrowth occur and it's just, it's my art; we have a sense that if I can achieve that to a high degree that that's my art within the community.

Soon after rain is an important time for the removal of buffel, when it rapidly responds by creating a green sward across the landscape. Claire describes the practice of her art in very embodied terms. She tells of regularly starting at 4.30 or 5.00 on summer mornings and removing buffel for three hours before the business of the day begins, coming inside drenched in sweat and satisfied with her exertions. This physical, almost sensual, engagement and investment of labour is similar to those described below by passionate gardeners who are planting things, and lawn mowers who are removing things.

Narratives of redemption are expressed frequently by CNGs, who often describe themselves as purists, or sometimes as 'indigenous fascists'. Jennifer, for example, from the northern suburbs of Wollongong contrasts the purity of nature with the impurities of culture.

> *I love the Australian bush. I've been a bush walker all my life. I like walking in it and although I have grave doubts about Australian society, the bush itself to me is pure.*

For Marie, also from the northern suburbs, a purist approach has developed as she gradually became more familiar with the environment she was living in and the bush adjacent to her backyard.

> *Yes, I've decided to become really pure. I wasn't quite so purist at the beginning and I'd be tempted to have a little exotic here and there but as time has gone on, I have really appreciated how the native garden looks and how I feel about it, I've decided that I'm going to be purist and if anything foreign comes up, I'll take it.*

In calling this group 'purists' we are referring to their own identity and aspirations. In fact their backyards are as hybrid as any others. It is interesting that their dogs, cats, vegetables, houses and human selves are exempt from their ideal.

As might be expected, CNGs who live next to bushland are more likely to have unfenced or physically or visually permeable boundaries, and to discuss their planting strategies in terms of bringing nature in to the domestic environment (Table 4.1). Kris advocates 'a merging of the Australian natural environment and our living environment rather than being this discrete thing'. Indeed CNGs form a higher proportion of the edge sub-sample (21%) than they do in our total sample (13%), and often talk about 'connection' to the bush as the reason they bought their properties.

General Native Gardeners— the Pragmatists

We have named those who choose to plant both natives and exotics 'general native gardeners' (GNGs). We studied sixty-two of them—23% of the total sample. For this group 'native plants' are usually eucalypt and/or hybrid cultivars such as Grevillea, Callistemon and Banksia. The most common proportion of natives in their tree and shrub layers was 41%–60%. Their main reasons for planting natives relate to aesthetics, attracting birds and suitability for Australia's dry climate.

> *And the reason why we've got natives on the front and the back of the house or on the land is because we love caravanning and we love the birds as you can see over here and we've put them in because they're maintenance free sort of thing, they look after themselves.*
> *(Keith, northern suburbs, Wollongong)*

> *I wanted all natives out the front. For a start they will virtually look after themselves and I very very rarely water them . . . I might change all this and I might end up with all natives there because I've started to find this gorgeous little honey eater that's coming in . . .*
> *(Margaret, Forest Grove)*

> *I can stand in my kitchen there and . . . the honey eaters and the silver eyes . . . it's just so beautiful to be able to stand there and watch the birds and hear the birds . . .*
> *(Irene, Port Kembla)*

> *I suppose we try to have an impact on that [the environment] by planting a lot of native plants around our backyard; a lot of the plants over there are natives, and try to encourage the native animals to the backyard.*
> *(Emma, West Wollongong)*

Keith and Emma typify the GNGs, with their position closer to the centre of the diamond on the diagram. It indicates a pragmatic approach

Figure 4.4: Janine on the creek boundary of her property, outer northern suburbs, Wollongong

Figure 4.5: Chris's daughter on the trampoline with open fencing and pond behind, Alice Springs

in the choices they make, compared to the moral passion of the CNGs. However, many people in this group change their attitudes over time as a result of their engagement with and observation of birds. Many GNGs also appreciate the spectacle and showiness of grevilleas, callistemons and other flowering natives. Generally the GNGs love flowering shrubs and trees, even if they are not natives. The most popular non-native shrubs for them are hibiscus and camellia bushes, and jacarandas at the tree layer.

GNGs tend towards a more emphatic separation of what they see as domestic and natural spaces, and they sometimes employ complex boundary makings even when involved in restoration activities in the bush adjacent to their backyards. For example, Janine has a fence which separates the more domestic part of her backyard from the bush. On the inside are grass, vegetables, garden beds and homes for her extensive menagerie of pets. On the 'outside' of the fence, but still on Janine's land, is an area that she is regenerating, extending down to the creek.

> *The inside of the backyard I've got a mixture . . . but on the other side of the fence everything that I plant out there is like local and what belongs there. There's actually three old camellia trees out there that are quite big which I'm going to have to cut down because they just don't belong there. (Figure 4.4)*

Janine would have no qualms about leaving the exotic camellias if they were a few metres away, inside the fence.

Chris, who lives on the outskirts of Alice Springs, has an extremely manicured backyard including lawn and rose beds, as well as native beds, bordered by an open mesh fence that backs on to bushland extending up to the range behind the line of houses (Figure 4.5). Although there is a striking contrast between inside and outside, Chris sees it as more of a continuum, enhanced by the fact that she can see through the fence: 'we like to think of our backyard as being an extended

Figure 4.6: Non-native garden with emphasis on floral display

backyard in that it goes into the bushland and up to the range'. The fence marks the legal boundary, and is there to keep the kids and dog in and larger bush animals out, but is transgressed when for example bearded dragons come in through the fence and are attacked by the dog. A pond that they maintain outside the fence provides water for kangaroos and euros[9] that the family enjoys catching glimpses of. Like Janine, Chris is active in weed removal beyond the fence, seeing different types of nature as belonging in different places.

Non-Native Gardeners—Earth People, Flower Lovers and Native Haters

Non-native gardeners (NNGs) choose not to plant natives but may have inherited some when they moved to their current address. They were 51% of our sample. The group of 136 participants is understandably diverse, and it is in some ways misleading to define it in terms of something it is not.

Nevertheless, just as you do not have a totally native garden by accident, nor do you have a totally exotic one. Some are adamantly anti-native. Others are better characterised as passionate about other plants, such as exotic flowers or vegetables (Figure 4.6).

Camellias are by far the most popular choice of shrub for NNGs, with around a third of NNG backyards containing camellia bushes. Hibiscus bushes are also popular, as well as mature rose bushes. For NNGs, in fact for all types of gardeners except CNGs, Orange jessamine (*Murraya paniculata*), a fashionable landscaping plant over the last decade, is a popular choice.

Some NNGs actively dislike native plants, often seeing them as 'straggly' or 'scraggy'. Others distinguish between what is desirable in their backyards and out in the bush. Alison apologises for her dislike of natives, saying, 'bush to me should be bush and . . . you know, if you want to plant a hibiscus, put it in your backyard.'

> *I love going out in the bush, and going and looking at wildflowers and things like that. But I just felt what I wanted out here was a nice, very flower garden, more like your cottage type garden and the natives just didn't do that for me. (Monica, inner Sydney)*

> *There's a lot of native plants I don't like . . . I don't find them attractive and I didn't like them when we grew them on our farm. My husband liked them . . . and I probably always liked exotics. But I also loved the bush; I love the bush and I've spent time in the bush, you know and I could spend a week walking in the bush. So it's not because I don't love the bush. (Christine, inner Sydney)*

Alison's apology, and comments such as 'I don't like natives; probably that's a sin to say that but that's just how I feel personally' (Beverley, Forest Grove), alert us to the moral terrain of nativeness. Guilt is experienced by NNGs such as Beverley, and Susan of inner Sydney, who says, 'It's probably the worst thing I could say is, I'm not a big fan of natives.'

NNGs who have a boundary with bushland tend

Figure 4.7: Honey production is the focus for this non-gardener. Sheets of tin are laid on the grass to cut down on mowing

to extend the domestic space outside, like Lennie at the beginning of the book, and a couple who have an open boundary with a national park (Figure 4.9):

> **Wife: There was no point getting all complicated with the garden . . . The focus is out there anyway.**
>
> **Husband: That's part of our garden.**
>
> **Wife: Yes, that's the way we treat it yes. he's been pruning the natives out there and they do come good. They've got the straggly.**

Figure 4.8: Backyard on the edge of a national park, North Shore, Sydney

Non-gardeners—Indoor People, Entertainers and Stylists

We classed thirty-three participants (12%) as non-gardeners, including those who describe themselves that way, and those who are not involved in gardening. While some lack strong feelings, positive or negative, about garden space, others can be passionate about other dimensions of the backyard. Maria, Alexandra and Linda exemplify this group. Family is the issue for many, and the moral space of growing happy children. This group includes people we describe in the next chapter as 'stylists', who emphasise the visual design aspects of the backyard, often in association with its use as an entertaining space. A lot fewer of them have trees in their backyards than among the other groups (24% constrasted with over 60%).

> Well, we have just finished our garden and I'm finally feeling more relaxed and we're both more excited. It's just taken us so long to get to this point and now we're excited actually. We feel things are getting done and that finally the kids can go out and play. We're at a good point. And we can't wait to use it. Like we're going to get a table and use that whole space. We just need a table . . . We've got cushions for all those chairs, and a barbecue and we're set. We're going to do a pergola too. But slowly. We also want to do, for Christmas, we'll probably get a swing set for the boys. We haven't decided. We think probably down here, and a cubby house. *(Maria, Hills District, Sydney)*

> But it's a pretty bomb proof garden and I must say my parents were never gardeners, they were never cultivating the garden, they just dealt with it. But I mean it's nice to look at but I didn't actually do anything towards this

garden per se; I did not envisage how it would look, it's pretty much as it has been since we got here . . . But I suppose my passion is not gardening per se . . . I like painting (Alexandra, Eastern Suburbs, Sydney)

I've got my mondo grass that I don't have to do anything with, my frangipani which I just love frangipanis and my bird of paradise. And they look attractive but I don't have to do anything to them. (Linda, Hills District)

Yeah we just try to make it look green and nice. I would have liked heaps more but I'm not very good with plants and they kind of die on me. (Marilyn, Alice Springs)

The Gardening Passion

When asked about backyard activities, people talk frequently about gardening. This is not surprising. The 1999, 'National Physical Activity Survey' found that gardening and yard work are reported to be the second most popular physical activity, after walking, among Australian adults (Armstrong, Bauman and Davies 2000).

Gardening can encompass many different things when people talk about it. Most of our participants engage regularly in at least one gardening related activity, frequently associated with maintenance such as weeding or pruning. This is not remarkable in itself, given that backyards and gardens need at least some level of maintenance. However, people who get a high level of enjoyment from these tasks far outnumber those who consider such activities a chore. The passion they share for gardening, though it varies from one person to the next, is generally very welcoming to plants. For some this includes natives, while others actively dislike them. Thus the term passionate gardeners encompasses both GNGs such as Jo and NNGs such as Vi. The gardening passion differs from the distinctive passion of CNGs, derived more from a moral position. Although CNGs spend a lot of time

'in the garden', and are active in planting and weeding, they do not tend to talk about themselves as gardeners.

The need to garden, whether for production of food or more generally, is related by a number of people to the earth itself. The physicality of soil is connected with the physicality of work. The integration of labour and restoration of the soul are felt to be so fundamental to life itself that one elderly woman declared 'I belong to the universe when I am out in the garden'. The quotes below are from people of a range of ages. They show among other things the very physical nature of the connections, particularly between person and soil, or as they would mostly have it, 'the earth'.

I was very, very tiny about four, five years of age when I first picked up a shovel and a hoe. I've never put them down since. It's in my blood . . . It's never been work, never. I've always considered that the earth heals. If you handle soil, handle the earth, it heals. You don't get things the matter with you, you can come out into the yard feeling depressed, down in the dumps, the whole world is on your shoulders. You work with the soil for half an hour and your whole attitude changes. (Vi, northern suburbs, Wollongong)

I always had a garden. You see I have to get earth under my nails (laughs); it's always been like that. (Kirsten, North Shore, Sydney)

So I dug the garden, I brought the manure and new soil to enrich it and I worked it over. I turned over the soil and the manure to make it more richer and then when I planted the chillies. Oh the chillies—you should have seen back then—were nice and big. (George, Port Kembla)

I think there's something about the earth than just the feel of it and—I mean I've got nails at the moment because I'm not digging around in the dirt—but I don't know, I just get a really good sense about our country and just our environment and how we need to look after it from being involved in my own backyard. (Barbara, Port Kembla)

For me it's a bit of sanity, a day in the garden or sometimes if I just get my fingers in the garden. I absolutely love the compost, I love turning and I love the worms . . . I'll go shopping with the little ones and then realise we've got dirt all over us and oh they were my best jeans but I just happened to pass the garden on the way . . . and see that something needs pulling out. (Shooshi, northern suburbs, Wollongong)

For other people this engagement was time out from busy lives, as shift worker Leanne, from Albion Park, explains:

So planting trees, being with nature, getting totally away from the things I do at work, my yard is almost the opposite of that, it's being with plants, pottering around, not having to think intellectually, to be able to just relax and dig dirt, get my hands dirty, dig dirt, water it and just fiddle around with some sort of project.

Amber, a young retail manager from inner Sydney, talks about being able to 'pull everything back to now and this moment'. She goes on to say:

So yeah being in the garden and the physical work is great because it just gives you a release [from] having to think sometimes. You can just switch off and just do.

I sometimes think weeding and tidying up is work. But once I get into it I really like it. I like puddling around in the dirt. (Margaret, Campbelltown)

I love pruning and it's always dangerous because I keep going just for the pleasure of it. I don't do it enough but there is something nice about the actual tangible. I mean so much of our work and work lives are slightly intangible things that you do. So it's nice to go and get your fingernails dirty and watch things grow. (Catherine, Eastern Suburbs, Sydney)

We both work with people all week and for one of my jobs I don't see concrete results . . . This is concrete. Gardening, you can actually see results within days or within hours even. You can have a good day kind of gardening. (Lis, northern suburbs, Wollongong)

For these people, having a garden is about engaging with it closely—with the earth, with growth and change. It is also about a different experience of time to the one that dominates their daily lives and that they often equate with stress. In the garden, by contrast, people describe either a loss of a sense of time, or the therapeutic role of 'pulling everything back to now', to use Amber's words. This pulling is not achieved by doing nothing, but by the sorts of rhythmic activities they described. In this emphasis on processes, change is inherent. For gardeners, Maria's notion that the garden could ever be 'finished' would be incomprehensible.

Figure 4.9: Rebecca hanging washing in her unfinished backyard, Albion Park, Wollongong

I think a backyard has got to be changing; you can't have it static. As a gardener, if you had it static it would become boring. Well I think the thing about a garden is that it should change. So I think there will always be some little changes made to it, but I just think that's part and parcel of enjoying a backyard.
(Jo, northern suburbs, Wollongong)

A garden should be productive; it should be something you can constantly go to and work on. Gardens are never finished I don't think. They are kind of like art, like a lot of people describe paintings as they are never finished. You can look at them twenty years later and still want to do something to them. So a garden is a constant work in progress. (Amber, inner Sydney)

Well for me, it's kind of a work in progress and things will gradually change. (Shooshi, northern suburbs, Wollongong)

While the notion of 'pottering' and the relaxation and aimlessness it implies are important for many gardeners, there are some who think of a moral purity associated with gardening. For them, engaging with plants and soil is contrasted with the impurity of the city or the human race, in a way that invokes the yeoman ideology discussed in chapter two. This is usually implied, but sometimes overt.

You know the city, like Newtown is busy, busy, busy, you know it's busy and noisy, you know, it's like concrete sort of and it has lots of character and all that sort of stuff but [the balcony] it's like a little haven, you know, that's what I try to create and the plants give a sense of, you can have that quiet pottering around and something is growing . . . and flowering and doing things. (Mandy, inner Sydney)

So wherever there's a good garden, you've got a nice sort of a person. That's philosophical too. Where there's no garden, there could be alcohol there or there could be domestic disturbance. It's a sign of feelings. (David, Hills District)

Although the vision of nature these gardeners have differs from that of the CNGs, there are parallels in the way they both attribute moral power to the nonhuman world, contrasting this with the strife of the human world.

Lawn—Lovers and Haters

Lawns are controversial. Paul Robbins and Julie Sharp have studied the environmental issues lawns raise, in their 2003 paper. In our study positive and negative responses to lawn prompted some quite intense moral positions. Lawns are a further illustration of the diversity of engagements between people and plants.

Seventy-nine per cent of backyards in this study have lawn, varying from a small patch to extensive swathes. Twenty-five per cent of the backyards with lawn are 25% lawn or less (measured as the proportion of ground covered excluding structures, to the nearest 5%), 40% are between 30% and 50% lawn, 27% are 55%–75% lawn and 9% are over 80% lawn. Although many people mention the importance of lawn for children, these is little difference overall in lawn coverage between households with children and those without. For the 21% who have no grass or lawn, reasons include short length of tenure, lack of space and personal taste.

There is a strong polarity between those who love lawn and those who hate it. Lawn lovers focus on the sensory pleasures of grass, the pleasure of the labour of mowing and lawn's importance as a play area for children. Lawn haters see it as an ecological evil; a voracious consumer of water, chemicals and time better spent on other things.

We think of the lawn engagement, at least by the lawn lovers, as a variation on the gardening engagement. People mostly regard mowing, or at least the end result of a neat and tidy backyard, as a pleasurable experience. More than half the participants have some comment on mowing or lawn maintenance. Often it was to simply give information about who is responsible for specific tasks, but frequently they express attitudes, including the attitudes of absent partners. Many refer, often jokingly, to the ongoing negotiations within households—particularly between the male and female members—as to who will mow the lawn. Lawn duties primarily rest with the male partner and, despite the jokes, this relegation of duties rarely seems to be contested. Men's feelings about lawn mowing are surprisingly positive. They see it as 'time out' or a means to a pleasurable end. Karen, quoted below, is rare amongst women in voicing the same feelings. Of course, not everyone feels that way. Some people point to constraints that impinged on their ability to enjoy mowing—such as time, health and accessibility considerations, while others voice their opposition to mowing in terms of their anti-lawn sentiment.

Stan of Forest Grove acknowledges both the pleasure and the pointlessness of mowing with some bemusement.

> *I like to get out there on a hot day and mow the lawn and then I can have a beer at the end . . . You go out there in the summer when it's growing, like you encourage it to grow and then you mow it down. It seems a pretty senseless activity. Yeah you get out there and do something and it looks really good when it's greened up.*

> *I enjoy cutting the grass, there's something kind of therapeutic because I mean our lives generally are just so fast paced. Family life is very full and work is quite involved.*
> *(Joe, Hills District)*

> *There's always something to do and I love it. For me it's not a job. In summer I come home and before dinner I'll go and cut the grass and then I relax. (Bruno, southern suburbs, Wollongong)*

> *I do mow the lawn, I love the smell of mowing the lawn, I love the exercise of mowing the lawn . . . (Karen, northern suburbs, Wollongong)*

Those who are positive about lawn itself often refer to the sensory aspects of touch and smell. People with new houses are more likely to express these sensory responses. They are also more likely to landscape the backyard and lay finished turf rather than create a lawn from seed.

> *I think it's really nice to walk around the yard barefoot in the summer time and just feel the prickle in your feet; it just feels good. (Bob, northern suburbs, Wollongong)*

> *Everyone that comes here for a barbecue usually takes their socks and shoes off and stands on it and they say it's great. (Jim, describing the turf in his three year old house at Shell Cove, Wollongong)*

The desire for lawn is often related to a desire for control and order. Lawn areas are kept pristine and weed free, with participants talking about crawling around on their hands and knees removing broad leaved plants that marr their green oasis. Kellie and Rebecca describe plans for the backyards of their new houses and look forward to a time when they will be 'finished' —

> *I like grass, it's like carpet you've got to have, and then all that will be concrete from across there, so the whole lot of that will be cement. (Kellie, southern suburbs, Wollongong)*

> *I know that it would only take [my husband] a good, like if he could just have a couple of days off he would be able to get the gravel spread and put some turf down, and then I'd be happy. (Rebecca, southern suburbs, Wollongong) (Figure 4.9)*

In contrast, lawn haters voice their anti-lawn sentiment in terms of excessive water use, condemning lawns as environmentally un-sustainable in the Australian environment. A number have removed lawn from their backyards. These passions are not expressed only by committed native gardeners. Female lawn haters, like Kris—who describes herself as being on a 'mission' against lawn—are more likely to express their dislike in terms of environmental reasons, while male lawn haters just tend to dislike mowing.

Figure 4.10: Mark surveys his lawn from the front veranda, inner Wollongong

> *I can't understand why people water their lawns but they do and it serves*
> *no useful purpose unless you've got something grazing on it.*
> *(Heather, northern suburbs, Wollongong)*
>
> *I hate it actually, my ambition is to get rid of it, not in the backyard,*
> *but in the front yard I'll landscape so there will be no lawn left.*
> *(Mark, Wollongong) (Figure 4.10)*

Heather and Kris qualify their antipathy to lawn with the statement that they do not have young children at the moment. This reflects a commonly expressed feeling that kids need lawn.

> *All I want is for [my son] to play on the grass because he's had no grass*
> *for a year. (Rebecca, southern suburbs, Wollongong)*
>
> *I still wanted to leave lots of grass so that the kids could play on the grass,*
> *otherwise we would just have it all concrete. (Rhonda, northern suburbs,*
> *Wollongong)*

To return to the moral intensities of figure 4.1, attitudes to lawns reflect all corners of the diamond; passions for nativeness, sensory engagement, spaces for relaxation and environmental goods.

Customer type	Characteristics
Green Thumbs	Love gardening and have high maintenance gardens
New Seekers	Keen to learn, enjoy gardening and are establishing their gardens
Self-Expressionists	Proud of their gardens; see them as an expression of themselves and as a creative outlet
Not Confident Loyalist	Need reassurance in establishing their gardens and tend to see gardening as a chore
Time Poor	Busy purposeful shoppers who enjoy gardening but don't buy many plants and spend minimal time in the garden
Bargain Hunters	Enjoy shopping for bargains and will shop around
Prefer Cut Flowers	Likely to buy cut flowers rather than plants and do not spend much time gardening

Table 4.3 Customer types and their characteristics as identified by the nursery and garden industry. Source: The Nursery Papers Issue no. 2001/13 (www.NGIA.com.au)

Gardeners as the Market Sees Them

For a rather different set of gardener categories, table 4.3 shows the seven customer types identified by the nursery and garden industry in 2001, based on purchasing behaviour. The first four of these account for 82% of sales, and can thus be targetted with marketing strategies that emphasise, for example, individual creativity or time saving, or that offer simple and clear instructions and ideas. Like any categorisation, these have fuzzy boundaries, and consumers can behave out of type. It is estimated for example that 26% of nursery sales come from impulse purchases,[10] indicating the power of merchandising, such as a stand of 'potted colour' on special near the cash register.

As noted in the previous chapter, backyarders report media as a significant, but not the major, influence on their decision making, and while there is little evidence of slavish adherence, the increasing consumer culture of backyards and gardens is clear. It is important then to ask what messages about nativeness are presented in media such as the gardening magazines? In articles that focus on individual plant species or genera, or an assemblage of plant types, non-natives outnumbered natives three to one. In *Gardening Australia*, which has the highest coverage of natives, the ratio is still about two to one in favour of non-natives. This is consistent with their relative value in the industry, with Australian natives making up 35.4% of total sales by production nurseries compared to 64.6%

Figure 4.11: 'Get edgy' (Source: Burke's Backyard April 2002: p88)

Figure 4.12: 'Mix it up (Source: Burke's Backyard April 2002: p87)

exotics.[11] It parallels the dominance of exotics and exotic/native combinations in our backyards.

The wording of magazine articles on non-natives positions them as the *normal* garden choice. In contrast, natives are portrayed as unique, a fashion choice ('Natives: the Rebirth of Cool' trumpets *Burke's Backyard*, May 2003), and a recent addition to suburban gardens. (In fact they are not recent. There is a long if minority history of interest in using native plants in Australian gardens, as related in Neale's 2003 article.) Where magazines are encouraging increased interest in natives, they acknowledge that most people are likely to plant them in combination with exotics, rather than go the way of our committed native gardeners.

> Many of us now have native plants living side by side with exotic species in our suburban gardens, but we can take the challenge of planting natives much further. (*Gardening Australia*, May 2003: 27)

> Native inspiration—planting your own native garden, or simply adding some native plants to your existing garden, is a superb way to improve Australia's natural environment, and our endangered native fauna really will love you for it! . . . Mix it up—hey, its a post-modern world, and you don't have to stick to the 'purist' line, mix natives and exotics and enjoy the effect! . . . Get edgy—a neatly manicured lawn is the best thing you can add to a native garden. It tidies those shrubby edges instantly and is the ideal pathway to wander down your little patch of bushland. (*Burke's Backyard* April 2002: 86–87, 88, 89) (Figures 4.11, 4.12)

The notion that a native garden needs somehow to be tamed, for example by juxtaposing it against a neat lawn, can be seen in the backyards of many of our general native gardeners, whose natives are usually confined to separate and clearly demarcated garden beds.

The portrayal of natives as tough, messy and likely to disrupt the order of the garden resonates with the attitudes of the non-native gardeners, and the reasons they give for disliking them.

> After another dry season in the garden, Jennifer Stackhouse embraces a tougher kind of beauty. (*House and Garden*, June 2003: 194)

> Australian plant breeders have been busy creating tougher, more beautiful and better-behaved native plants. (*Better Homes and Gardens*, February 2003: 44-46)

The frequent emphasis on 'new natives', these 'better-behaved' ones that have been improved through cultivation, is undoubtedly attractive to many people, including our general native gardeners who embrace their bird-attracting qualities. Commercial developments such as 'Flora for Fauna', a marketing program for native plants, have been highly successful, with 16% of nursery customers reporting purchases specifically to attract birds, butterflies or other animals.[12] But the emphasis on the 'taming' of natives can also paradoxically reinforce the view that they are difficult, and that the real home of such messy nature is outside the garden fence. Only rarely are natives defined or promoted in this literature as plants native to the local area. Much more common is a generalised Australianness, in which natives 'typify the spirit of the Australian landscape' (*Better Homes and Gardens*, December 2002: 152).

Gardens and Nature

Contrary to the conventional environmental wisdom about settler Australians being alienated from nature, it is clear from these accounts that people are enmeshed in diverse engagements with the nonhuman world, as exemplified by plants and soil. Even the inorganic parts of this world are acknowledged to have agency and a kind of life, such as the earth which 'heals' for Vi. There is widespread recognition of the dynamism and constant change in the nonhuman world. Maggie, from inner Sydney, expresses this view that nature has a life of its own beyond human control.

> *A backyard is something you have, it's a space, but a home is something that is nurtured and has a sense of soul and I think a garden has that. I think also a garden has a sense of discovery and it has a sense of relationship, that you are having a relationship with nature; in a sense it's not yours, you are the keeper of it in a sense and things are revealed to you, nice surprises and nasty surprises like something is eating my lovely orchids.*

Most participants are comfortable with the hybrid reality of combinations of native and exotic plantings, with affection for their different attributes.

People respond in a variety of ways when asked whether people are part of nature, recognising the complexity of the issue. For many the ambiguity of the human position can be summarised as 'we are but we aren't'. Most think of people as in some way part of nature, sometimes including provisos such as 'yes but a destructive part' or 'only indigenous people'. This last response comes only from native gardeners (13% of our CNG participants and 5% of GNGs). While gardeners of all groups recognise humans as 'changers and destroyers' of nature, this tendency is slightly higher among CNGs. We take this combination of attributes to confirm the strength of scientific and ecological thinking in the native gardener groups, consistent with their higher educational status. Conceiving of humans as destructive also illustrates the deep ambivalence the committed native gardeners in particular attach to their own belonging, an issue we return to in chapters eight and nine.

CHAPTER FIVE

My *Place*

This chapter focuses on the ways people have of making their backyards into part of a place called 'home'. Themes of 'my place', home and haven are expressed with passion and considerable emotion in the interviews, leaving no doubt that the backyard is highly valued as an integral part of many contemporary homes. Backyards are also important landscapes of memory where connections between past, present and future are expressed.

Figure 5.1: Gerard with chillies, inner Wollongong

*F*red is an 85 year old widower from Wollongong, who migrated to Australia soon after World War II. Although he had to stop every now and then to get his breath, he insisted on taking us right to the back of his very steep backyard.

I never imagined we could have a place like this, never in my wildest dreams and when we bought this block of land, I mean it was heaven, and that's what we came to Australia for and that's why thousands of migrants come out here.

He reminded the interviewer that he had come from a classed society where people all knew their station, and that the migration experience provided opportunities beyond his wildest dreams.

In fact a surprising number of people answered the question about their ideal backyard with the words 'this one'. They might go on to add their plans for the future, or an object of desire such as a water feature, but high levels of satisfaction with the basics of current circumstances are common. This is not to say that they think of the backyard as a static place where nothing ever changes. Although a fenced outdoor area can suggest a fixed and clearly bounded space, most people have a much more dynamic understanding of their backyards. They are places of transition, change and possibility, and not only in relation to plants.

Backyard spaces are imbued with feelings, expressed through tangible objects and activities, and as intangible 'places of the heart'. We tried to get people to talk about this by asking them their main feelings about their backyards. One of the strongest emotional responses that emerged we named 'a sense of connectedness'. This might be linked to home ownership, but renters also talk about connectedness. Certainly investing time and energy to create something is an important contribution to this feeling. People sometimes link their feeling of connectedness directly to being close to nature.

I just get a feeling of tranquillity and serenity and it's just a little haven, especially when I go out sometimes and watch the frogs . . . you can just watch them and it gives me a great feeling of satisfaction because it's something that sort of puts you back in tune with nature which is sadly missing from our society and most of our lives, so that's something that I can, I'm very drawn to; it makes me feel a sense of well being. (Lynette, inner northern suburbs, Wollongong)

As we will see, socio-economic status influences whether the sense of connectedness is expressed more towards people or towards nature.

This chapter is structured around types of what we have called 'engagements'. Place making is a process which binds people to all sorts of elements in the nonhuman. These engagements also bind time and space together in quite dynamic ways. They both crosscut and overlap the gardener groupings used in the previous chapter.

We are *not* arguing that gardeners are more 'connected' to nature than other people. In keeping with the framework established in chapter one, we see all human lives as enmeshed with the nonhuman world. What is of interest is how people understand this and the practical implications.

Shared or Contested Space?

Different members of a household will engage in different, sometimes contested, ways. Some writers have argued that the backyard is a male space, distinct from the home as a female space. The evidence conflicts with this view both in historical sources and in our contemporary data. While some spaces within backyards may have been the domain of the male, it was never exclusively a male place.

Much of the historical discussion in Chapter Two relates to that important part of women's lives, washday. In the responses to the National Museum, men are mentioned more frequently as having responsibility for the vegetable garden, for example Maureen Everitt's father. Maureen's father was also involved in the heavy lifting of water in the years before full plumbing.

> **There was no drainage [from the washhouse] so the tubs would empty through a pipe in the wall to outside then into drums (which Dad had put handles on). These drums would then be emptied under the mandarin tree or whatever needed watering. The old Pope wringer would also be emptied into buckets and carted away. (Everitt 1992)**

Engagement with particular backyard spaces in our study echoes divisions of labour within the home, for example for mothers of young children who describe themselves as 'always at the clothesline'.

> **Washing. If you've got two small children that's what happens in the backyard . . . It's a wonder I didn't put a load on before you came. (Annie, Alice Springs).**

People who are passionate about their involvement in gardening sometimes mention either a delimited space or an agreed role in the organisation of tasks to avoid tension. For some passionate gardeners this was not a problem when their family members either were not especially interested in the backyard or when they were happy to allow one person creative rights to the space. But for other people a sense of negotiated space was evident, albeit often presented tongue-in-cheek. Both men and women talk about one person, often the male partner, working 'under instruction' or 'helping'. Or as one elderly Macedonian man described it, 'it's like a boss and a labourer'. Angus makes the following comment:

> **My dear wife is the creative one who's done all the plantings, and directs me where to dig, and has the natural creative flair for how the things would move forward. (North Shore, Sydney)**

We found few really contested spaces, although several uneasy spaces are described, evidenced by this comment about a spouse's perceived interference: 'whatever he does is wrong. So it's best he stays away.' There are also stories of shared spaces, shared ideas—but again with a gravitation to particular gardening-related activities that each person enjoys. As Tracy comments, 'we often work in separate sections of the garden at the same time; it's sort of a space to be with yourself really.'

Types of Engagement

We have identified a set of engagements that, while not clearcut categories, link different dimensions of connection, practice and attitude. We were particularly interested to trace the contrast between those for whom work in the backyard is a burden and those who enjoy its physical or contemplative aspects. The different types of engagement have implications for people's relationships with nature. One way to understand the differences is to examine how backyard work is described. Invariably, people who enjoy such labour, or do not see it as work, are quick to add positive comments. In contrast, we surmised that those who simply describe a list of tasks derive little enjoyment from them. People also respond to what they see as society's conventions about keeping the backyard, and particularly the frontyard, neat and presentable. This internalised expectation is sometimes expressed negatively as a sense of guilt. People who talk about their backyards as *work* can be characterised broadly as time poor, or age weary, or overwhelmed by the scale of mounting tasks of maintaining a backyard. Those who readily admit to not being 'gardeners' often find little pleasure in what they see as the repetitive tasks of maintaining a backyard. Rather, they want the time they do spend there to be 'relaxing'.

The Project Engagement

People who talk positively about work often talk about the backyard as a 'work in progress', or about change. The project engagement is about a constantly evolving space, but one which contains a conceptualisation of the future.

It's somewhere you come out to plan your projects. Backyards are great because they've got a future to them and it's always nice to have something with a future . . . It's not just like 'oh by Christmas I'll have everything done'. And they are always changing as a good plan always is and every time I come out here I do something but I know that I've got more to do and I'm in no hurry to do it. (Michael, Alice Springs) (Figure 5.3)

When people come to a house (usually as owners) they often have a clear vision of the things they plan to do to it. This involves creating enough blank space on which they can put their imprint. When asked to describe the backyard when they first arrived, the two most common responses are 'it was nothing, there was nothing here' and 'it was a total mess' that had to be removed. They either have a blank slate or have to create one. Their picture of the future is also tied into where they see themselves as a household.

So this was probably the flattest backyard and the most practical backyard where I could see a future with family. When we bought this house we only had one child but we had visions of more. (Glenys, Hills District)

Evan and Sonia had very intricate plans for their new backyard in the Shell Cove estate (Figure 5.2). Not everyone has. As we saw in the previous chapter, Kellie, who has a young child and a backyard full of mud, wants nothing more than a patch of grass to mitigate the mud. When people who have lived in the same house for many years provide an account of the changes they have wrought, the overwhelming impression is of how much cumulative effort has gone into the backyard over the years.

On the other hand, it is important to emphasise that people do not necessarily need a long time to express the affection and involvement that attach them to a place. So after only twelve months, with their backyard still developing, Sonia is able to say:

I love the fact that everywhere you look there's something different and it's been created, I've watched it grow. I'd come home from work and Evan had done something else and we'd go and sit and have a drink and you know, I'd sit down and say, 'oh this looks good', stand up and admire it.

This type of involvement is not just a function of the quantity of time, but the fact that it passes and changes can be observed. Sonia also benefits from the labours of Evan, who tells us that he cannot wait to finish it!

People engaged in projects may also express high levels of satisfaction with the labour involved. They describe their pleasure, love, enjoyment and other strongly positive emotional reactions to the backyard.

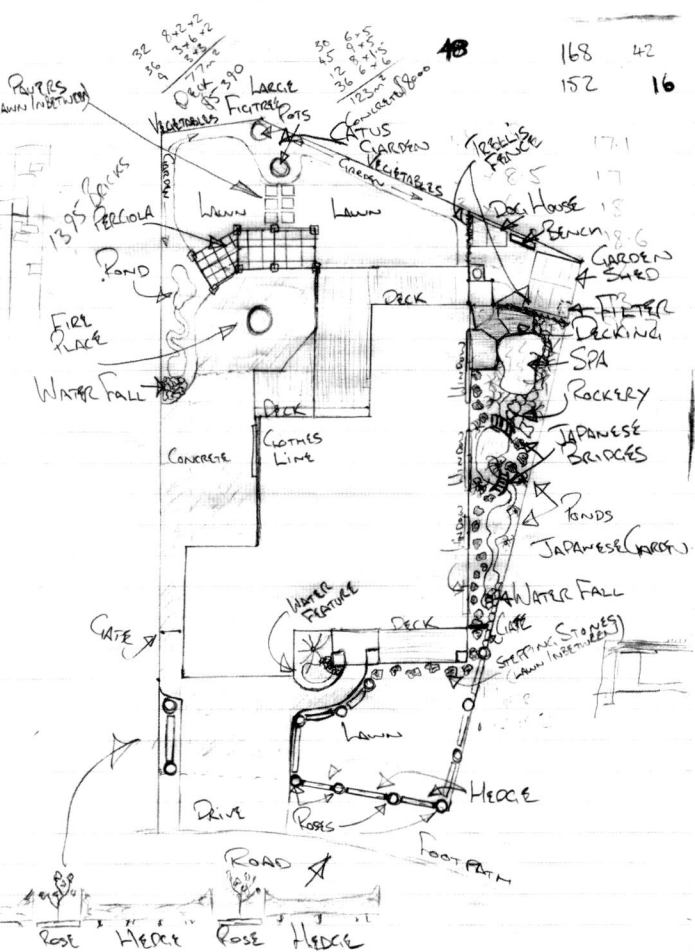

Figure 5.2: Evan's intricate plans, Shell Cove, Wollongong

Figure 5.3: Michael with projects ready to go, Alice Springs

The project engagement also relates to the work of tidiness and order, a project that is never finished.

> *A job has to be done, you have to cut the grass, you have to clean the hedge. If you want flowers or vegetables you have to work them in; there's always something to do and I love it. For me it's not a job. (Bruno, southern suburbs, Wollongong)*

> *If you've got a backyard, mowing the lawn is an interest. It's an occupation, a weekend occupation. If you work all the week and you come home, and you're home all the weekend, well what do you do, sit and read the paper? Some people do. Some people sit and diddle around with a computer. I'm sorry, the internet's not my cup of tea at all. The backyard is an interest, an occupation and a necessary one to keep it tidy and keep it in order. When it's tidy you feel better. It makes you feel better. It's part of your wellbeing program. (Leo, North Shore)*

In that respect it is also about work that doesn't get done, leading to feelings of guilt as well as satisfaction.

> *Mainly at the moment I would get out there and actually weed it and tidy it up again. It actually looked good at one time but I've just left it because I've been on shift work and just so busy lately that I haven't had time to actually do anything so it's just gone on to how it has at the moment. (Quentin, Albion Park)*

On the other hand the repetitive nature of some of the work involved is not necessarily construed as negative.

> *I feel as though I own it; I mean I do in terms of, not monetary owning, but owning in terms of I suppose because I've put work into it and I've mowed the lawn a million times or whatever it is, you know, as though there's a part of me in it. (Keith, Alice Springs)*

> *It's been my ideas. It's been my hard work that's gone into it. Hard work and when I say hard work I also accept the fact that there's been a huge amount of pleasure that's come from that. (Barbara, Port Kembla)*

> *It's a source of enjoyment. It's pleasurable. Even the work, even the hard work is pleasurable because you can see light at the end of the tunnel. It's really an enjoyment to see the natives come in. (Richard, Campbelltown)*

The Engagement of Finishing

When people talk about work without such positive indicators we were interested in why this work is considered differently. For another group of people the backyard is conceived as a finite project, as one day being 'done' or 'finished', or simply as work, as Julie, from the northern suburbs of Wollongong, reports:

> *Most of the time it's just normally work, not relaxation, unless we have a barbecue with friends over or something.*

Many people who talk about the backyard as work also talk about not having enough time or having competing priorities (small children, demanding job, hobbies). This includes those who bought new and are in the throes of getting it all together, people who recently moved into an established house and are changing the backyard, people with young children who only manage half an hour in the backyard before their attention is required elsewhere, and people who are juggling work or study commitments. It also includes retirees who have expended energy on a backyard for a long time and now want to scale down, and people who are not gardeners.

Maria encapsulates the idea of the backyard as a finite project and conceives of it quite differently to Michael, quoted above. While Maria and Michael are both young, have both had less than two years in their homes, and are both married, their family structures differ as Maria has small children. Finishing the backyard is a priority for her and her husband in terms of children's play space (Figure 5.4). Added to this are the pressures of purchasing in a newly established suburb where completion and display are a neighbourly expectation.

> *And my husband, he hasn't had a lot of chance to enjoy it because he's still trying to do things every weekend. That's why I can't wait till we're at that point where we do enjoy it, when we sit down and have a drink and have a barby and enjoy it, and have friends over, friends that we've made that can come around and share that with us.*

Central to the differences expressed by these two participants is how the backyard is used. For Maria it will eventually be a place to relax and enjoy with friends and family, while for Michael it is the combination of planning and execution, with enough flexibility to enjoy the shifts and changes that he anticipates will happen.

Maria's response is typical of occupants of new homes, who envisage their backyard transformation and pleasure in the future. It is similar to the feelings of other younger people:

> *I suppose after we do a few other things around the place, eventually we'll just, you know, just enjoy the backyard. Just a BBQ and just be able to relax out there on the veranda. (Quentin, Albion Park)*

> *We know it is going to take some time to get to where we want but I think once it's done then we'll be very happy with the result. (Lorraine, Campbelltown, Sydney)*

> *In the garden yeah, I had a plan I wanted to get as much done in six months as I could, mainly so I could sit back and then relax. I didn't want something that was gonna last a life time; I wanted to get all the main features and main work, I mean the main structure, I suppose you could say, down . . . the reason I'm putting so much work into it is so we can entertain, we can stay out here ourselves. (Evan, Shell Cove)*

The Stylistic Engagement

People who profess not to like getting their hands dirty are more likely to perceive the backyard in visual terms. The stylists are an important component of the non-gardener group identified in the previous chapter. They consider aspects of style and colour more important than other sensory experiences, with design and layout also important considerations. Bernadette, Joan and Linda articulate desires for visually pleasing plants, and position themselves as not being gardeners.

Figure 5.4: Maria's almost completed backyard, Kellyville, Sydney

No I'm not much of a gardener. I'd just like to have a few things out there to look at. (Bernadette, inner city apartment, Sydney)

I wish it had more flowers but then you've got to grow them and I don't look after them and I'm not too good at that. I like them to be beautiful but I don't want to do anything. (Joan, Eastern Suburbs, Sydney)

**I like a bit of colour and a bit of flowers but I'm not a gardener, so it's got to be simple, and things that'll look after themselves as well.
(Linda, Albion Park)**

Minimisation of work is important for many of those who perceive the garden in very visual terms. This was particularly apparent during interviews with couples, where one partner would describe himself or herself, or be described by the other, as 'more of an inside person'. So Gita, from Sydney's Hills District remarks:

I'm not an outdoor person. I do the designing but he does the execution.

While particular people consider themselves non-gardeners and talk more specifically about visual aspects, all participants value the visual quality of the backyard as a primary sensory pleasure. However, the obsession with visual style is perhaps best exemplified by the gardening industry's emphasis on 'impact' plants. Impact plants are promoted as feature plants. People talk about impact plants in the context of landscape gardening, media influence and purchasing from nurseries and garden centres. We asked one participant who worked within the horticultural industry for his views on what trends he had observed.

> **See the plant there, that's a Dracaena draco, the dragon dracaena there in the pot. That is a striking plant. It gives you a, it has an effect. Now the trend at the moment is to plant all those around the pool with those other cordyline things which are accent and impact plants. And hedges. People love hedges because they're very defined. They have a sense of order. It makes a statement. But it doesn't change. It's not horticulturally curious. But the virtues of those plants are very defined and very strong. That's what people are responding to at the moment. You know, the makeover type approach.**
> **(Bill, Campbelltown)**

The less spectacular visuals of many native plants mean that many people do not 'see' them easily. For example, one gardener said her visitors were much more likely to comment on a showy pink azalea than a planted area that is 'just indigenous'.

The stylistic engagement is also connected to notions of time in that there is a demand from time poor people for instant gardens.

> **If you look around us, which we observe, people leave home at 6.30, 7 in the morning, and they're back home at 6.30, 7 in the evening. Then when you work out the weekends and the kids sport and everything, there is no time. So backyards are becoming an ornamental place, which are not functional. We've seen around us, what they're doing is they come in, they build a house, they bring the landscape gardeners in, they get it all turfed, plant a few trees and that's it. (Brian, Hills District, Sydney)**

An example of how the project and stylistic engagements can intersect is provided by Leanne's backyard in southern Wollongong. This also reminds us that an emphasis on the visual does not necessarily exclude other bodily engagements. Her space contains many of the fashionable design elements found in the backyard media—delineation of separate spaces, a freestanding pergola, a shade sail, strongly coloured paving and blue enamel pots (title page). Leanne is in their target demographic of young, houseproud home owners. Her conversation is peppered with references to the TV program 'Ground Force' and she describes conversations with work colleagues in which they suggested she install a water feature. Visual aspects, particularly colour, are important to her: 'My garden and backyard are a little bit like an artist's blank palette and it's like painting in a picture'. But this single mother with a demanding job in health services is far from being a slavish follower of fashion 'not just the idea of how to do something . . . but more giving me the belief that I can actually do some of this work myself'. She goes on to explain in great detail the way she plans out her projects, pinning a list on the fridge of goals for the next twelve months, and working through it. Part of the planning is financial, 'because you wish you had a bit more money to get it done a bit quicker.'

The Tidying Engagement

For perhaps the majority of people, but for different reasons, neatness and tidiness are associated with order, beauty and happiness (and sometimes the front yard as distinct from the back). This engagement intersects with the others, in that there are various ways by which tidiness can be achieved, and indeed a variety of perceptions about what constitutes tidiness. For example, a passionate lawn mower and a passionate native gardener who removes exotics are both 'tidying up' in the sense of creating order in their environment. This engagement can be summarised in the words of the participant who said, 'as long as it's tidy I'm happy'.

The backyard is an interest, an occupation and a necessary one to keep it tidy and keep it in order. When it's tidy you feel better. (Leo, North Shore)

I like neat and tidy things and flowers. (Lyn, North Shore)

To me when it's all neat and tidy I really think, yes, I've got a great backyard. (Denis, Hills District)

It is a very inviting area for me to look at visually and like I say, we don't like clutter, you know, there's no junk anywhere or anything and it always looks a neat, tidy area. (Kathy, southern Wollongong)

Our driving force is that the thing looks neat, tidy, pretty, colourful, we haven't been afraid to spend money on the place. (Ted, northern Wollongong)

The Pottering Engagement, or the 'Small Walk'

The pottering engagement was also shared, albeit in different ways, across all the types of engagement discussed above. On one level this could be considered a passive engagement, but we prefer to think of it as being actively still—listening, watching, touching, being. The pottering engagement is always pleasurable. Indeed pottering is one of the most talked about activities people engage in and it can range from a ritual wander around the backyard picking out the occasional weed, to losing track of time in nightclothes and gumboots, or forgetting to come in for lunch. This was the activity associated with well-being in the sense that the backyard or garden provided the space, while the unstructured engagement gave people a time of just 'being', or a time to think.

Figure 5.5: Arthur discussing the engagement of the senses in his backyard, Campbelltown, Sydney

The first thing that I do of a morning is I get out of the house, I go and walk through the backyard, it's like a small walk . . . I like to be the first one to see how the thing's grown a little bit more comparing to yesterday or I would like to be the first one to see the first chilli coming off the plant or the first tomatoes. (Blaguna, southern suburbs, Wollongong)

I love it and it's thinking time as well, you know, you're sort of pottering and thinking and making space for a thing to grow properly. (Mandy, inner city apartment, Sydney)

This engagement includes things like sitting in the backyard, often with a cup of tea or a drink, perhaps talking, watching children or animals, or reading, but sometimes seemingly doing nothing. One man described his backyard as a place to 'dream' in, while a Vietnamese participant spoke of it as a place to 'consider' things. Mark, whose backyard edges the Illawarra escarpment, speaks of it as a 'regenerative' space.

. . . it's lovely to have that space and we're glad we overlook the bushland. So for me it's like a regenerative, restorative sort of place to be in; just sit out there on a sunny morning with a cup of tea and just watch the kids playing in the sand. It's somewhere I can recharge my batteries which is one of the reasons we wanted to live in a place like this. (Mark, northern suburbs, Wollongong)

Having space to relax, think, recharge was important for everyone we talked to, not just those that considered relaxing more important than the 'doing' aspects.

Backyards are undeniably sensory places; they engage us with scents, sights, sounds, tastes as well as our sense of touch. Comments from avid gardeners were full of references to sensory experiences in the backyard, as this comment from Arthur, long term inhabitant of his backyard, illustrates:

Figure 5.6: Long time resident Ernest in his rose garden, inner Sydney

Well I guess it's very much an extension, your garden becomes very much an extension of yourself. I'm very aware of it. I don't have to close my eyes to think about it. I know what's there. I know what's been there before. I know what I can anticipate, but you can't anticipate everything. But I do feel very close, very close to it. The closeness it's tactile. There's a Banksia serrata, it's got a beautiful bark . . . I don't actually have to feel it. I sense it. There's that tactile quality. (Arthur, Campbelltown) (Figure 5.5)

The gardeners were more likely to talk about tactile senses (the contact with the earth, the feel of it under their fingernails, the smell of flowers), the stylists to talk about visuals. But the categories are not so separate; non-gardeners such as Julie can say, 'you know, I find it quite relaxing to come out for half an hour and pull out a few weeds and tidy up things'. Sometimes pottering has a spiritual aspect, as committed rose gardener Ernest muses:

> So if I want to do something I just go down into the garden and just have my music on and yes, that's my space, my sacred space if you like. (Ernest, inner city, Sydney) (Figure 5.6)

Disengaging the Outside World

It is clear from the examples above that time pressures are influential in the type of engagement. So many people talked about the backyard as a retreat, a haven, a contrast to everyday life, a private space, that we also conceptualise an engagement that disengages the outside world. One woman described her backyard as 'a bit like paradise really' while other people described their backyards as an 'oasis', a 'sanctuary' or a 'haven'. Central to all these metaphors is the notion that the backyard is a refuge where the outside world is temporarily disallowed and people literally and metaphorically 'close the gate'.

> So it's nice to come in and shut the gates. Like coming to the house and shutting the door. That's your tiny little plot that you can fiddle around in. You're closed off from the rest of the world. (Karen, North Shore, Sydney)

> I just love it. I suppose it's almost a companion. Because I'm never lonely. I love people and I love being with people but I also like my own space. (Alma, Penrith, Sydney)

> It's my private world. It's ahh, in a sense safety because no one can come in and change anything that I've done to it. (Gerard, inner Wollongong)

> So I don't see anybody, so I'm in my own little paradise (laughs). That's how I want it so that I can't, nobody can actually interfere with it. (Victoria, Sydney)

Class, Order and Community

The passions expressed above for the backyard as a haven from which parts of the outside world can be excluded raise the question of whether this is a landscape of exclusion. Analysis of responses to questions about the broader suburb and community revealed some class differences. As discussed in Chapter Three, the influential aspect of 'class' here is education, and age is also a factor.

When discussing their backyard activities, participants with low education/skills talk about a place to work and relax in, with activities such as weeding, mowing and watering, but not particularly as a place to disengage from the 'outside'. They value keeping things 'neat and tidy'. The lawn engagement of the previous chapter, and the satisfaction people describe in completing the task, is a good example of this. Native wildlife is generally not encouraged, with the exception of birds, an affinity with which is shared by both ends of the socio-economic spectrum, a theme we take up in chapter eight.

In terms of the wider community setting, these participants value a safe area, with good facilities and strong community support. The focus is on people and infrastructure. A strong sense of community as highly connected with place is expressed for example in the inner Sydney suburb of Erskineville both by older working class residents and the newer gentrifiers. 'All the world needs an Erskineville', comments one.

For high education/skills participants, the backyard is more a place to relax in than work. They are more likely to 'just sit', with a cup of tea or a book, than necessarily 'do' things. Women in particular talk about a 'sense of peace', 'time out' and 'nurturing'. Although the keen gardeners amongst them discuss it in these terms, this group more frequently wants a 'low maintenance' backyard. For example they have only token vegetable or herb production, which is typical of people of white Anglo-Australian backgrounds. In the wider setting they value natural phenomena, the trees, the landforms and the existing vegetation, rather than talking about the social aspects of the community. They are more likely to adjoin open land or bush and be active there in some sense (walking, bush regeneration, maintaining fire breaks), as well as encouraging native wildlife into the backyard.

This is not to say that human sociality is unimportant, but that it is not as strongly connected to physical place. It is encapsulated more in the notion of community as 'people like us', with more affluent people not expecting to have their main, or necessarily any, social connections with neighbours. They discuss social life explicitly, however, in terms of entertaining. The backyard is an important site for welcoming friends and family, and thus becomes an extension of the house, which 'spills out' into it, and requires the same level of attention to décor and design as the house does. This is the sort of sociality that both reflects and feeds the culture of consumption seen in the media.

An exception to this is children. Parents across the socio-economic spectrum express an aspiration for their children to have a place-based sense of community, to be able to run in and out of each other's backyards, even if the parents do not want it for themselves. Even upper middle class people who would see adult transgressions as an invasion of privacy, or as a disturbance to their retreat, generally accept that kids should feel free to transgress such boundaries. Often they would refer back to their own childhood as the standard for this. One example is in the 'old east side' of Alice Springs, which has very large blocks with physically open boundaries.

. . . someone two doors down will say, come on kids it's tea time. And someone will yell out, we've fed them. And that happens. So it is porous . . . But I think because of the big blocks and the way that the kids roam through all the different yards, and the fact that we're in this triangle, it is a bit of a community. (Brad, Alice Springs)

The situation Brad describes has a number of contributing elements; the physical configuration, the outdoor lifestyle, presumptions of safety, parents with shared expectations and children around the same age. Some elements of that are possible to predict or plan for, others less so.

Both ends of the socio-economic spectrum express a need for control and order, but in slightly different ways. Emphasis on neatness and tidiness fits with previous research on class-based aspirations to respectability. For example Madigan and Munro suggest that the English working class experiences 'tension between the home as a warm, friendly comfortable place designed to suit the needs of the occupants, and a place in which certain "public" standards have to be maintained'. Such public standards have also been invoked to explain middle class American obsession with the front lawn (Robbins and Sharp 2003).

I'm ashamed of it now because it's a bit of a mess.

The concept of this estate is to keep everything on a nice even keel, keep it tidy, keep it clean, get people to look after their yards . . .

We'd rake the yards to keep around the house as tidy as we could. Well it was pleasant to go home and see everything neat and tidy. I'm afraid Dawn and I both like things a bit tidy.

For upper middle class participants in our study, for whom there is no question about their own respectability, control and maintenance issues in the backyard have more to do with its role as a place of peace, leisure and/or entertainment. That is, it cannot perform this role if it is a mess, and will become rather a place of stress (another set of demands in already busy lives) and work (or guilt, if the work is not done). These emotions are particularly experienced by women.

It irritates me if I see it looking too scruffy.

This year I've got back into the garden again but I really resented it, I resented the mess and the constant need.

Figure 5.7, left: Theresa's father Nino in the vegetable garden in 1955, inner northern suburbs, Wollongong
Figure 5.8, right: Nino in the same backyard in 2002, inner northern suburbs, Wollongong

> **I think a lot about the plants I should plant, and the stone I should move, and bits and pieces I should tidy up.**

Once again, children are an exception. Some messiness is always tolerated for kids, who are expected to be able to 'just run and play and make a mess'.

Landscapes of Memory

Memory implies the past, but the sorts of time we want to invoke in this section extend in several directions. At any moment in time a backyard carries within it evidence of the work and dreams of previous owners, the activities of present inhabitants, and the seeds—both literal and metaphorical—of future changes.

Memories of backyard changes are often measured by points in the life cycle, such as the age of children when the family arrived. For example Lillian of Berkeley says, 'I have a rose bush that is as old as Mark; it is forty years old. I

was pregnant when I was digging the hole for it.' The process is often documented in photos, that themselves also punctuate the memories in the same way as remembered events do:

> **I've got photos when that wattle was three foot high and that was it; it was completely and utterly barren. It had grass and that was it. (Anne, Hills district, Sydney)**

> **We have photographs of me constructing this wall (laughs), to give us a flattish backyard. I'm constructing the garden beds. (Grahame, Eastern Suburbs, Sydney)**

An important dimension of backyard evolution is the value people put on labour they have invested there. In this context, a number of participants commented how they would hate to have the 'instant' backyards common in TV makeover shows. For Jim of Shell Cove the process of growing a backyard is comparable to that of bringing up kids: 'that's it, the same sort of thing as you do with kids like, you get them and you bring them along'. Irene, who had lived in her Port Kembla home for 26 years and seen a number of changes as her children grew up, described her ideal backyard as:

> *like this, one that would evolve as I saw something that I liked. I could not sit down and plan a garden. There's so many things in my garden that people have given me bits of, and you've got (to) have room for those sorts of things. You can't sit down and, you know, (say) I'm going to have this, this and this. Well for me it wouldn't work.*

Angus described his attempts to develop the garden progressively to reflect

> *the natural attributes of the environment rather than having somebody come in and say we will create something particularly special. So in other words, the garden has evolved rather than being created according to some grand plan. If a landscape architect had come in here, [they] would probably have done something completely different. So it has evolved through our feeling for the area, and our knowledge of what grows where. (Angus, North Shore, Sydney)*

Over time, then, backyards become places capable of invoking complex and detailed memories of past events and people.

> *My father used to grow a lot of vegetables and fruit trees because he had seven children to feed. So he had to feed a family, so it was useful, and my father loved his garden, loved gardening . . . I would say about at least half or two thirds of the garden was vegetables and fruit trees. We also had some chickens in the backyard so we had fresh eggs as well. We had them for about maybe twenty years, maybe ten years of my childhood. And we also used to play a lot in the backyard as children, play in the street and in the backyard and with some of the other neighbours, other children in the neighbourhood as well used to come around.*

Figure 5.9: Mum's tree in Joyce's backyard, Forest Grove, Wollongong

Figure 5.10: Paul in his sunken courtyard garden, inner city, Sydney

So the backyard was useful in my childhood . . . My father was out here just about every day gardening, growing his vegetables and attending to his fruit trees and now that only two people live here it is not used very much, just occasionally. (Theresa, northern suburbs, Wollongong) (Figures 5.7, 5.8)

Memories can be particularly strongly invoked when the changes have been most dramatic. For example, Janine's house in the northern suburbs of Wollongong has been through several dramatic renovations, leading to almost cyclical changes in the house and backyard as her family has grown and then shrunk. In describing the cycle of renovations, she invokes the hydrangeas as a surviving symbol of the original house:

You just can't kill hydrangeas, I've decided. A lot of people say that they can't strike them but every time it gets dug up it comes back again and I think it's really cute that it's the one thing, because there's only about one thing in the whole that is original. I think it's a window in the background from the original house we bought.

Memories testify also to the changing ecology of the suburbs. Patrick of St Ives describes the evolution of his North Shore backyard in Sydney, from the original orchard when they bought the place forty-three years previously—

Patrick: in those days the birds didn't come and bother us for the peaches. Gradually it got all built up and the birds came around and they ruined the peaches before you could pick them.

Interviewer: It's interesting that you got more birds when it got built up.

Patrick: Well of course they feed the parrots.

Residents who have a strong historical sensibility about their suburb are likely to value vestiges of past environments and occupants that remain in the backyard. This is less of a blank slate approach than one that is very aware of connections to the

past. Stuart and Catharine, who live in an old and now affluent suburb near the entrance to Sydney Harbour, have an ongoing issue with water coming into their backyard, particularly when wet periods coincide with high tide. Rather than seeing this as just a 'drainage' issue, they are conscious that

this back part of the garden used to be part of the natural inlet from the beach into the lagoon which is the old park there . . . very little has changed from what it was a hundred years—a hundred and fifty years—ago, the water used to run through the back here and into the lagoon.

In a related vein they are very keen on what they describe as the traditional historic plants of the area, for example camellias and frangipani. They (and other locals) have a grapevine grown from a cutting from the first grapevine in the area, originally (but no longer) in the house next door.

It has been around in Watsons Bay for a long time and that connection, well we value that connection . . . I think it gives you a sense of the place rather than just the houses that are around . . .

Maggie of Balmain, who has an 1880s house and is eager to retain the historic nuance of her area, kept the backyard dunny 'because it's a reminder of the way people lived'. She also expresses regret at not keeping any of the 'tiny pieces of china and stuff' found during excavation of her backyard.

Memory is an intensely personal and often invisible influence. When people are asked to describe the changes they have made over time, they discuss a broad range of things, including major structural changes. But themes of memory and emotion, whether in response to questions, or raised by study participants, cohere more tightly around plants. Perhaps this is because of the links to cycles of life and death that connect plants and people.

Further, memories can have profound implications for the configuration of plants in a garden. They lead to physical transplantation of species from distant areas that are often otherwise unrelated. Ecologically, the mixtures of plants created are potentially quite unruly. Here we summarise three different aspects of memory that arise most often.

Memories of childhood are both a connection to the past and a motivation for plantings in present backyards.

> **Every time I look at the hydrangeas both at the front of the house and the back of the house they remind me of my paternal grandmother who had a lot of hydrangeas in her garden at Coogee. (Helen, Eastern Suburbs, Sydney)**

> **According to my seven year old, this is a good fairy garden and I have done plantings of things that remind me of my childhood in some places, like the peppercorn tree when I was a kid on a farm in Queensland; that's what we had . . . I've got a fig tree which isn't probably what you would plant by the sea but it came from where my mother grew up on a different farm and it's an offshoot of that and it's here. (Alison, northern suburbs, Wollongong)**

> **We took a mulberry out of the front yard because it was just becoming a nuisance which made me cry because I have an emotional attachment to mulberry trees too, from my grandmother's backyard. (Dianne, Wollongong)**

> **The mango tree has lovely shade and it's very nice to sit under on a hot day but I also planted it because it reminded me of my childhood. Where I came from we had lots of fruit trees in our garden being a tropical country so, even though they don't produce a lot of fruit but it's a pleasure to see it growing and flowering and you just hope that one day it will produce some fruit on the tree. (Emily, northern suburbs, Wollongong)**

> **I want to grow the fruit trees so I can remember in my country we had those fruit. (Nhan, Fairfield, Sydney)**

Transplantations and memories from different countries are explored further in chapter six.

A number of participants describe sections of their backyards which are in effect *memory places*—particular plants are remembered as having been gifts from friends, or as commemorating beloved friends, relatives and pets. They also commemorate major life events of celebration and grief. Potted Sesanqua camellias from twenty-first birthday parties are eventually planted out into the garden. Bushes are planted, and not moved, for a baby that miscarried. One woman knows that 'the previous owners . . . planted a camellia in the front which is dedicated to their Poppy, which I will be leaving there'.

Joyce of Forest Grove described what she calls 'Mum's tree':

> **We planted that at ten o'clock at night, the time that they were burying mum in England. My sister was here from England at the time. We had a planting ceremony. And when we used to make tea in a pot we always used to go and pour it there and say "good morning Mum" and when my friend comes she'll go out and say "good day Mary, how are you?" (Joyce, Forest Grove) (Figure 5.9)**

Paul created a formal remembrance garden for his partner, that started with plantings at the wake (Figure 5.10). He also makes the connection between the life cycles of plants and people.

> **Well it's got a lot of memories in it for me, a hell of a lot of memories. I suppose that's the nature of watching anything grow for a long time. I remember when things were planted; I remember who gave me what plants. So yeah the hardest thing I think you have to learn about gardening is that things die, [laughs] you just can't, you know they die, so get used to it. (Paul, inner Sydney)**

> **And I wanted to transmit all those feelings of pain and anger and resentment into something and I thought I will find something that I find very beautiful and it will be my forgiveness tree and it's a buddleja and I just bought it up at Woolies . . . people love it, it hangs over**

Figure 5.11: John in front
of his pool, Campbelltown,
Sydney

*in summer and you can see people stopping to take in the scent. (Maggie,
inner Sydney)*

More common than the formal process of memorialising described above
are plants that invoke *memories of friends, family and relationships*. There are
many examples in the study of plants that have come as gifts. Sometimes
this creates rather random and unreflective mixtures within a garden; at
other times people know exactly who gave them what, and where it still is.
These informal practices often involve saving money, but that is not the sole
motivation.

> *I've got a port wine magnolia in the front that a girlfriend Ann gave me, and
> as I say Betty gave me the jacaranda. The Kaffir plum was I was working at
> B . . . School . . . and the council were having some promotion of plants and
> . . . there were a few bits and bobs left over and the Kaffir plum was one of
> the ones that I bought back here. And then so many other things that are
> in the back garden are things that I've taken cuttings from other peoples
> gardens and put them in and they've multiplied . . . I think that connectivity
> with other people and other people's gardens—you know, that sharing—it's
> very good. (Barbara, Port Kembla)*

I like to do my own cuttings not just for price wise but because I get bits and pieces from sister's garden or my mother in law's garden and I get part of their life in my garden. (Veronique, Wollongong West)

I've got hanging hoas in baskets which Mum really loved and a bleeding heart and there's a few of those older fashioned plants which I think remind me of my mother. (Helen, Wollongong West)

A lot of the plants around the front of the deck were planted by Bob's mother. So it's a very different garden now to when she lived with us but there are a lot of things that remind us of her and some of them really aren't appropriately planted now because the Japanese maple is gone. But she planted hydrangeas and every Christmas we think of Granny, you know, when we see hydrangeas. (Jo, Wollongong West)

But if I took the Norfolk Island pine down that my son planted, I would be without a son. He sees that as his tree. (Janine, northern suburbs, Wollongong)

Figure 5.12: Slave and Blaguna with chillies and cucumbers, western suburbs, Wollongong

Engaging with Nature

What are the links between how people engage with their backyards and how they think about nature? When asked specifically for their understanding of nature, around forty per cent of people position nature as spatially distant from the backyard. The rest express more fluid and dynamic understandings. These include the view that nature is 'something we've pushed around a bit', and a more relational view:

In a way nature is sort of a relationship, anything that is in relation to another thing in some ways, from the natural world, like from the living world.

People who define nature as spatially distant, such as wilderness or bush, hesitate to include their backyards in the way they think about nature. This is most evident in people whose primary concern in the backyard is with neatness and order and those interested in restoring native plants. They consider the backyard as either part of the built environment, or a manipulated nature that is, at its heart, different to pristine nature.

Oh. Gee. Well. Okay nature to me is the original landscape, basically untouched. That goes for the fauna as well. It's just pristine. That's my interpretation of nature. (Richard, Campbelltown)

*But nature is the bush. It's the bush to me. It's a natural environment . . . I'm not a greenie or anything like that, but we need to leave the bush and nature to its own devices.
(John, western suburbs, Sydney)*

Richard and John do not consider people as part of nature. John sees a separation between the suburbs and the bush, enjoying the neatness of his own backyard and the like-mindedness of his neighbours.

So everybody takes pride in their properties. You won't see any overgrown stuff in the street. Everybody takes pride in their property which is good. You're proud of what you're doing, what you're mowing, what you've built. (John, western suburbs, Sydney) (Figure 5.11)

Are Richard and John expressing a negative view of nature? Not necessarily; for John it is important, but belongs somewhere other than where people live, and humanly created landscapes have a value and beauty of their own. Richard is more inclined to a negative view of human impacts.

It is people who speak of a connectedness with the backyard—through physical and sensory engagement—whose perception of nature en-compasses all living things and, occasionally, non-living things. Their view includes an awareness of nature as an active participant in the backyard, sometimes acting in unforeseen ways. This recognition of nature having agency is very strong in the gardening engagement, spoken of in the previous chapter, and expressed here by keen vegetable gardeners Slave and Blaguna of Wollongong West:

We go around and come back and makes you feel nice, satisfied that you are among your things, you are in nature and it makes you in a way better prepared for the day. (Figure 5.7)

Some people, such as Sue, recognise this power in even the highly humanised landscape of the inner city:

But nature to me is like everything and the thing I really like about it is that men and machines can concrete things; like eventually the sun and the shifting of the earth will crack the concrete and the seed will get in there and then a plant will grow. As much as people try you can't actually kill nature, you can't get rid of it, you can't keep it down, it will keep coming back. (Sue, inner Sydney)

It is fair to say that what we can call the 'wilderness ideal' has enormous appeal to a whole range of people with different backyards, including those who see it as spatially and conceptually distant from the city, and those, such as the committed native gardeners from the previous chapter, who want to bring it back in and purify the city.

CHAPTER SIX

Production and
Reproduction

Food production is linked with reproduction of tradition
and practice in the migrant experience. Our case studies
are the backyards of Macedonian, Vietnamese and British-
born migrants, a group of first generation Australians,
and Alice Springs residents mostly from 'somewhere
else'. There is no fixed template for a sustainable human
presence in Australia; these are examples of possible
pathways, each with costs and benefits.

*M*any things are produced and reproduced in backyards, from
the highly material such as vegetables to more abstract things
such as family values. In this chapter we link the theme of
food production with that of the reproduction of tradition and practice in the
migrant experience. Migration is complex and not a unitary phenomenon.
Migration within Australia is considered in our Alice Springs case study.
Most of our Alice Springs people come from 'somewhere else', usually a much
less arid environment, and recount their experiences of learning to live and
produce a garden in a very different environment.

This chapter is also relevant to discussions about settler Australians'
'coming to terms' with the Australian environment. There are three key
issues. One is that those discussions have previously focused most on Anglo-
Australians. There is a pressing need to consider the diversity of non-Anglo
immigrant encounters with the Australian environment, a project we have
only scratched the surface of here, but one that deserves considerable research.
Fortuitously, our case study groups of Macedonian and Vietnamese immigrants
are comparable with those chosen for two New South Wales National Parks

and Wildlife Service studies of immigrant use of National Parks. This broadens our opportunity to discuss cross-cultural understandings of nature and environment.

The second issue is that there is no pre-determined, ideal way for humans to live in the Australian environment. This may seem an obvious point to make, but the tone of some critiques of contemporary environmental practices suggests otherwise. Expressions and terminology such as 'living within the constraints', or 'accepting the limits' of Australia can perhaps unintentionally convey the deterministic view that this environment has something in mind for what the ideal human presence might look like. Let us be very clear here. There are good reasons why Australians should, say, reduce their consumption of water, among other necessary improvements to environmental practice. But there is no single way by which this can or should be done, nor is there a magic sort of land use that is in itself better than any other. The ethical struggles of Alice Springs residents over whether or not to grow vegetables are a good example of these dilemmas.

The third issue follows from the second. 'The Australian environment' is not an entity in itself distinct from social processes. To follow the example of Alice Springs and water, people are adapting not just to 'the desert' or to 'arid conditions', but to a network of actors which include the Roe Creek borefield and

the technology of extraction, purification and distribution that links the Mereenie aquifer with the lawns of Alice Springs. It is possible to see this network, as many participants do, as supplying an abundance of water.

Production of food has, with the historical development of cities, become increasingly removed, physically and conceptually, from many people's daily lives. What are we to make then of the finding that vegetables are grown in 52% (137) of our 265 backyards? (This varies from a few herbs to extensive vegetable gardens that dominate the backyard). Only a small minority of participants would be anywhere near self sufficient in their vegetable production, but the ways in which people talk about their reasons for growing or not growing food demonstrate concerns with productivity and creativity. We use the terms production and reproduction to connote this wider context, which includes the exchange of ideas and practices between generations.

The numbers above are biased by the subsistence characteristics of the ten Macedonian and sixteen Vietnamese backyards (which account for most of the backyards with 80%–100% of the herb layer given over to vegetables and herbs). However, that leaves well over a hundred other backyards also producing vegetables, and many more with other expressions of food production, such as lemon trees (22% of all sampled backyards have a lemon tree). Six per cent of participants keep chooks or ducks, usually for eggs.

Percentage of herb layer allocated to growing vegetables and herbs	Number of backyards with vegetables	Proportion of all vegetable producing backyards
0-25	70	52%
30-50	25	18%
55-75	12	9%
80-100	30	21%
Total	137	100%

Table 6.1: Backyards growing vegetables and herbs by percentage of the herb layer. The herb layer is defined as the area under growth of less than 1m excluding lawn, to the nearest 5%. These 137 backyards with vegetables constitute 52% of the total sample. These figures exclude vegetables and herbs in pots.

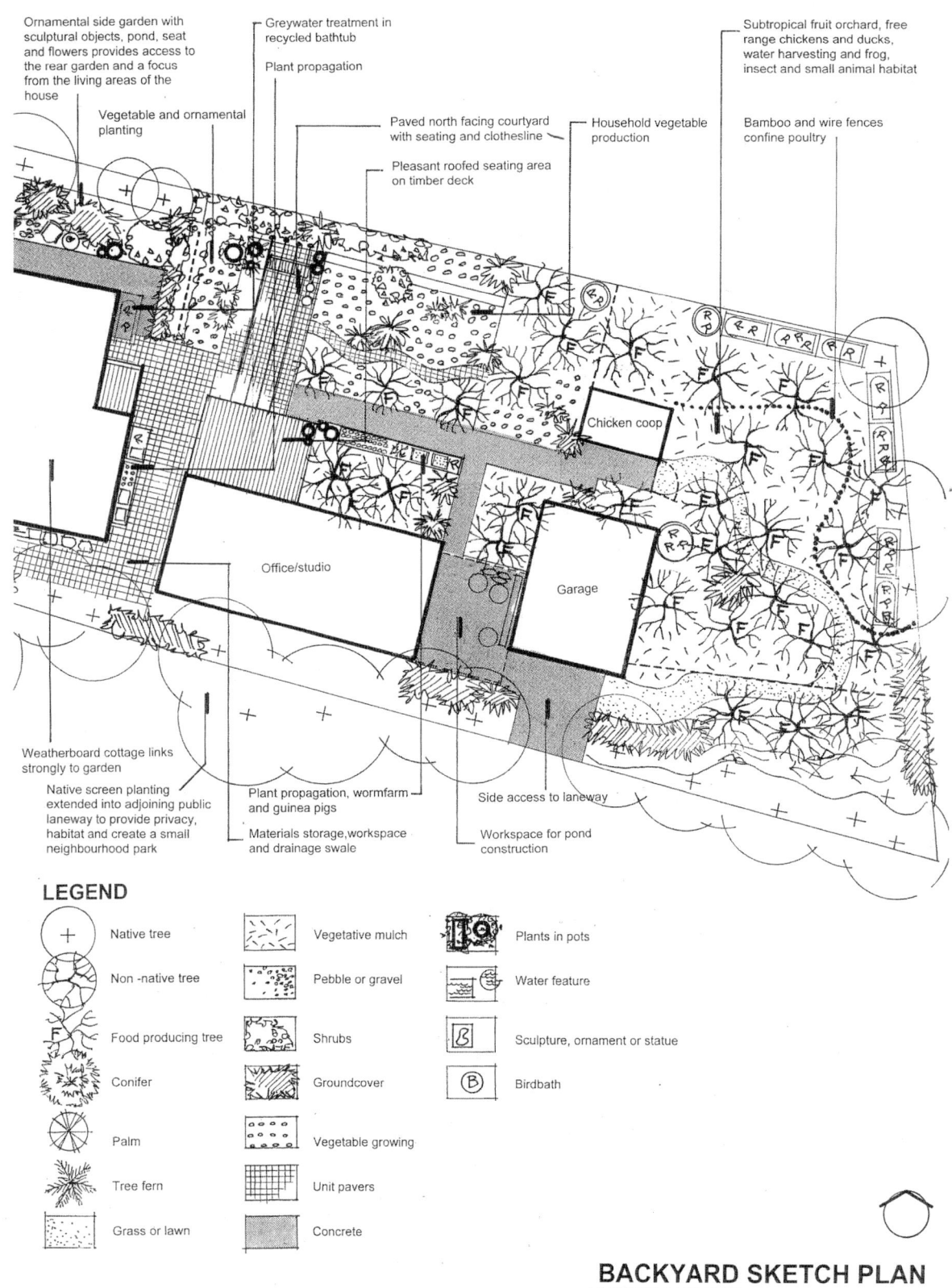

Ornamental side garden with sculptural objects, pond, seat and flowers provides access to the rear garden and a focus from the living areas of the house

Vegetable and ornamental planting

Greywater treatment in recycled bathtub

Plant propagation

Paved north facing courtyard with seating and clothesline

Pleasant roofed seating area on timber deck

Household vegetable production

Subtropical fruit orchard, free range chickens and ducks, water harvesting and frog, insect and small animal habitat

Bamboo and wire fences confine poultry

Chicken coop

Office/studio

Garage

Weatherboard cottage links strongly to garden

Native screen planting extended into adjoining public laneway to provide privacy, habitat and create a small neighbourhood park

Plant propagation, wormfarm and guinea pigs

Materials storage, workspace and drainage swale

Side access to laneway

Workspace for pond construction

LEGEND

Native tree	Vegetative mulch	Plants in pots	
Non-native tree	Pebble or gravel	Water feature	
Food producing tree	Shrubs	Sculpture, ornament or statue	
Conifer	Groundcover	Birdbath	
Palm	Vegetable growing		
Tree fern	Unit pavers		
Grass or lawn	Concrete		

BACKYARD SKETCH PLAN
DAN SUE PORT KEMBLA

Figure 6.1: Plan of Dan and Sue's backyard, Port Kembla, Wollongong

Productivity and Creativity

Although many participants produce food in their backyards, it is not usually at a level that can be relied on for subsistence. This section discusses some of the variables influencing their food production decisions.

An important characteristic of keen vegetable gardeners is age. Elderly and retired participants like Vi have more time to spend in the garden.

> *I generally start about seven . . . I love to chip so I'll go and chip my vegetable garden. I love chipping, always have, and I chip around the vegetables and mulch those with straw or dried grass. Plant anything that needs to be planted, dig up a bit of ground if it's needed and plant something in it . . . and I work to about lunchtime . . . and then I call it quits for the day . . . (Vi, northern suburbs, Wollongong)*

(Chipping is hoeing to break up and remove weeds).

Their consciousness of temporal rhythms extends into a keen awareness of generational differences, including their own ageing. Elderly people are concerned that traditions are unlikely to be continued. They comment on the pace, demands and affluence of their children's lifestyles. This is not confined to recent migrants. Older people are more likely to emphasise the importance to them of hard work, self reliance, community support and thrift, and to contrast it with the twenty-first century lifestyles of their children and grandchildren. They express this for example in the way they speak about making do with what they had rather than going to the shop:

> *what we did was playing outside with a bit of newspaper and a bit of rope around it and play football with that, because there was no money to buy a ball, you know. (Jhon, Forest Grove)*

However, younger generations also express interest in growing food, illustrating the physical connection with place that many value. A set of mostly younger food producers consistently mention environmental sustainability and organic methods as reasons for growing vegetables. Dan and Sue, activist permaculture gardeners of Port Kembla, have given over the whole of their suburban block to ecological practices that include fruit growing, vegetable and egg production, recycling of vegetation and water, and creation of wildlife habitat (Figure 6.1).

When asked to describe a memorable backyard from his childhood, Dan, who lived as a child in nearby Warilla, describes that of his Italian neighbour:

> *there wasn't a square inch of ground that wasn't under production. There wasn't a blade of grass in the backyard and the only trees that he had in the garden were fruit.*

Dan, Sue and Karen (below) are rare examples of people still in the workforce who produce significant proportions of their food in the backyard, at least at certain times of the year. Most younger food producers rely less on their produce as a major part of their food supply than the older generations mentioned above. The issue of time, particularly the time constraints of jobs and children, collides in various ways with the aspiration to organic and environmentally friendly practice. Thus younger people talk about wanting to grow vegetables as often as they talk about actually growing them.

Karen (aged in her 40s) in Wollongong's northern suburbs, finds the time to produce substantial quantities:

> *I can be almost self sufficient in the summer time growing lettuces, and tomatoes and beetroot and anything that I could possibly think of. I try and grow a new vegetable every year that I've never grown before . . . I spend time out here growing things, coming out here everyday and seeing where the weeds are, checking how the vegetables are. I don't think you can grow vegetables if you don't spend a lot of time checking how they are. Because I*

grow them organically I'll look at my cabbage to see if the cabbage moths are there, squash the caterpillars, do all that sort of thing.

On the other hand, people commonly talk about wanting to grow food rather than actually doing it:

it takes a lot of time and yeah as I said it's depressing because you want it to be nice you think I'd really love to get out there and do it but you just don't have the time it's really hard. (Judith, northern suburbs, Wollongong, describes her empty vegetable beds.)

I'd like to get back to nature and be able to put a spade in the garden and to get the satisfaction of seeing something grow, something productive and something that you can eat, instead of just going to a supermarket and buying everything in a plastic bag and hopefully we won't be using pesticides. (Lynette, northern suburbs, Wollongong, describes her plans for the future)

The idea here that food production must be understood as also producing a variety of social goods echoes Andrea Gaynor's 2001 analysis of postwar home food production, which she claims was more prevalent among the middle class than the working class, and could not be explained by necessity alone, since it was sometimes more expensive to produce than buy. She writes 'where food is produced by a household, it is often produced not as "food", but as "home-grown food", a distinctive category of produce.' (p. 27). Karen, Judith and Lynette all understand domestic food production as a kind of social good, and as an important way to connect to nature. But with various combinations of jobs, children and other commitments, the extent to which aspirations come to fruition varies considerably.

This is not to say that backyards with just a few tomato plants are not considered productive places by their inhabitants. The productive aspects are also expressed in the cooking, eating and sharing of food across generations. This includes the sharing of produce:

The other great pleasure is that I'm growing things both for myself and for my neighbours and friends and it's wonderful to be able to share things with people who either haven't got a garden or haven't the time to cultivate things . . . My father would lean over the fence and say to the elderly couple next door, 'have a punnet of blackberries' or 'have you got any gooseberries, would you like some of ours, have some apples', you know, this was ingrained I think. (Sylvia, inner Wollongong)

But altogether, this year I've got nearly twenty [chickens]. And we get about four or five eggs a day; there's not much this time of the year. But for the family and when we've got more we give them to our children and grandchildren; they are very good eggs. (Lennie, inner Wollongong)

As we discussed in chapter three, the outdoor eating and entertainment area is often the major social focus of the backyard. Bruno describes his spit:

I'm the one who cooks . . . I like chicken, piece of lamb, quarter lamb, little pig; you can't do this on the barbecue . . . So this way is very efficient and when they come they enjoy the food. But its hard work which I don't mind doing. You have to provide the wood, put the wood away until it dries . . . (Bruno, southern suburbs, Wollongong)

Bruno's and Lillian's son Mark continues an aspect of this tradition with his own family:

I like to cook, I don't see it just as a barbecue area, I see it as an eating area as well and that's something I'd like to develop further . . . So I've got a gas cooker and it's somewhere that's an extension of the kitchen and we can sit out there and drink beer and fry sausages . . . when we socialise we just sit out there and have a cup of tea . . . (Mark, northern suburbs, Wollongong)

Figure 6.2: Blaga shows interpreter Verica the vegetable garden in her backyard, Port Kembla, Wollongong. Rows of vegetables in a typical Macedonian production backyard include chillies, tomatoes, cucumbers, spinach, lettuce and onions

The Reproduction of Place and Practice— the Migrant Experience

Here we focus on the backyard gardens of three migrant groups within our broader study (Macedonian, Vietnamese and British born), and a fourth group of first generation Australians with both parents born overseas. Helen Armstrong explains migration as a process—rather than a trajectory with a clear beginning and end. Traditions are not maintained, translated or reworked in any sort of linear or predictable way. The complexities of the process reveal themselves in the domestic garden landscape (Armstrong 2004: 241).

The Macedonians are the most cohesive of the four groups. They are all elderly, most are retired post-World War II migrants, and a number of the men worked in the Port Kembla steelworks. Our British and first generation groups are drawn from the general survey. They vary in age, location and socio-economic status.

Macedonian Backyards

Nine of the ten Macedonian backyards are in older suburbs with houses built in the 1950s or sixties. Most of these backyards are relatively large, between 200 m² and 299 m². The exception is a new house built for an extended Macedonian family, which has a very large backyard extending onto farmland. Flowers, vegetables and herbs are all important in the backyards of this group. The main flowers are dahlias, chrysanthemums and geraniums, valued for their showy colourfulness. Seven of the ten Macedonian backyards have vegetable gardens, and they tend to occupy a large proportion of the available space. All these vegetable gardens are used to grow chillies and tomatoes, with salad greens (cucumber, lettuce, spinach) common. They are highly structured and ordered, with bare earth between the rows, often channelled, and plants chipped around to aerate the soil and keep weeds down. Matting to suffocate weeds was observed in at least two backyards, and soil is frequently discussed.

I always try to keep the soil clean around the plant because if one [weed] is allowed to start growing between the plants it takes all the goodness from the soil and from the plant. (Blaga, Port Kembla) (Figure 6.2)

Shrub and tree layers are dominated by fruit or nut trees, most frequently stone fruit (nectarine, peach, cherry), followed by lemon and mango. Only two backyards had native trees. Apart from fruit trees, trees are usually limited to one small flowering tree, such as a camellia, crepe myrtle, frangipani or oleander.

The Macedonians' discussion of their shrub and tree layer is inseparable from discussion of production—from the notion that the backyard should yield food. Participants talk about grape and passionfruit vines and nut trees (chestnut, walnut), as well as melons (watermelon, rock-melon, honeymelon) and fruit trees. The emphasis is on stonefruit, but they have mixed success at growing these fruit trees in the variable and humid Wollongong conditions. Menka, however, has only good things to say about her trees in Port Kembla.

Happiness is the only thing I feel. The trees are like, the fruit trees around, I go there, I pick the fruit that I like, I eat it. I go at the back, I pick a plum and look around, look at the sky, the trees, the grass and I feel happy, content.

Menka is less content with the banksia and melaleuca, purchased by her daughter from the local council's Greenplan, describing how the banksia was moved because of sprawling branches and another tree has been removed because it grew too large. George has a similar comment:

Figure 6.3: White foam boxes used as herb planters were photographed underneath Hoang's grapefruit tree in Green Valley, Sydney

Figure 6.4: Le tending vegetables in his Fairfield, Sydney, home where almost the entire backyard is planted with vegetables, herbs, fruit trees and vines

> *I said big trees are not to be grown in the back-yard, you grow a fruit tree or something small that look nice and something that can give you fruit, peaches, plums, lemons whatever. Nothing that grows big.*

These participants with vegetable gardens all talk about the first walk around the backyard each morning to check how everything is growing, the 'small walk' we mentioned in Chapter Five. With some exceptions, the backyard is not generally used by the Macedonians to sit or eat in.

Vietnamese Backyards

Thirteen of the sixteen Vietnamese participants live in detached houses with backyards and three in townhouses with small courtyards. The interviews spread across older inner western suburbs of Sydney, with moderate sized backyards (100 m^2 –199 m^2). Most of the houses were built in the sixties, some in the nineties or later.

Herb layers are dominated by edible herbs (several kinds of Vietnamese mint, menthol, lemongrass) and vegetables (sweet potatoes, chillies, taro, bok choy), with minor plantings of non-native flowers and shrubs. High proportions of available space are utilised for vegetable and herb production (Figure 6.4). White foam boxes are frequently used as starter boxes for seedlings and herbs (Figure 6.3). There could also be a seasonal reason for Vietnamese participants emphasising vegetable production less than the Macedonians, as the Vietnamese interviews were conducted in winter, July and August 2003. Macedonian interviews were in spring.

Fruit trees dominate the shrub and tree layers, mainly tropical fruits (mangoes, pawpaws, loquats and longans), followed by citrus trees (grapefruit, mandarin, lemon) and bananas. Two thirds have at least one fruit tree in the backyard, for half, more than 80% of shrubs and trees are fruit bearing. (Figure 6.4). Vietnamese participants do not deliberately plant any other shrubs or trees in the backyard, but have retained some left by previous residents.

When asked to describe their backyard, nearly all the Vietnamese participants begin by describing the type of fruit trees grown. One sole parent laments that a lack of time means she cannot grow fruit trees. (In contrast to this, the Macedonian responses begin at the herb layer with a description of the types of vegetables they produce, and then move on to fruit trees). In informal conversations they take pride in the quantity of fruit produced and the practice of bringing citrus seeds from Vietnam, believing the fruit from these seeds to be superior in size and flavour. Discussion about other types of shrubs and trees is minimal.

Gardening for food production is the most frequently discussed backyard activity with sitting and relaxing also important. Eating is less important, with messy cooking done outside, but most eating occurring inside, except for gatherings of extended families.

British Backyards

Backyards of British migrants are more diverse than the above two groups. Sixty per cent contain flowers, most frequently geraniums, agapanthus and impatiens. Colour is important to them in discussions of flowers.

Shrub and tree layers combine natives (most commonly *Eucalyptus*, *Pittosporum* and *Leptospermum*) and non-natives (camellia, jacaranda, frangipani and hibiscus) and palms (mainly cocos or date palms with some native bangalows). Fruit trees are primarily citrus (lemon, lime, orange) and stone fruit (peach, plum and nectarine). In comparison to the other three groups, British-born participants grow the fewest fruit trees in their backyards and the emphasis on citrus usually translates to a single tree, most frequently a lemon tree. There is little discussion about the relative benefits of having such trees or the use made of them, rather a straightforward listing of such trees occurred in the course of describing the yard. There would seem to be less investment in fruit trees, in

Figure 6.5: Tam with fruit trees in a paved section of his Bonnyrigg, Sydney backyard

terms both of productivity and attachment, than amongst the Vietnamese and Macedonian participants.

Seventy-one per cent of British participants have native shrubs or trees, speaking positively about them in terms of attracting birds, or because they need less water and are perceived to be low maintenance. However one third of this group either does not like or does not want to grow native plants.

> We started off with just a few little things and we put the natives in as you can see but we've also put the trees in that we like . . . So we've got flowers and things coming out all the time, flowering things, but in spring and summer

Figure 6.6: Pat and Bill in their Forest Grove, Wollongong backyard, with extensive native and non-native shrub and tree layer planted behind the retaining wall to attract birds and to admire the flowers

Figure 6.7: Flowering annuals planted in hanging baskets are a reminder of seasonal change for British born Maggie, inner Sydney

it's beautiful because nearly every tree has a flower on it, it's very nice. (Pat and Bill, Forest Grove) (Figure 6.6)

We don't have a huge amount of natives in the garden. We've both come from elsewhere and we're mad on seasonal change. Not to say that natives don't give you that . . . but the whole nuance of the garden was to kind of awaken to the nuance of different times of year. We love colour, we love scent so we try to create that. (Maggie, inner Sydney) (Figure 6.7)

They talk about gardening frequently, not specifically in regard to food production but rather as a more general activity, including weeding and pruning. Sitting, often with a book or a cup of tea, is also frequently mentioned, as well as eating with family or friends. British participants also mention mowing as an activity more than other migrant groups (Appendix 2.9).

First Generation Backyards

There are twenty-two first generation Australian participants with parents all born outside Australia. Most of their parents (thirteen couples) were European. Participants with an Italian parent or parents comprise the largest group (five) among them. Six Australian-born participants had one or both parents born in Britain.

Ten of them talk about why they grow vegetables, but it was never on the scale of the dominant vegetable gardens observed among the Macedonian group or several elderly Italian vegetable gardeners in our sample. Of the four groups selected for migrant backgrounds, the first generation Australians have the highest proportions of native plants, in both the herb (e.g. prostrate grevillea, native orchids) and shrub/tree (*Eucalyptus, Callistemon, Casuarina*) layers. Every one of these participants has at least one native plant, but in only nine backyards out of the seventeen had it been a deliberate choice to grow natives, many participants having acquired natives with the purchase of their house. Flowers (geranium, agapanthus and impaties) are popular, as well as flowering non-native trees and shrubs (hibiscus, jacaranda, camellia and orange jessamine). Fruit trees, mostly citrus, were present in half the backyards of these participants, who link their desire to grow fruit trees to memories of production backyards of their childhood.

The memory of backyards under heavy subsistence production influenced participants both for and against becoming producers themselves.

> *You get things from your parents. My parents are migrants from Europe, from the Ukraine after the war. To them having a garden was all about getting some food out of it . . . We had the typical migrants' garden in the western suburbs of Melbourne—potatoes, sunflowers, corn, peas. (Toly, Alice Springs)*

For Desiree, however, whose Italian father is a keen and generous vegetable gardener, there is little incentive to do it herself:

> *I just think they're too much effort trying to keep the bugs out of them and everything.*

Thus those who grow vegetables do it because they value the traditions of an older generation, rather than being driven by thrift and necessity. They still talk about saving money, and relaxing in the vegetable garden, but the emphasis changes from need to more of a desire to continue particular practices. There is a sense that participants value the benefit of having fresh vegetables or fruit but treat it as a choice rather than a need.

Memory, Tradition and Change

> *it's not just the difference between there and here as it is from before and now.*

The transplantations that we are speaking of include practices, ideas and, sometimes, plant varieties. Slave, who comes from Macedonia and now lives in the western suburbs of Wollongong expresses the common response of migrants to displacement. Isis Brook describes this in her 2003 article, "Making Here Feel Like There", as making 'here' feel like 'home' through the use of familiar plants.

> *And every tradition from there we brought it here so that's why we are making gardens and trying to produce chillies and tomatoes or something little, in a way to remind us of there, but somehow to have the taste from there brought here, and to continue the tradition of making produce and something from the soil. (Slave, Wollongong West) (Figure 5.12)*

Macedonian participants' memories of child-hood are of land; useable land and what was grown on the land and by whom. As nine out of ten came from villages, their definition of backyards was extended to include work in the surrounding fields. Their memories were about helping to do chores, and seasonal changes. There were few play stories. Vietnamese participants' memories were about the different types of fruit trees and vegetables grown, with blocks of land commonly remembered as smaller than the backyards of western Sydney. Chickens and pigs were the animals described. There is little discussion about what they did in their childhood backyard in terms of chores or playing space. Eleven of the sixteen had a backyard in Vietnam; the remaining five lived in the city.

Elderly people of different nationalities share the concern that traditions are unlikely to be continued.

> *And probably the tradition will die off as this generation are slowly dying because when we talk with other people of our generation they said we gave up the gardening, but why, the reason being that the kids didn't want to participate in it they didn't want to continue making a garden. (Slave, Wollongong West, Macedonian)*

When my daughters-in-law were living together with me here in the house, every time I would get the chillies and bake them then I need to fill them, to do something with them, they would hide themselves in their room and go to sleep instead of come and help me . . . They don't like home made they prefer to buy it in the shop. (Menka, northern suburbs, Wollongong, Macedonian)

My mother sold a few eggs, sold the milk to buy the socks and the shoes. There was no money. In Australia the parents and the children have too much money and they spend too much. In my country we worked in the garden and we did not spend much. I grew the grapes, I made the wine. (Theresa, Port Kembla, Italian)

Some elderly participants recognise that conditions have also changed in the places they left behind, as encapsulated by Slave saying 'it's not just the difference between there and here as it is from before and now'.

People are working. They have no time. They are time bound to take the kids to school or to activities, to go to work . . . and there's no time or not enough time to devote it to growing a vegetable garden.

It is clear that the shift in practices between migrants and their Australian-born children is heavily influenced by the profound socio-economic changes of the last few decades. Younger generations do gardening only as a relaxing leisure activity. A desire to reduce maintenance is mentioned by the British participants and the participants with migrant parents, wanting to keep either the back or front yard low maintenance, or having a backyard that looks after itself and is easy to manage. Choosing plants because they need little maintenance is not a consideration of the Macedonian or Vietnamese participants. Macedonian participants speak about the need to look after the plants they put in the ground, and the time and care expended.

Production and Productivity

The importance of productive activities in the daily rhythm is particularly poignant when elderly people can no longer manage independent living, as Julie reveals:

Interviewer: You must like spinach.

Julie: No, I don't; there's a Yugoslav man who lives across the road who lives in a unit . . . he had a farm in his home country and now he's living in a small unit and he just hates the fact that he's not growing anything and so he comes over and plants all of these vegetables and tends them and all the rest of it and takes what he wants for his family, and I'm happy to have him do that because it helps me to keep the place in some sort of order. So no, I don't like spinach much. (Julie, inner Wollongong)

For the Macedonian participants, the notion that we refer to here as productivity encompasses three distinctly physical engagements: (i) between the gardener and the soil, such as described by George in chapter four, (ii) the importance of smell and taste, and (iii) the temporal rhythms of life.

In Macedonia even the wild things in the mountains in the valleys that would grow by themselves, they have a nice smell, a nice look. Even though they are wild they look like they've been grown by someone, maintained and everything is ripe and ready to be eaten. Everything smells, the flowers, even the fruit trees when you go by. (Slave, Wollongong West)

It grows here as well as it grows in Macedonia but the difference is in the taste. When you taste it, it never tastes as good as it tastes in Macedonia no matter if it's the chillies, the tomatoes or the cucumber. (Menka, northern suburbs, Wollongong)

For the elderly women isolated by their lack of English, the productivity of the garden goes with the notion of life itself. For Menka, 'the main feature in the backyard is the garden that in a way keeps me alive.'

> When you are alone but it gives me a reason to get up in the morning and get out here and have something to do. It's my entertainment, my pastime for the whole day.
> (Blaga, Port Kembla)

Our Macedonian participants are divided on the cost factor, some saying that the cost of enriching the soil and dusting or spraying makes the produce more expensive than shop bought vegetables. One of them grows no vegetables for this reason. On the other hand, Blaga grows far more vegetables than she can consume, and sometimes sells them in the neighbourhood.

Freshness, Food, Peace and Happiness

So, how do the Vietnamese experiences of backyards and backyard production compare to the Macedonian ones discussed above? There are similarities in themes of tradition and pride in self sufficiency. There are also differences, since as a group the Vietnamese are significantly younger than the retired Macedonians. The Vietnamese interpreter used one participant's response to a question on garden influences to articulate a broader Vietnamese philosophy of food production:

> Because the Vietnamese people, when they go to anywhere they grow trees there. So to make it look nice and it has fruit to eat. So they can also save money because they don't have to go to the shop and buy vegetable. And they grow without chemical fertiliser. They just use natural fertiliser.

The comment was triggered by Le's response to one of our questions. Le, an elderly participant, has virtually the entire garden space devoted to food production, and is proud of the fact that his extended family (of at least eight) does not need to buy any vegetables at all (Figure 6.4). Another participant, Ken, reinforces the utilitarian purpose of these gardens.

> Actually my mum, she planted. Plant is for food, for eating. The main point for eating, not for . . . looking good . . . Good for your health. You can eat fresh food. Don't need to pay. (Ken, Fairfield Cabramatta)

Like the Macedonians, the Vietnamese express the need to be able to get outside, to do things, to observe and to think. They talk consistently about the backyard as a place that makes them happy. Since most of this group are of working age, those contemplative moments are often found after work.

> Interpreter: He happy with the garden. Sometimes after work, he come home and go to the garden, look at the plants and he feel happy with it. (Hoy, Fairfield Cabramatta)

> So when I feel a bit tired or a bit, I want a bit of moving [from computer study] so I come to backyard and have a look and then go around and see how they going. And try to understand, try to find out how this plant going. Something like that. A sort of possession. The thing that I have. (Chi Vuong, Fairfield Cabramatta)

> My main feeling in my backyard is connect to me in what I'm feeling happy, I am sad. Or sometimes if I am angry or I go to outside there, maybe when I see my backyard I feel the angry gone. (Son, Fairfield Cabramatta)

A strong sense of thrift and 'making do' is not explicit in the Vietnamese interviews but is inferred from numerous makeshift structures in backyards constructed from recycled materials, and the widespread practice of using polystyrene boxes as seed planters.

Attitudes to Nature and Environment—Comparisons with Public Open Space

Recognising its responsibility to a multicultural community, the New South Wales National Parks and Wildlife Service recently commissioned research on attitudes to and use of national parks by members of the Macedonian and Vietnamese communities. Among elderly Macedonians, there are striking similarities with our research in terms of the importance of smell. Martin Thomas in 2001 recorded cases where smell emerges in memories of Macedonia, as well as people who regard the Australian bush as not having a smell.

> *You can rub grass there and it has a different—an earthly smell. I rub grass here, it smells nothing, unfortunately. It's not Australia's fault. I think we are in a topography where all the goodness is washed out. (Paul Stephen, Macedonian, quoted in Thomas 2001: 62)*

Thomas reports strong attachments to Australian plantations of introduced *Pinus radiata* as the nearest equivalent to the 'intoxicating' smell of Macedonian pine forests—to the extent that Macedonian people buy holiday houses near them. Associated with these memories is 'great nostalgia for the rural life, where the food was healthy, the water pure, the air clean' (2001: 67). In strong echoes of the reasons our study participants gave for growing vegetables in their backyards, Thomas reported that 'the flavour of the earth, as manifest in fruit, air and water, seemed important to all the informants' (p. 68).

The importance of sounds and smells is also frequently mentioned in relation to the densely populated Vietnamese landscape. 'That the Australian bush is scentless and soundless is often commented on' (Mandy Thomas 2002: 81). Rice paddy fields figure strongly in memories of Vietnamese life and landscape. Since most people in Vietnam live in rural areas, there is a strong relationship between subsistence and nature.

For both groups, the daily integration of people with the environment in village or rural life translates into different understandings of parks from the wilderness ethic that has underpinned much of the Australian national parks movement. This is expressed by the centrality of people in family photographs of Macedonian national parks, and in descriptions of beautiful places in terms of the actions that took place there. 'There was no sense of photographing a mountain, a tree, a river, for its own sake,' writes Martin Thomas. Nature 'is something in which people are always imbricated' (2001: 69).

> *You rarely hear people talk about the beauty of a physical place, at least in the sense whenever our parents talk about it. It's not just a beautiful river but it was the beautiful river where we did this and this. (Novica, age 27, quoted in Thomas 2001: 82)*

Mandy Thomas reports that for most of the Vietnamese group, 'the flora and fauna of Vietnam is equated with fruit, flowers and farm animals, and not "wild" animals. Rather than a "wilderness" the landscape was domesticated and viewed as a resource' (p.71). This sense of a domesticated landscape has several related expressions. On one hand 'they try to grow Vietnam in the backyard!' (Cuong, quoted in Thomas 2002: 76). On the other, people are not interested in parks or in walking too far from human settlement. 'This reflects their experiences in Vietnam where it is unlikely even in rural areas that people were very far out of earshot of others' (p. 98).

> *You don't need to go far, your backyard is your national park. (Minh, quoted in Thomas 2002: 59).*

Nevertheless, members of both groups talk of a gradually increasing affection for the Australian landscape that they had first experienced as empty, dry and lacking in smell.

The process of migration is inscribed on the post-World War II Australian suburban landscape through the food producing activities of

Macedonian, Vietnamese and Italian migrants, among many others. Particular combinations of foods result in distinctive landscapes that can be identified with particular ethnic groups. For example extensive plantings of chillies and tomatoes indicate Macedonian, or at least southern European, influences; tropical fruit trees and polystyrene planters of Vietnamese mint and lemongrass denote Vietnamese. Yet the details of daily interaction as described by our participants support the argument of Tim Ingold, that

> nature is not a surface of materiality upon which human history is inscribed; rather history is the process wherein both people and their environments are continually bringing each other into being . . . human actions in the environment are better seen as incorporative rather than inscriptive, in the sense that they are built or enfolded into the forms of the landscape and its living inhabitants by way of their own processes of growth.
> (Ingold 2000: 87)

In their daily interactions, ethnic groups as diverse as Vietnamese and Macedonian bear this out. Among Macedonian participants, their strongest memories, and thus strongest experience of the difference of Australian conditions, is the smell and productivity of the soil—'the flavour of the earth' as Martin Thomas puts it (2001:68). Vietnamese participants combine very utilitarian attitudes to garden production—'plant is for eating . . . not for . . . looking good'—with a valuing of even small green spaces for their contemplative possibilities. For all their differences, these two groups reflect a shared rural subsistence background in which humans are embedded in their environment through physical labour. Ingold's term 'incorporative' reminds us of the importance of the physical body—through senses, labour, daily rhythms—in these environmental relations.

When we have a sample group that is more diverse with respect to factors other than ethnicity, as in our British born group, the gardens are also more diverse. Indeed it would be difficult to ascribe 'Britishness' to any particular garden landscape or feature. The British seem to split between those who enthusiastically adopt Australian plants, and those who maintain an ordered, ornamental approach to their garden, incorporating the occasional flowering native.

Gardens of intensive food production virtually disappear within a generation of migration. Among the first generation Australian born they are more likely to be reflected in motifs that echo tradition—pots of herbs, a few tomato plants, an outdoor oven as centrepiece of an entertaining area, favourite flowers—than in any intense day to day engagement. This has less to do with adapting to unique Australian environments than with the socio-economic conditions of contemporary urban life.

Reproduction and Adaptation—the Example of Alice Springs

Most of our Alice Springs participants grew up somewhere else. Some had come to the Centre for specific work opportunities, others arrived on a youthful journey and never left. As a migrant case study, it is a story then of people who have generally had more economic and political choices than the Macedonians or Vietnamese. Nor did they have to change their cultural position or learn a new language in the process. Probably for these reasons, people talk less about making Alice Springs 'like home' than about adapting to its environmental demands—the need for shade and water.

For the most part, this is the colonisers' view of the Alice Springs environment rather than the indigenous people's view. Two (8%) of our twenty four Alice Springs backyards belong to Aboriginal people, an under-representation of their proportion in the population of the town (17% at the 2001 Census). There are three backyards with an Aboriginal owner in our total sample (1%,

Figure 6.8: Sue in her vegetable garden, Alice Springs

compared with 2.4% of the Australian population identifying as Aboriginal at the 2001 Census). We have not tried in this study to do justice to the full variety of Aboriginal gardens seen throughout Australia, for example the communal gardens in Alice Springs, which fall outside our scheme.

Another important part of the Alice Springs landscape not included is the houses and gardens maintained for the predominantly American staff of the Joint Defence Space Research Facility at Pine Gap, outside the town. Many of these have very lush lawns, evidence of an intensive watering regime.

Wide-ranging attitudes are expressed towards water usage. With only 286mm annual rainfall,[13] Alice Springs can exist because it utilises water from the Mereenie aquifer in the Roe Creek borefield to the south. Water is currently being drained from this aquifer more quickly than it is recharged, and the projected lifespan is about twenty years under current water use practices. Average household water consumption is 1600 litres per day, 63% of it used on gardens.[14] For comparison, Sydney Water's summer consumption target for an efficient Sydney household of four is 694 litres daily.[15] Debates about water supply are not then so much about actual lack of supply, as about the capital cost of developing a new borefield. The interpretation of this situation by our participants led to diverging attitudes to water; some see this as a situation of chronic water shortage, and evidence of a continuing frontier mentality, while others argue that 'there's plenty of water there'. This leads on to divergent attitudes to things like lawn.

In terms of gardener types, both committed native gardeners and non-gardeners constitute proportionally more of the Alice Springs case study than the total sample. This reflects several related characteristics of the locality. Our sample has on average high educational levels. The generic natives favoured by 'general native gardeners' in the Sydney region are much less likely to survive in Alice Springs than local arid zone natives. Many exotics are impossible to grow (citrus and roses are notable exceptions), and the harsh conditions and transient population mean many people just don't bother. On the other hand, the generally large suburban blocks in Alice Springs encourage experiment. 'When we first moved here', says Brad, 'we thought, great, a huge backyard.'

'We Don't Live Where we Came from'

The gardening challenges that people face in Alice Springs are most obviously environmental ones; too much heat, not enough water and a substrate that is basically sand. There is an initial hesitation when 'you get over the idea that you can't do it, you can't grow things here'. A number of participants like Brad describe great enthusiasm when they arrive, followed by disappointment the first summer, and a gradual process of accommodation. As Sally says somewhat wearily—

Maybe when you first come to town you plant things over summer, then you get so disappointed. It's such hard work . . .

Chris, who with partner Paul has developed a garden including natives, vegetables and fruit trees over seventeen years, describes 'an evolutionary period of kind of realising that we don't live where we came from'.

I had always grown up around water, I probably had quite an abusive attitude, you know, the Murray River it's big and there's always going to be water there and when I first came, you know, it was what you were used to. I mean living on the east coast for a while, and everything is green and lush and grows

Figure 6.9: Shade and water create a haven in an Alice Springs backyard

at the drop of a hat, and it is much more of a challenge to grow a garden here. But it was that process of realising that, oh, I don't live on the east coast, I don't live in Victoria, I live here and these are the sort of things that grow well without having to be looked after too much and they do look nice . . . . I came back [from a visit to Victoria] thinking more about how to live in the environment in which I actually am living in, rather than trying to bring in other environments into the backyard; sort of making that sort of bush connection, I suppose.

The Ethics of Lettuce

For participants conscious of adapting to local conditions the key dilemma is not so much the question of local natives, but in whether and how to have a vegetable garden. For those who came from the east and south with what they would think of as an environmental sensibility, when confronted with the possibilities of a large backyard the obvious choice was some combination of native plantings and food production. For those interested in native plantings, obtaining local natives has become relatively straightforward now that the Alice Springs Desert Park propagates them commercially. Vegetables create a lot more uneasiness as people realise that it is a choice between depending on the technology of water extraction and distribution in Alice Springs, or the technology of vegetable transportation from other parts of Australia—

but it got difficult with the soil and with the water. You just can't justify it. It's not ethical to spend that much water on lettuce for example. So we've now just started to concentrate the vegies in one area. Realising that we can't have a food forest. We can just have a smaller area that's ethical and manageable. So now we're planting more natives because you just see how hardy they are and how little energy you have to put into them. And they are very, very

beautiful plants. So our knowledge of what we like and what we're doing has just grown. (Brad, 3 years in Alice Springs)

I mean we are so dependent on that infrastructure to our daily existence. Now for me I can live without my vegie patch because I can go down to the supermarket and buy it but I don't know, maybe there's something innate or something primordial in actually having my own vegie patch and growing it. (Michael, 2 years in Alice Springs)

You can tell yourself you're providing yourself with organic fruit and vegetables, but you're doing it at a cost to a water system. We're just living off bore water that's going to run out one day. So it's a contradiction . . . Growing vegetables in summer is not an environmentally sound thing to do. (Sue, 7 years in Alice Springs) (Figure 6.8)

Sue goes on to describe her dilemma over whether the ground itself needs to be watered:

if the ground isn't getting watered regularly it dies. All that nice compost you've put in, its hard for those living organisms to keep going if it dries out . . . So I'm starting to wonder if I should leave the water on it even though there's nothing growing there just to keep the soil alive. Alive for gardening I mean. It doesn't need to be alive to grow a local plant in it.

A longer period of residence in Alice Springs seems to bring greater equanimity, and a recognition that there are limits to how much an urban culture, dependent on agricultural produce and fossil fuels, can 'adapt' to desert conditions. This is expressed most succinctly by Toly, whom we met above as a first generation migrant. His backyard combines influences from his Ukrainian parents in Melbourne, his Aboriginal partner Alexis, who also has Chinese ancestry, and their twenty-five years living in the Alice. The garden is an eclectic mix of plants, providing perhaps its most distinctive feature, lots of deep shade. Toly describes a long period of living and working in the bush, but at the same time accepting that 'we're not really desert people. No one is.'

> *That's a roundabout way of saying that I've learnt a lot about this environment; but I also know that I'm not from here. And I'll make all sorts of adaptations and adjustment but I still like to retain the things that are important to me in my relationship to nature. Often that's water and shade and those sorts of things.*

So, while these gardeners make certain decisions that they think make ecological sense, such as not having a lawn, they do not describe this as replicating nature, or bringing the bush into their backyard. Indeed Toly differentiates his soothing garden from the harshness of desert bushland. Rather it is about creating a home, a place of comfort, cool and restfulness (Figure 13). At the risk of reading too much into their discussion, it expresses an interesting dialectic between belonging and not belonging. Investment in the garden was an important part of their creation of a comfortable home. Toly, though he says 'I'm not from here', adds

> *That's the trick about living in central Australia. You don't want to feel like your life's on hold till you go back and live somewhere else.*

Coming to Terms

The notion of 'coming to terms' with the environment is often used to denote the cultural shift that is required for all settler Australians to develop sustainable lifestyles, including those who have been here for generations. The potential usefulness of the concept is undermined if those terms are taken to provide a readymade template for what an appropriate and sustainable human presence in Australia might look like. To start with, there is not one but many Australian environments. More to the point, the 'environment' is not a stand alone phenomenon separate from human existence, but a configuration of connections in which humans and nonhumans are already embedded. The people in this chapter illustrate just a few of the many pathways by which human beings can negotiate their presence in a 'new' landscape. The networks of connection can link the 'flavour of the earth' with the labour force participation patterns of second generation migrants, the Mereenie aquifer with the making of home. None of these fits a predetermined template. Each offers environmental costs and benefits that deserve detailed consideration. While the possible pathways are infinite, the processes have certain things in common. They are grounded in everyday experience and activity, they gather together people and food, and they enfold past, present and future together.

CHAPTER SEVEN

Water and the Power to Make a Difference

People use a variety of strategies to reduce water consumption, symbolised by the bucket in the shower. On the other hand, they voice desires for more water in their everyday environments. The younger and more affluent are losing an older ethic of frugality; this makes them more likely to behave in ways that actually increase consumption. However, urban Australians have begun their much needed culture shift in relation to water, and are waiting for governments to go with them. Gardens help rather than hinder this process as people can see the full cycle of production and consumption, understand where and how to make a difference, and are prepared to work to save them.

Figure 7.2: 'The trouble with Sydney', (Source: Cathy Wilcox and Sydney Morning Herald)

n May 2005 *The Sydney Morning Herald* ran a detailed set of reports, 'The Trouble with Sydney', examining various woes besetting the city and its future. These included many environmental issues, such as transport, air quality, water, and urban sprawl versus urban consolidation. The Wilcox cartoon on the editorial page (Figure 7.2) encapsulates the key contradiction of this special feature. In the rest of the paper, it was business as usual, with regular advertising supplements exhorting the reader to buy more cars, real estate and 'lifestyle', thus exacerbating the environmental problems at issue. Pulled between these two forces, the cartoon character sighs and trudges off for a coffee. An abdication of responsibility for trying to resolve the tension is implied by the latte, signifier of people affluent enough to be the target of the advertising, and educated enough to contribute to solving environmental problems.

In this chapter we focus on water, an issue brought to the fore by the drought of 2002–03. How do people understand and use their own power and agency in relation to water and other environmental issues?

We find water closely related to practices that entwine with other aspects of domestic life, such as the allocation of time and the division of household labour between the sexes. These practices do not correlate in a straightforward way to consumption patterns. There is disruption, resistance and breakdown of messages—in the case of water, quite intense messages—from the public sphere. Nevertheless we have found that all sorts of people have been inclined to change some aspects of their behaviour in relation to water consumption. Why has this been more marked than for other issues? Is it just a reflection of the visible crisis of drought? Are there other influences?

In *Comfort, Cleanliness and Convenience*, Elizabeth Shove argues for a shift in the focus of social environmental research 'so as to comprehend the collective restructuring of expectation and habit' (2003: 4). Through a detailed focus on everyday practice, she shows how changes in what is considered 'normal' in personal cleanliness and laundering have implications for water and energy consumption. She uses the metaphor of the ratchet 'to represent the locking in of technologies and practices' (p. 194). For example, once American homes began to be designed for air conditioning, home owners had to use it to be comfortable. In a general sense, the consumption of energy is inevitably ratcheted up. To illustrate alternatives, she uses the metaphor of the pinwheel, which 'can move in different directions but is momentarily held in place by a particular configuration of sociotechnical considerations' (p. 194). Her example is the way in which the construction of basic needs affects how and how often people have a bath or shower, and thus patterns of water consumption.

If we understand that 'much consumption is customary, governed by collective norms and undertaken in a world of things and sociotechnical system that have stabilising effects on routines and habits' (p. 9), we realise that changing environmental behaviour is not just a matter of giving people 'knowledge' and expecting them to do the right thing, as is the tone of a lot of public environmental education programs. Rather it is important to understand how practices, expectations and ways of life become customary. Further, from this perspective, neither the dispirited latte drinker nor the future of air conditioning is inevitable. Certainly there are examples of ratcheting along a fixed pathway, but there are also examples of destabilisation, change and resistance. If habits are pinned in place they can be unpinned. If practice is variable, we have visions of other ways of doing things.

> Looking ahead, what people take to be normal is immensely malleable. There are no fixed measures of comfort and cleanliness and it is perfectly possible that future concepts will be less resource intensive than those of today. The real environmental risk is not that services will be redefined (this happens all the time), but that there will be sweeping, cross cultural convergence in what people take to be normal ways of life, and a consequent locking in of demand for the resources on which these ways depend. (Shove 2003: 199)

One of the things we find in this chapter is that multiple attitudes and practices, in this case with respect to the use of water, are in fact widespread.

We also build on Maria Kaika's study of how the denial of nature in the city extends to denying nature in the home. In *City of Flows* (2005) she argues that

> the social construction of the Western (bourgeois) home as an autonomous, independent, private space is predicated upon a process of visual and discursive exclusion of undesired social (anomie, homelessness, social conflict, etc.) and natural (cold, dirt, pollution, etc.) elements . . . (p. 7)

She makes the point that while social exclusion in and around the home has been extensively studied, the exclusion of nature and socio-natural processes has not been adequately researched or documented (p. 52). Using the example of water, she observes that

> Natural elements are not in fact kept altogether outside the modern home; but rather are selectively allowed to enter after having undergone significant material and social transformations, through being produced, purified, and commodified (p. 64)

Thus water is purified to become 'good' nature before it enters the house, and once it becomes 'bad' nature, in the form of sewage, it must not only be removed, but be visually excluded. Both the purified water and the sewage are hybrid forms dependent on complex material and social networks. The familiarity and comfort of the bathtub or swimming pool, Kaika argues, require those networks to remain invisible, and the space of the home to remain clean and pure.

As Shove also showed, these processes of spatial cleansing and purification are intensified by consumer capitalism. Advertisements for washing powder, air conditioners, for houses themselves, all tap into fears of dirt and desires for pure spaces. Imagery promoting 'cleanliness, purity, whiteness and spatial order, images reflecting the idea of a pure inner self' (Sibley 1995: 78) are particularly widespread in homemaking media. The visual representation of homes and gardens in these magazines always excludes the impure—the dirt and the mess (unless in a before and after shot that illustrates the process of cleansing). In presenting domestic spaces as static, a further set of exclusions occurs. The labour required to create the space and keep it clean, becomes invisible, as many feminist commentators have noted. The messiness of human experience is also invisible. The kids, the dirty laundry, the ebb and flow of paper (junk mail, bills, school notices, packaging), the constancy of food preparation, and the rubbish bins are never seen. Even as the text might talk of the kitchen as the hub of family life, the kitchen bench is never buried under more than a stylised bowl of fruit. Here of course is the attractiveness of so-called 'decorator porn'; it provides a fantasy for the usually female readership that such spaces are possible. Here also is its role in increasing consumption; it builds on anxieties of what the ideal should be.

For most of that readership, the home in lived experience is likely to be more like an intestine— an organ that is continually processing inputs and outputs of goods and services. While this experience can lead to anxiety, it is also an important source of understanding of how things actually work. We argue here that householders are in a better position to change their water usage when they can see the full cycle of production and consumption. It may be that this is generally more the case in the garden than the house, and it is important to extend Kaika's analysis of 'home' to include outdoor spaces.

It soon became clear in our interviews that water is an essential component of any conversation about contemporary backyards. Most backyards cannot operate without water, but few are self sufficient in it, a consciousness exacerbated by having done the fieldwork during the 2002–03 drought. Everyday knowledge and practice are important for water managers in the Greater Sydney region, with garden use accounting for 25% of all household water use (Sydney Water 2003). The proportion for Alice

Springs is more than double that. The drought was intense throughout much of Australia, and by the end of winter 2002 there was considerable discussion in the media. However, people had already been talking about water well before this, and it seemed to us as interviewers that the drought exacerbated an existing consciousness rather than creating a new one.

Media influences in relation to water consumption and the drought were diverse and pervasive at the same time. Messages came through all media, even down to the reporting of dam levels on the TV news. With the imposition of water restrictions there was extensive advertising in the daily press, as well as mailouts to households.

Our discussion is not about actual levels of water consumption. Rather we seek to understand everyday practices and habits, and the processes that reinforce or change them. A further issue, particularly on the narrow coastal plain of Wollongong, is that the necessity of disposing of excess water during short-lived flood events is of ongoing concern even in periods of drought. Intense storms and flooding, such as those of August 1998, are strong in people's memories. In parts of Sydney, local council regulations stipulate that stormwater runoff has to be contained on the property, so people have detention basins in their backyards. Our Kellyville participants describe their dual water systems, in which a separate supply of recycled water is used for flushing toilets and watering gardens.

Participants' responses to the water shortage indicate detailed observations and understanding of entangled social and ecological systems. They talk of daily and seasonal weather patterns; the behaviour of ants, birds, mosquitoes, soil and plants; managing the time and habits of everyday life; and the strengths and weaknesses of the networks of water transport within their houses and gardens. As a dimension of everyday life, water practices are tied closely to division of labour between the sexes.

Figure 7.3: White plastic buckets are left out to catch rain in Maureen's Wollongong backyard

Environmental concerns over conservation and the dryness of the continent are a factor in 110 responses. Examples of the practices include planting native plants, mulching to reduce water loss or installing a water tank. Another strong theme is 'desire', which encapsulates wants, needs, dreams and desires surrounding water. Some desires are for water tanks and other water saving devices linked to action in the near future, but many more were desires for a water feature or dreams of having a swimming pool. When asked to imagine an 'ideal' backyard, more than fifty participants include water in their musings. 'Saving and waste' figure in thirty-nine responses, representing a continuation of family traditions, a disdain for waste and a means to save money. Finally, in twenty-six responses, 'pleasure' is mentioned—an investment strongly associated with 'time out' while watering the garden, as well as the often cited tranquil effects of having ponds and water features. Pleasure is closely linked to desire.

The themes presented in the section below summarise the most consistent and widespread discourses about water. Each is connected to examples of specific everyday practices in ways that both increase and reduce water consumption. Individuals sometimes express contradictory opinions; the tensions between desire and pleasure on the one hand and reducing water consumption on the other are particularly notable.

Women and Informal Water Gathering

'Water gathering' refers to a loosely defined set of practices that are informal, irregular or unstructured and differ from participant to participant. They include collecting water in containers of varying sizes from overflow outlets such as downpipes, hot water systems and leaking taps; setting containers out to collect rainfall; and manually collecting water from the kitchen, laundry and bathroom. Buckets are the main tool.

These activities are usually but not solely described by women. Their informal and ephemeral nature makes them difficult to document formally. They are sometimes highlighted by opportune moments; in Wollongong, Maureen was prompted to talk about her water gathering practices by a sudden downpour, which interrupted the interview.

> We've actually got the garbage tin there, there's not a lot of rain but we're trying to collect a little off the drain pipes there and I've got plastic buckets there . . . so that we can use that on the garden instead of using the taps. (Figure 7.3)

Accounts of buckets in the shower, such as Sue's in Marrickville, are common—

> I have a shower in my bath . . . and I put the plug in the bath when I have a shower, and then I take buckets of water out to water any plants with. And I also use that water in my toilet and my washing machine.

Menka, an elderly Macedonian widow, speaks of manually bucketing greywater from the washing machine, in response to a question about how she spends her time in her Wollongong backyard.

> From all the washing that I did yesterday and today I was collecting all the water and I was using it in the garden because it's not allowed to water the garden, so I try to make use of that water, the washing water for the plants . . . I'll go to the trouble of taking the water in buckets to the garden so I can make use of it . . .

Menka and other elderly Macedonian women share a similar generational practice of collecting water in buckets for use on their extensive vegetable gardens, and an ethic of not wasting water. But with limited English and a fear of government surveillance, they had also interpreted the media campaigns about reducing consumption. They worried that their water consumption was being monitored by neighbours or authorities.

Figure 7.4: Polystyrene boxes on Kirsten's veranda are used to collect rainwater for plant and animal use, North Shore, Sydney

> *I'm afraid of being fined for using too much water. It's not for the money that you pay for the fine, it's the actual knowing that you've been fined, punished in a way for doing something that shouldn't be done.*

In Wollongong's northern suburbs, Emily details her water gathering practices when asked what she would like to change in her backyard. She begins by talking about creating a waterfall with rockeries and a fishpond at the bottom to collect the water.

> *But all the water that we use here we try to not to waste . . . Even from the washing machine I tend to collect the water with buckets, you know, for the garden. Water the trees and the lawn and at the moment because of the drought we haven't had much rain for many months so even when I have a shower I have a bucket underneath it to collect the water and water the garden. The other thing is even when I wash the vegetables in the house or I wash my hands I tend to have a bowl or a basin underneath it to collect all the water.*

Emily refers to her Malaysian upbringing as having fostered a belief in not wasting resources.

> *I can't remember how long I've been doing this. It might be because of my upbringing and my family, we've always believed in not wasting. Really it frightens me when I see people doing the washing up under the tap, you know they have the tap running constantly and there's so much waste you know and we need to conserve the water.*

Investment in informal water gathering does not always proceed from a rationale of water conservation. For Kirsten, on Sydney's North Shore, who has several polystyrene vegetable boxes lined up against the veranda to collect rainwater, the issue is rather one of water quality (Figure 7.4).

> *I have been collecting them because I wanted to collect the rain water for my plants, because I believe rain water is better for the plants than tap water. And I think I can prove it because now I have a cat and two dogs and they don't drink tap water, they drink this water or the spring water I have in the blue bottles. But tap water, 'no thank you then I'm not thirsty'.*

Vietnamese participants and Alice Springs residents also expressed a belief in the relative purity of rainwater.

The Sensory Pleasure of Watering

Hand watering the garden is work, and thus generates a spread of positive and negative attitudes. Those who express real pleasure are mostly women. 'I love water,' says Jacqui of Wollongong West, laughing—

> *I think I have a fetish about watering gardens . . . I just get extreme pleasure out of being in the garden . . . I do remember my mother . . . I still remember her sitting on this chair in the*

driveway at the house at Fairy Meadow hosing the garden and she would sit there for hours and . . . I do the same thing here . . . I often sit on this garden bench down here, it's not just there for looks . . . I sit there and I can hose quite a lot of the garden by sitting on that bench.

Susan: I like the feeling of just doing the watering myself. It's relaxing.

Mary Anne: Yeah you do it every second day.

Susan: When I get home from work.
(Inner Sydney)

Several women made deliberate decisions not to install drip irrigation systems in at least part of their garden so that they could continue to enjoy hand watering. These are certainly not universal feelings; Joyce of Forest Grove, for example, says 'I hate watering. Some people love standing there with the hose and I hate it.' For those women who enjoy watering, themes of pleasure, tranquillity and meditation came through in their conversations.

I water a lot in summer and when I'm miserable I talk to the plants; I go out and let the plants cheer me up. And they tell me when they're thirsty or over watered.
(Barbara, inner Sydney)

Men from diverse backgrounds also describe the pleasures of watering. These pleasures were just as sensual as those of women.

At least a few times a week I get out there in the morning and I water the garden. For me that's before I start my day and that is a very pleasurable activity, and as I water the different pots that are on the wall I check on the well being of the plants just to see how they are travelling . . . and they're like my babies. And so I start my day with that uplifting experience and that's a major activity for me . . . I jog around the street, come back here and while I'm cooling down I'll water the garden and just check on the health of everything. (Peter, inner Sydney)

When asked what he likes about hand watering, Frank connects his own need for liquid refreshment with those of the plants.

To me it's, obviously, you know, that I like a drink. To me it's something that I've done for the past thirty years that I can remember, even when I was at Punchbowl. I love—particularly after I've mowed the lawn—to water and have a beer; have a beer and water; it's just something, it's just, I don't know.
(Frank, Campbelltown) (Figure 7.5)

This is also a time when detailed observation of processes occurs. People don't just water, they accumulate all sorts of detailed ecological knowledge, such as Brenda's description of the activities of ants.

> *I was watering the front last week . . . and the ants made a beeline for the water, the moisture on the rocks along the garden, and I thought gosh they must be feeling the drought, they all came charging, millions of them just poured out just for the water. (Brenda, Penrith)*

When asked why she enjoys watering, Tra Mi says she enjoys watching the plants grow from small seedlings into large trees. This is something that is lost if watering is an automated process. These are factors that should be considered in the implementation of policy related to the regulation of watering.

Men and Water Redirection

'Water redirection' refers to more structural ways of managing water, such as channelling stormwater from guttering or greywater from the house, as well as drainage and irrigation. Construction of drainage and storage systems to utilise water is an activity that provides a different sort of pleasure relating to water; the pleasure of construction, resourcefulness and practicality. This is mostly a male pleasure.

> *The other time I enjoy coming down here is just before summer kicks in, just come down and play with the watering system; I get a buzz out of that. I've been told by the bloke at the irrigation shop . . . 'irrigation systems are big kids' Lego', that's what he reckons. (Drew, northern suburbs, Wollongong)*

For Drew, the playfulness is directed towards a useful purpose, as various pipes are configured to direct the stormwater run off onto different levels of the garden. Elaborate systems such as those described below are not usually primarily constructed to harvest water during droughts, or to water gardens, although they can serve those purposes. In fact more often they start as a means

to manage the drainage of stormwater. Most of the Wollongong area has annual rainfall in excess of 1000mm, much of it falling in intense storms. The narrowness of the coastal plain exacerbates the tendency to flooding.

While women also speak about these aspects of water management, they are usually not the material actor in the process of redirection and they speak of their husbands or partners putting in place systems to redirect the flow of water.

> *We've just had to do a bit of drainage work underneath here because we've just filled this in you see, this was all open and all underneath there was open to there and to that end. So he's just done all that himself, yes, he's just done all that and had to do some drainage because when it really rains it's like a creek running down there, it's just incredible. (Jo, northern suburbs, Wollongong)*

Vi, the passionate gardener we met earlier, talks about her deceased husband building long open drains to redirect the water in their extensive backyard; 'Everything from here drains right through to the back and everything this other way goes out onto the street' (Figure 7.7).

Theo from Sydney's North Shore describes the drainage system he put in. 'I just put in some agricultural drains to cope with the excess water in times such as we've had right now and that has been very successful.' Similarly, Graham's concern is to redirect water in more appropriate ways in his backyard and utilise the stormwater run off through the use of a soak pit.

> *It's a boardwalk but it's a boardwalk that's been built for a purpose. It's a boardwalk that is actually a soak pit. So, we're hemmed in by neighbours, so what do you do with the run off? You put it down a big long pit full of rubble to disperse it across your land and that's what this thing is; it's a long soak pit . . . we have a plan, that's why the big pipe is sticking out the far end of it to pipe out, downpipes our guttering runoff, stormwater into this soak pit and it will also*

Figure 7.6: Graham and Veronique standing on their boardwalk, with ag pipe drainage protruding, Wollongong

Figure 7.7: Long drainage channels redirect excess water in Vi's inner northern suburbs backyard, Wollongong

Figure 7.8: Chi Vuong with downpipe and drum for water collection, Fairfield Cabramatta, Sydney

help water Veronique's plants from time to time whenever it rains. (Graham, Wollongong) (Figure 7.6)

Conversations about drainage are thus often about managing excessive water with little or no investment in its conservation. Schemes for utilising greywater, however, are firmly linked to conservation.

One of the most elaborate examples of water conservation utilising different forms of water redirection is Dan's and Sue's permaculture backyard in Port Kembla, where they recycle greywater from the house, and harvest and reuse rainwater for growing their produce. Dan, asked to describe his front yard, includes his drainage solutions (Figure 7.9).

We dug out a channel and big holes in the ground and dropped bath tubs in. And then we picked up the run off from our roof, and we passed that through a series of baths and then flowed it to another bath, so that every time it rained these baths would fill. It'd flow along a gutter and a gutter to a bath and then into a series of troughs and baths and just basins which we then packed with rocks and basic(ally) created a dry creek line with like little ridge lines on either side so that the water would actually flow through and then go down the drain if it ever got to it. (Dan, Port Kembla)

Mark and Denis also reuse greywater through a concern for the environment that acknowledges the cost of purifying and processing water. Mark says

I can't believe we use first grade water to water palms and or water grass and things so I'd, rather than put it down into the system, I just pump it [the greywater] all out onto the front yard and water my lawn and trees that way. (Mark, Port Kembla)

Denis uses greywater holding tanks and a drip system to water his backyard—

In all my little projects I kept the environment in mind, the climate and the fact that clean city water is so valuable. (Denis, Kellyville)

Women also talk about the importance of using greywater, but only two refer to structural changes that allow for the regular diverting of greywater from the house into the backyard. Most refer to manual methods such as bucketing the shower water or washing machine water onto the garden.

Water and Desire

Participants had a number of opportunities to express their desires and aspirations in relation to the backyard, most fully at the end of the interview when they were asked to imagine their ideal backyard. Water emerges here in a number of ways; desire is expressed, in order of frequency, for swimming pools, water features (including fountains and streams), water tanks and automated watering systems.

Water is very clearly connected to visions of a nature that is tranquil and peaceful (Figure 7.10).

Figure 7.9: The front yard at Dan's and Sue's, with drainage channel hidden by dense lomandra, Port Kembla, Wollongong

In speaking about water features, people refer to beauty, the sound of running water, soothing natural sounds and the notion of creating a restful place within the garden.

Having been in a city, close to the water, every day I passed the water and there's something tranquil and relaxing about that. Again, that's nature. (Debbie, North Shore)

John describes his swimming pool as not being about swimming, but 'about having water, being around water'. The restfulness of water is also implicit in Maureen Everitt's description of afternoon times in the vegie garden while her father watered, discussed in chapter two; 'you'd go out to talk to Dad while he watered'.

Bill, a garden centre manager living in Campbelltown, comments on this in relation both to his own desires and those of his clients.

Interviewer: Do they want a water feature because it's on every second lifestyle show, or

is there actually more a subliminal need to be near water?

Bill: *The answer is probably both . . . The Chinese say that you should see water. That's one of the first things you should see each day. It's probably enriched our life living here. We feel great. I go in there and do some work on my laptop and I look out on water. And I wake up every morning before breakfast and I see water . . . But just back to your question. It is . . . being driven at people in these programs. And it's not about natural things either. It's about human emotion as well, and that is prestige . . . If you go back twenty years to the western suburbs people might never have heard of a water feature . . . You needed professional people to install them and you needed thousands of dollars. Now you can go into a nursery, and for five or six hundred bucks, which is within people's scope, they have a choice of ten . . . I think the other factor is the prestige . . . They equate the accumulation of some of those things in their garden as success.*

Danny, a landscaper, commented on what he sees as the crazy commercialisation of good and natural watery desires. He described being in a café the previous weekend where there was a beautiful fountain on the back patio. A woman went to show it to her child.

She didn't say let's go and have a look at the fountain. Do you know what she said to this four year old kid? Let's go and view the water feature. No one even thinks of the word fountain or pond now. It's water feature. It's so beaten into us by Jamie Durie and Don Burke and by the magazines and everything that you must have water. You know that huge craze with feng shui. You must have water. It's gone mad, but it's good. I fully agree with it. I think water is incredibly important for movement and sound. (Danny, inner Sydney)

Women rather than men speak of wanting an automated or semi-automated watering system—

a system that works. The aim is both a working ecosystem that does not use too much water, and one that, once set up, does not require too much human intervention. Sylvia already has a semi-automated system and when asked what her ideal backyard would be, says, 'I'd love to have all those water saving gadgets; I wish I'd had them years ago, a kind of more self-sustaining garden.' Her perspective on the female labour associated is quite different from the watering discussed above.

Two main reasons are given for wanting water tanks; the conservationist perspective of saving water and the related economic one of saving money. There is no apparent distinction between women and men in this, with a number of couples clearly having discussed and considered this issue together. Participants who desire a swimming pool rarely elaborate on their reasons; it is often presented by both sexes as self evident that an ideal backyard would contain one. There are also people—not so many—who explicitly do not want a pool.

Thus desires relating to water go in opposing directions in relation to conservation and reduced consumption. Desires focused on water features and swimming pools see watery attributes as enhancing the relaxing and soothing aspects of backyard space. If acted on, these would increase the consumption of water. Desires that go in what we would presume is the opposite direction include the good feelings engendered by saving water, for example through installing a water tank.

Technologies and Networks of Water

People express frustration at the way the existing infrastructure impedes their efforts at water conservation (for example, many Alice Springs residents cannot install water tanks easily because they have no roof guttering to channel the water into the tank). They also think of creative ways to work around it. Some examples below emphasise ways in which technological systems are active in the process, most notably in that they can create rather than save work. They are also used in different ways from those which were originally intended. For example watering systems are usually promoted as a way to reduce water consumption, but a number of people use them essentially as a time management tool. Either they do not have time to water by hand, or they are not around at the best times for minimising evaporation, i.e. early morning and evening.

In Maria Kaika's reading of urban environments, networks of water supply are hidden from or ignored by domestic consumers until something goes wrong. Yet, for the participants who speak in this chapter, in the context of a backyard there is often quite detailed knowledge of and involvement with these networks. Several participants also visualise the pipes that bring the water to different parts of the house, and recognised the issues, particularly in transporting hot water.

> *Because our ensuite is right at the front of the house, you can use two and a half litres of cold water before you get your hot water through. So we trap that water as well. The same at the sink here at the back. It's just the set up of the tap. You turn it on. You hear the water coming through. You do what you have to do, you turn it off and it keeps on running. So again we've got a bucket in that sink and we trap all that water. For quick rinsing and stuff like that I just rinse my hands in that. So you get four litres of water in no time. (Richard, Campbelltown)*

The technology does not always deliver the peace and tranquillity envisaged, as Bill the garden centre manager explains in a critique of water features.

> *The reality is a lot of those, you put them in your garden, you spend all your time running to the toilet because of the noise of them . . . I used to be involved with design, and I'd often say to people—this was in Mosman and Vaucluse—*

[They'd say] 'I'd like to get something in the courtyard.' The first thing I'd say is, have you considered the noise? Because I knew other people had them—when we'd go to maintain them and they'd be all grotty, because they wouldn't turn them [on] because they couldn't stand the noise. Or the people would be running to the toilet. You have a glass of wine and you spend all night running to the loo. So that's the reality.

The work demanded by the technology itself is a big issue in Alice Springs, where Sue describes the active role of drip irrigation systems in facilitating garden establishment.

> *There's a rule if you want to be a good gardener you put the dripper on before you plant the plant because every little plant needs its own little dripper. Otherwise it's going to die. You'll try and hand water it, then after a while you'll forget and then it will die.*

In Sue's garden, like many others, there is an underground network of pipe so fine grained that when digging in the backyard she has to be careful to remember where the pipes are. This system allows water to be directed appropriately towards different types of plants.

> *Sue: If we walk around there's black pipe, 13 mm pipe. Things that need more water like the fruit trees have their own line. Then things that need water more often like the groundcover at the back have a separate line. These two vegie gardens are on their line. So there are four systems.*
>
> *Interviewer: You have to remember which tap to turn on?*
>
> *Sue: No. It was all connected to different taps originally but we got it automated so that we can go away every summer for Christmas. So it comes on with the timer. It's good because that way you can water things like the natives, like I can water them for twelve hours once a fortnight. Then when they're established that's*

Figure 7.10: Water pot, inner Sydney

enough. Then you can have it separate. Like the citrus need water every four days or so. The vegie gardens, in the height of summer they get watered twice a day.

Thus this technological system frees the owner, both from making mistakes like forgetting, and from being chained to the garden. It is a common practice in Alice to go away for several weeks at the height of summer, often to spend Christmas with relatives elsewhere and escape the heat. This three or four week holiday was commonly described as a make or break period for gardens, prompting some people not to bother, and others to configure their drip systems accordingly. But this is not so simple, as the systems themselves require a lot of maintenance. Peter and Wendy attribute their decision to give up on their system to the difficulty of maintenance. While still a prominent feature of their garden, it is not operational.

Wendy: It doesn't work anymore.

Peter: Yeah, I think it's probably clagged, it's now twelve years old and we haven't used it for about ten years. I think drip systems are only good for getting gardens established, because I mean ants get in and they need a lot of maintenance. And so once the garden got established we let it go.

Brad, a relative newcomer to Alice Springs, was still in the throes of working out his system. His detailed technical description shows how much work is required, challenging the notion that such systems actually save time.

We've been continually doing bits and pieces. Whether it's fixing the irrigation. That's a big job all the time. Because of the extremities of the weather the irrigation system is always failing. So you're constantly running around putting in joiners. Then we started using the clip lock things but they corrode. So now you put twist wire or non-break chicken wire around the pipes and you move the problem somewhere else. So you spend all of summer fixing the irrigation.

Interviewer: Has everything got irrigation?

Brad: Everything has irrigation. There's a six valve, six section irrigation system at the front. Everything gets watered from that system. But whoever put it in didn't do a good job. Some of the trees are on sprayers rather than drippers. Because they're on sprayers you can't mulch because you're only wetting the mulch. It should be dripping underneath. Gradually we've been having to retrofit all of that. (Figure 7.11)

Gardens create their own demands—they own you. George of Kingswood in western Sydney speaks of his decision to let his vegetable garden go because it was too demanding—

like they [the vegetables] mainly need water between six and eight in the morning or a certain time of the night . . . I find some nights you might be out at that time or in the morning you might go out early.

Figure 7.11: Brad with drip irrigated winter vegetable crop, Alice Springs

Graeme's description of his Alice Springs lawn makes it sound almost deliberately petulant:

I mowed it about four months ago and you really have to pour the water in. If you forget after two or three days it starts to go. I haven't cleaned up the back, but last weekend I mowed the lawn because it was as high as that. We had rain about three weeks ago. It just poured. And because of the heat it just came up.

And self-sown plants in his garden demand his attention and change his practice—

If a tree grows or a little bush grows and you think it needs water, I whack a dripper on it and leave it there.

Consciousness of a Dry Continent

Consciousness of saving water, while it may have been promoted by the drought, is not a recent thing. When asked to connect their backyard to broader environmental issues, many people immediately name water as the key issue. 'The biggest problem this country has is the lack of water', says Diana of Sydney's North Shore. She goes on to connect her present water saving practices to a childhood on the land and the normality of scarcity. Rural or agricultural childhoods and living with tank water were common. Several people relate their awareness of the harshness of the Australian environment to a more specific experience.

We've just driven to Adelaide and back and to see the country as brown and as bad as it is, it just goes to show us that maybe somewhere along the line we've got to be able to control water. (Bill and Helen, Hills District)

Dave and I went travelling around western Victoria and New South Wales on a motorbike before we had kids and there were a lot of areas out there that were badly affected by drought . . . I was totally shocked and just seeing animals that were dying in paddocks,

and I can still recall the smell, it was just so bad. And I think we came back here and I think we were just like 'that's amazing', we just take it for granted so much and we are living in the driest continent so we're looking at water tanks for the front and the back and for recycling of as much water as we can. Yeah, and I think even when the drought breaks, I think we'll continue doing it. (Maureen, Wollongong)

We travelled across the Tanami last year and I gained a sense of the real fragility; it gave me such a deep sense of kind of touching almost the womb of the land and realising how fragile it is, how precious things like water is and we're looking at a way to put water tanks in. (Maggie, inner city Sydney)

(The Tanami Desert is a very arid part of the Northern Territory and Western Australia).

These stories demonstrate direct links between a specific experience and a willingness to change consumption patterns. At first glance Maureen and Maggie seem to have used their experiences to 'come to terms' with a dry Australia in ways that Alice Springs residents, with less than a quarter of the rainfall and more than double the average household water consumption, have not. But this needs some examination, because it concerns the complex relationships between perception, practice and power.

The first point to note is that people living in a constantly arid place such as Alice Springs rely heavily on their personal environments, both house and garden, for respite. For example, the provision of shade is a much stronger theme in their backyards than in the east coast ones. Water is important in creating a cool haven, whether through watering plants, or having a water feature. In a milder climate, like Sydney's, surrounded by greenery, people need less water to enhance their surrounds.

Second, the connection between the Tanami and Sydney in terms of water is, in a material sense, far fetched. When Bonnie of Penrith tells her teenage daughter in the shower to 'save some water for the farmers, Jess', she is expressing a broad consciousness of the arid continent rather than a belief that if Jess showers for less than twenty minutes the farmers will actually get more water. There is no strong relationship between water availability in the two places, either in terms of where the rain falls or where the storage and distribution infrastructure moves it to. The same applies to western New South Wales and Wollongong. The connections made by Maureen and Maggie are totally symbolic, although no less powerful for that.

We met Maggie in chapter six as someone who loves her flower garden; 'we've both come from elsewhere and we're mad on seasonal change'. So the trip to the Tanami, though it powerfully affected her sense of water, did not prompt her to come back and plant natives in her garden.

To describe Australia as a 'dry continent', while clearly true in that it is two thirds arid, is to overlook the wetness of many places where people are concentrated. As the drainage systems of Wollongong backyards show, the east coast is sometimes very wet indeed.[16] The dry continent is often invoked as a contrast to the European homelands of Australia's immigrant population, and the environmental sensibilities developed in a wetter environment.

> *It makes me so cross to think that even two hundred years down the track people are still thinking in terms of the European landscape where you get so much rain. And you can have green lawns. (Danny, inner Sydney)*

A further example of how this has been absorbed into public consciousness is provided by the following exchange between Graham and his Belgian-born wife Veronique. Graham is describing who does what in the backyard:

> **Graham:** *Veronique plants the flowers and watches them die.*

> **Veronique:** *Because I don't often water, that's my problem.*

> **Graham:** *They don't need to water in Belgium you see, it rains so much, they don't have droughts.*

In fact in Belgium the average annual rainfall is about two thirds that of Wollongong.[17] The point of this is not that Sydney and Wollongong have abundant water to be poured on gardens; they have not. Rather it is to emphasise that sustainable practice needs to be built on more resilient perceptions and understandings than those of Maureen and Maggie. Public education campaigns that depend on the dry continent theme to change people's practices risk colliding with their lived experience of abundant, if variable water, unless they have had a life changing travel moment such as those described above. An experience of abundance may incline people to change practices back once it starts raining. To repeat a theme from the previous chapter, the environment we must 'come to terms' with is a complex one that includes in this case the social and technical infrastructure of water storage and delivery. The rainfall environment of Australia is only part of this equation, a part that varies considerably with place and time. Droughts may indeed be more frequent in Wollongong than in Belgium, even though Wollongong is statistically 'wetter'. And of course the issue of dryness is affected by the relationship between rainfall and evaporation.

We could argue in fact that the residents of Alice Springs have a better understanding of the total socio-environmental network by which they get their water than the average Sydneysider has, and they have formed their habits and practices accordingly. By the same token the households in this chapter have demonstrated detailed responses to the alternating abundance and scarcity of water. Although it would be a bit glib to say that men deal with excess and women with scarcity, there is an element of truth in that generalisation. Male and female have both shown considerable willingness to change their practices towards reduced water consumption

Figure 7.12: Old cans become decorative fence art in this Wollongong backyard

in the backyard. We return below to consider whether water is different to other environmental issues in this respect.

The Declining Power of the Waste Mentality

A common sense point that has come up several times in this book is that for people old enough or poor enough to have experienced material scarcity, an ethic of frugality and disdain for waste has become second nature. (We think this also applies to the generations parented by those people in the post-war decades.) For them waste is self evidently a bad thing; people talk about 'hating waste'. It is wrong to waste things, regardless of any other considerations.

Among younger and more affluent study participants the virtual absence of any discussion of waste is a striking feature. When talking about saving water or recycling, they would talk of the environmental imperatives and the importance of conservation. We draw two points from this. The

first is that, on the pathway to sustainability, the younger, more affluent and well educated parts of the community have lost, or are losing, a useful moral resource—an ethic of frugality. Second, this makes them more likely to adopt behaviour that actually increases consumption.

The commercialised nature of recycling illustrates this. While there is much discussion in Australia about recycling in the household context, most debates focus on the disposal of end products and many participants practised recycling in this form. They composted, mulched and reused old materials. This is a very time and place specific way of thinking about recycling—as the endpoint of a consumption chain in an affluent, materialistic society. This sort of recycling can be disconnected from the issue of reducing consumption in the first place, indeed in some cases it can help people rationalise high levels of consumption. In lifestyle TV shows, 'recycling' is often repackaged into another way to consume. Thus the display of milk cans and jugs decorating a fence in southern Wollongong

(Figure 7.12) recycles old containers but required the purchase of new lattice and spray paint.

A further example is that in relation to water, desire and the 'pleasure principle' are stronger for more educated participants at the upper end of the socio-economic spectrum. This is not in itself surprising—these people are more likely to be able to spend money on their backyard and when asked to imagine their ideal backyard have no trouble thinking big. Nor is it surprising that they might desire swimming pools and water features. But what it does mean is that even within their environmental thinking they tend to latch on to actions that cost money and consume resources, such as installing watering systems or tanks.

We are not arguing that watering systems and water tanks are not a good response to the issues of reducing water consumption, quite the opposite. Rather we are pointing out that restraint, self discipline and frugality are not the environmental options that first come to mind for more affluent and educated Australians. They have lost a useful weapon that previous generations had, and it will be that much harder to disengage themselves from the ratcheting up of demand discussed by Shove. As Michael Redclift points out, 'we will not be able to undo, through environmental management, what we have done through naturalising our consumption' (Redclift 1996: 148, cited in Shove 2003: 8).

Agency and Power

So how do the study participants understand and experience their own agency and power to accomplish change, within and beyond the backyard? Are they, like the Wilcox cartoon character, trudging off for a latte because it is all too hard? When canvassed on their attitudes to the environment, participants are most likely to speak of water as a precious resource that has been mismanaged by successive governments. Around half of the participants who talk about water as an environmental issue make observations on 'big' water issues such as farming use, drought, falling dam levels and water quality. They express concern, but also a disconnection between water in the environment and their own use of water. Overt or implied responsibility to 'fix the problem' rests with the government. 'Wish we could get some of these politicians to put in another dam or two. It's ridiculous,' said one participant.

A sense of personal agency defines the other half. They explicitly link water as a major environmental issue with their practices in the backyard. Ninety-two participants describe a range of practices—some new, many embedded into daily routines—that illustrate a conscious change in the way they use water. Some of them are quoted above. Fifty-two participants discusse the impact on their water use of restrictions brought in during the drought. They describe a number of creative responses to these enforced changes. However, while their positive interventions sometimes contribute to a sense of feel-good activism, in certain cases they obscure other activities of intense water consumption. One discussion focused solely on the water hardy natives in the backyard, with no mention of the adjacent swimming pool.

Tensions arise when participants compare their own level of concern with that of neighbours, the general public, authorities and government. People position themselves and others as responsible users of water or as water wasters. For example, wanting a water tank accords a sense of environmental responsibility, if only by implication. The relative health of lawn is seen as another marker of environmental responsibility, with green lawns signifying waste and dead grass signifying water conservation. Imperatives to change how the Australian public thinks about water are articulated as a unified 'we', such as 'we just take it for granted, there should be more education on how not to use water.'

The question of water shows people to be involved in many activities that they believe to be environmentally beneficial. Intention collides with the rhythms of daily life for many people.

Anne from Sydney's Hills District expresses a common view that infrastructure changes could support rather than work against such intention.

I'm concerned about things; I'm slacker than I should be. But I'm probably not as slack as a lot of people in terms of actually doing something positive. I'd like to see more structural changes to make things really easy for people. I think stuff like recycled water is brilliant because people don't have to think and if you make sure people don't have to think, they'll do it. Having the recycling bins is great because people don't have to think, they just lift a different lid and that's when you are going to get stuff happening. So you know, we've got our little worm farm and you know we try to sort of use mulch and all of those things.

The tensions between personal habits, watering technologies and wider environmental issues are illustrated well by one incident we encountered in a backyard in Sydney's eastern suburbs. As was common in our interviews, the wife had taken the opportunity, early on, of the time we spent sitting on the deck, to set the sprinkler on the lawn. Towards the end of the interview, when her husband was actually criticising the way Australia manages its water, she suddenly realised that the sprinkler was still going because she had mistakenly left it on too long—she rushed to turn it off!

For many householders environmental issues are both physically and conceptually distant. In such cases the backyard is disconnected from major environmental issues. For example, participants who bemoan the clearing of trees for urban development might live in a new suburb with a paved backyard without a tree or bush. People are particularly likely to distance themselves from responsibility when they feel they lack knowledge and understanding:

I don't feel like we actively go out of our way to promote environmental awareness in our lives. ut that's not up to me. I don't think I've got the expertise to change any of that.

Well I feel strongly that the environment is important but then, my actions, I don't do anything actually to protect the environment. So I feel a tension between what I feel and what I actually do. So I feel quite powerless to what's going on.

Well as far as managing the environment, pollution and problems with the waterways that really worries me. Because I don't know how to deal with it and I just have to hope that somebody else knows what to do about it.

I don't have a great knowledge on what to do or what's involved but it's nice to read about it in the paper that things are being done and see on TV that things are being done.

Level of education is a strong variable in people's sense of their own empowerment. As could be expected, comments such as those above come more frequently from people with lower education and skill levels. For some, the backyard itself can become an equivalent of the latte in figure 7.2. I can't do anything about the outside world, it's too big and too difficult, but here is a space that I can do something about.

Other participants explicitly connect the backyard with bigger issues, seeing their own practices as a contribution to the wider world.

Peter: It's really down to what is the smallest footprint we can make in our own way on the landscape of Alice Springs. And so a lot of what we do around here sort of flows from that.

Wendy: I think that's a good way of putting it, that making as negative impression as we can on the environment. And I think what you do in . . .

Peter: In your own backyard

Wendy: Well I think you have control over what you do in your own backyard and I guess that's where I feel it's as far as I can go really because you can only do what you feel you can do and you hope that people will change their attitudes. But that is going to be a really slow thing and yeah, I guess it's something that you feel you have power over. So our rainwater tank is the newest thing that we have done as far as the environment.

Sometimes such a consciousness leads to involvement in local environmental initiatives, particularly projects to restore native vegetation. Active Sydney bush regenerators Debra and Peter highlight the dilemmas of connecting individual action to larger environmental issues:

Peter: I retired about eighteen months ago . . . and I wanted to be doing something active and . . . it was in my local area and so on.

Debra: So think about doing things locally. You can't always influence other things broader, you can't do much about salinity other than donations.

Peter: My public service career would be way up there in the abstract dealing with environmental questions. To come back down to something kind of grass roots level and work on something where you can actually see the changes happening and,

Debra: And that's why bush regeneration is so rewarding, you actually physically see things actually improving. That's why it can be very rewarding but you often feel frustrated about the bigger issues, the bigger land care issues.

A number of participants were employed or working as volunteers in different land and environment occupations. They frequently talk about 'making a difference', not just in their own backyard spaces but by educating other people, and setting an example for others. Some criticise colleagues and neighbours whose practices do not match an environmental understanding they assume is shared. Their missionary zeal, and the social boundaries it sets up, are discussed in the next chapter.

The Bucket in the Shower

Backyarders express a range of sensual and physical engagements with water. It is a part of nature that is usually a source of pleasure. Their responses to a situation of water shortage indicate detailed observations and understanding of the networks that convey water within their houses and gardens. They speak about their strategies, both creative and banal, to conserve and reuse water: the jug beside the sink, the bucket in the shower, the basin of vegetable washing water, letting the lawn go, not planting annuals, water saving shower heads, rain soaker crystals, mulch, and water tanks. They think the state government was tardy in bringing in water restrictions, and that 'they' should do more to fix the long term problems. While a few think the government should have built more dams, none contests the idea that as a society we need to change our ways when it comes to water. On the other hand they want more water in their everyday environments; swimming pools, ponds, streams, and water features to bring serenity and the touch of water. Such desires are both fed and gratified by the lifestyle industry. What are we to make of this key tension—an obvious willingness to make significant changes in everyday practice to reduce water consumption, combined with throbbing but partially leashed desires to create more watery environments?

Further, why is water different to other environmental issues we have discussed in this book? Interest in restoration of native biodiversity is a minority commitment. Almost no one in the study voiced anxiety over where their Cowra pebbles came from, or where their landscaping supplier sourced their soil. A commitment to water conservation is the nearest thing to a shared commitment for the whole study population, crossing age, gender, ethnic and socio-economic divides.

We can address these two questions by critically reconsidering the work of Shove and Kaika, the scholars quoted earlier in the chapter. Before we do this, there is a caveat. We are not suggesting that these urban Australians are water saints. By their own accounts, practice falls short of intention, and different habits counteract each other. Their willingness to change is conditional, particularly on government and industry altering their practices. Voluntarism is fragile when the kids are screaming for dinner, when work patterns dictate time scheduling or when injustice is perceived:

> I get really angry with the people up the road who you see out there, and they've got a wonderful flower garden and grass, and ours is brown because we're trying to do the right thing, and they are just blatantly wasting. (Bonnie, Penrith)

But urban Australians have begun their much needed culture shift in relation to water[18] and are waiting for governments and industry to go with them. Much of this change is hidden in the daily rhythms of household life, encapsulated in the metaphorical and material symbol of the bucket in the shower.

Our sample is short on people who hose their concrete, teenagers like Jess who take twenty minute showers, households with five bathrooms, and people who would prefer not to think about these issues, so it could be argued that our optimism is overstated. Two points are relevant here. One, that we discuss further below, is that people who value their backyard garden are prepared to work hard at saving water inside the house to put on their garden. Second, recognising the need for a changed water culture is one of the few environmental attitudes shared almost universally across our otherwise diverse sample population. (Another, the welcome accorded to birds, is discussed in the next chapter.) It is also likely that there are significant differences between cities in 'water cultures'. For example, in Perth systematic watering of nature strips ('verges') is common (Figure 7.13), although it is rare in many cities, including Sydney and Wollongong.

We should think again about Maria Kaika's analysis of the modern home in light of what people are saying. Nature, she claims, is allowed into the house only once it has been purified, and is removed once it becomes 'bad'.

While the dweller experiences the familiarity and comfort of his/her domestic tap, bathtub, or swimming pool, the intricate set of networks that produce this bliss remains invisible to him/her, hidden underneath and outside the house. It is precisely this visual exclusion of production networks, of metabolised nature and of social power relations, that contributes greatly to the production of a sense of the familiar inside one's home . . . although the modern home is ideologically constructed as independent and *disconnected* from natural processes, its function is heavily dependent upon its material connections to these very processes . . . (Kaika 2005: 65) [emphasis in original]

The creation and maintenance of this purified nature are driven by and drive increasingly consuming practices, assisted by technology, as elaborated by Shove (2003), whose concept of ratchet motion rules out backtracking from over-consumption. Veronica Strang makes a similar argument in her anthropological study of *The Meaning of Water* (2004) in the Stour Valley in England. In her analysis, the privatisation of supply, water technology that encourages visions of an unlimited resource, and increasingly individualised social lives, have together created a situation where 'domestic users are . . . impervious to efforts to conserve water' (p. 208).

Our Australian evidence has certain parallels, but the more striking conclusion is that urban Australia is cracking apart this false separation of nature and culture. When it comes to water, urban Australians are not blissfully ignorant of the networks that produce their domestic comfort. They are catching water off the roof, struggling with the connectors on their drip systems, and digging in drainage systems. They can see that the water cycle has been disrupted when it has not rained for months and street trees are dying. This is not perfect or full knowledge, but it is detailed and ecologically specific and they engage with it on a day to day basis. In an echo of earlier times in history, busy women are prepared to become water carriers.

Figure 7.13: Pop-up sprinkler system for watering nature strip and adjacent road, Perth, December 2002

Further, urban Australia has shown itself prepared to tolerate 'bad' or 'dirty' nature at home, within certain limits. The bucket in the shower catches and holds soapy bodily water rather than insisting it be immediately expunged from the house. Used washing machine water, also containing bodily wastes, goes onto sites of food production. Basins containing dirt washed from vegetables and hands are allowed to sit until someone is free to empty them on the garden. These practices are not universal, but they are widespread throughout our diverse sample. They bubble up through the interview transcripts, whether from Sydney, Wollongong or Alice Springs.

The presence and the value of the garden are not just a coincidence when it comes to these practices. It is in the relationship between house and garden that people see, understand and participate in the network of water storage and distribution. They know their own power and they understand where and how to make a difference. To the extent that the garden, or favourite plants, are particularly valued, they are willing to make sacrifices, and to inject their own labour into the water network. This may explain why recent per capita water consumption in detached houses with gardens in Sydney is little different to that of apartment and unit dwellers (Troy, Holloway, and Randolph 2005).

So, people are just as keen on latte, but at least as far as water goes, they do not use latte as a substitute for action. They might enjoy their coffee on the back deck, while keeping an eye on the greywater hose.

In the following chapter are cases of people not being so welcoming of the nonhuman world.

Figure 8.1: A large cactus lifts the concrete path in Jessie's Wollongong backyard

CHAPTER EIGHT

Boundaries
and Belonging

Humans construct variable boundaries around parts of the nonhuman world. These have material consequences for what is allowed to belong. The question of belonging is not at all straightforward in an ecological sense. Among the people in our sample, birds are almost universally welcome. The two issues of greatest contention, and social conflict, are trees and cats. One person's pet is often another's pest. Even among cat owners, the standing of cats is unstable and directly connected to the increasing value placed on visits by birds.

his chapter explores the boundaries that people think of as existing between themselves and the plant and animal parts of the world, using the theme of belonging. David Sibley's argument that 'the boundaries of society are continually redrawn to distinguish between those who belong and those who, because of some perceived cultural difference, are deemed to be out of place' (Sibley 1995: 107), can be extended to cover nonhumans as well as humans. We need to think about related kinds of belonging that have expression in terms like indigenous, native, exotic, feral and alien. The key theme of this chapter is that divisions between humans and nonhumans which may appear natural are anything but. They are:

- Variable. Different people think about the world differently, and for different reasons. This can lead to social conflict, and intersect with the neighbour-neighbour boundary.
- Contingent on circumstances rather than being subject to essential characteristics of either the people or the others. Axes that form criteria of belonging include those between native and introduced, between aggressive and good behaviour, and danger and safety, among others.
- Worked out in practice and interaction, and therefore subject to contradiction and change.
- Relational, i.e. worked out in relation to one another. So the position of cats is constituted in relation to that of birds.

While there are some shared understandings, we show that the question of belonging varies more along cultural lines than previous research (NSW NPWS 2002) indicates.

To compare animals with plants is to invoke rather mobile understandings of belonging, in which the humans do not have all the power. Plants have particular sorts of mobility; they invade, creep, grow, blow in, are deposited by birds. Animals come and go, reside and visit, fly, crawl and wander in different ways.

Engaging with animals is an important recreational, and in some cases, productive activity for more than half the people we talked to. Traditional pets such as dogs and cats are the most popular, with dogs in ninety-two backyards and cats in fifty-seven. Caged birds other than poultry were present in thirty-two backyards and twenty backyards were home to chooks. Many others were adamantly anti-pet, for a variety of reasons.

Among animals that are not pets, birds are particularly important. We found in chapter 4 that birds are often invoked as positive reasons for, and outcomes from, planting strategies, particularly of native plants. This is not confined to one or two types of gardens or gardeners. Birds are more than welcome visitors to or residents of nine out of ten backyards that we studied. They are the nonhumans with which people have overwhelmingly positive relationships.

A wide variety of other residents and visitors are reported; possums, echidnas, foxes, lizards, wallabies, euros, kangaroos, bandicoots, sugar gliders, bats, deer, cows, frogs, butterflies, insects and spiders. People with higher education or skill levels are more aware and encouraging of native fauna, and more likely to spend time observing their activities. They are more likely to draw the welcome line between native and non-native species.

Others had an ethic of total welcome, voiced as 'everything has a right to live'. Jessie of Wollongong voices this view, and her power to change her own practices as a consequence, in relation to a path that was being broken up by the growth of a very large cactus (Figure 8.1). Her grandson suggested this would threaten the pipes, and he was probably also worried about her safety. But Jessie feels she can cope with the problem and accommodate the right of other things to live—

the lizards live there and my legs go where I direct them. So when I get there I direct them out on the grass at the other part of the path.

Most people, however, are less than totally tolerant. Various strategies are used to negotiate the boundaries, ranging from changing one's own

Figure 8.2, above: Jo with her vegetable cage, Wollongong

Figure 8.3, below: Lattice forms a physical boundary between what is safe and dangerous for Sarah in this outer northern suburbs backyard, Wollongong

practices as Jessie does by walking around the dodgy bits of path, to structural measures such as Jo's vegetable cage (Figure 8.2) which facilitates more peaceful coexistence with the birds.

> **We tried growing them without a cage but the bower birds which interact very much in our garden, decided that they like the tomatoes very much, from the time they were very tiny.**

Sarah, a British migrant, describes the tension between her fear of poisonous creepy crawlies and wanting to let her two year old daughter explore. She derives a comfort that she acknowledges as illogical, from having placed some physical boundaries in her backyard.

> **I was in the garden the other day and she came down to where I was and she had taken her shoes off and you know, she's of the age that you can't think 'don't poke in that hole with that stick' [laughs], you know, those are the things that worry me and . . . I don't know whether I think perhaps spiders can't climb through lattice fences but I just think, you know, if there's a fence, that they are going to be a bit safer. (Sarah, northern suburbs, Wollongong) (Figure 8.3)**

As is clear in the case of spiders and snakes, humans are not the only ones who create and police these boundaries; one participant notes, that

> **the dog rules this area of the yard and doesn't allow too much else to come in.**

Scientific Understandings of Belonging—Ecology, Biogeography and Evolution

What belongs is not at all straightforward in an ecological sense. Not only does nativeness intersect with other criteria of belonging, but the very question of nativeness depends on the context. The concept of 'invasive alien' (or exotic, or introduced) species combines two criteria that need to be teased apart if management solutions are to be most effective. Invasiveness relates to the behaviour of an organism, particularly in relation to other species and ecosystems. Alienness (or its converse, nativeness) refers to belonging or not belonging in a certain place. Invasives take over, but they may take over places they belong to. Aliens are in the wrong place, but they are not necessarily taking over. The idea of nation in notions of ecological belonging, for example, being native to Australia, adds a third layer of variability. Nation, in sociopolitical terms, may or may not make ecological sense, and in any case operates at a variety of scales. In a European context nation may be too small, in the Australian context nation may be too big.

To say that a plant or animal is native to Australia says very little about its ecological requirements. Nevertheless, the boundary of the Australian nation is more or less coterminous with that of a relatively isolated, ecologically distinct continent. The biota that have survived here have something of a shared evolutionary history. The melding of nativeness and nation continues in much popular gardening literature, for example Snape's *The Australian Garden: Designing with Australian Plants*. In the prologue to Snape's book, Seddon tempers his enthusiasms with a caution to the reader that 'Australian plants' is 'a convenient fiction, sometimes useful, sometimes not', because 'plants know nothing of nationality' (2002: 8).

Giving a resounding yes to his question 'Can some Australian plants be invasive?', leading plant ecologist R.H. Groves (2001) notes that this differs from his own findings twenty years previously, when relatively few weeds were native. Both a shift in consciousness and an exacerbation of the native invasive problem had occurred in the meantime. For example, in 1991 invading species were defined as the converse of native species—by the Australian National Parks and Wildlife Service, in the report *Plant Invasions* (1991: 20). Yet the same report recognises that native species can constitute environmental threats;

> native species naturalized outside their natural geographic distribution can be as ecologically serious as any alien introduction . . . and the likelihood of hybridization is probably higher. (p. 30)

Australian plants can be weeds outside Australia, for example eucalypts in California. Plants can become weeds in different regions within Australia. These typically include those native to the southeast or southwest corners that have crossed the barrier of the Nullarbor Plain with human assistance. And plants can behave as weeds within a biogeographic region when they experience cyclic expansion within or adjacent to their normal range.

So there has been a shift in understanding particularly in the last ten years or so. Instead of dealing exclusively with the indigenous versus alien distinction, ecologists more broadly analyse invasiveness and ecosystem health. Evolutionary biologist Stephen Jay Gould finds the primacy of nativeness an impossible position to support:

> 'native' plants cannot be deemed biologically best in any justifiable way . . . 'Natives' are only the plants that happened to arrive first and be able to flourish . . . Speaking biologically, the only general defense that I can concoct for natives—and I regard this argument as no mean thing—lies in protection thus afforded against our overweening arrogance. At least we know what natives will do in an unchanged habitat. (Gould 1997: 17)

Gould discusses how evolutionary theory fractured the idea that 'God made each creature for its proper place' by 'introducing the revolutionary idea that all anatomies and interactions arise as transient products of complex history, not as created optimalities.' (p. 13)

> Thus the first-order rationale for preferring native plants—that, as locally evolved, they are best adapted—cannot be sustained . . . This is because natural selection is only a 'better than' principle, not one that operates towards universal improvement. Once a species prevails over others at a location, no pressure of natural selection need arise to promote further adaptation . . . For this reason, many native plants, evolved by natural selection as adaptive to their regions, fare poorly against introduced species that never experienced the local habitat. If natural selection produced optimality, this most common situation could never arise, for native forms would be 'best' and would prevail in any competition against intruders. (p. 15)

The second-order rationale that Gould challenges is that species occupy the area best suited for their attributes, put forward as the idea that there is a 'right place' for all species.

> Since organisms (and their areas of habitation) are products of a history laced with chaos, contingency, and genuine randomness, current patterns (although workable, or they would not exist) will rarely express anything close to an optimum, or even a 'best possible on this earth now' . . . Consequently, although native plants must be adequate for their environments, evolutionary theory grants us no license for viewing them as the best-adapted inhabitants conceivable, or even as the best available among all species on the planet. (p. 16)

These are radical claims since the strongest advocates of nativism are people who invoke the authority of science and ecology. In the scientific milieu, nativeness is still supreme. Gould argues not against a preference for natives, but that the rationale must lie in cultural values—aesthetics, ethics and lessons in humility.

How does this argument fare in the domestic context?

Trees—Love, Danger, Mess and Nativeness

The example of trees cuts across boundary making between areas and species. Certain types of trees are considered to belong or not, and trees are considered to belong in particular places. Questions of tree belonging are also closely tied to social relationships with neighbours.

This section is based on eighteen of our interviews with twenty-one participants, thirteen women and eight men, analysing the way they discuss removing, planting or taking no action against trees.

The reasons most frequently given for removal relate to danger, disease and size, while the most important reasons for planting relate to aesthetics and creating habitat for birds. The associations are not always causal. For example, the association between removal and aesthetics includes having to remove beautiful trees that died, as well as choosing to remove ugly ones. The association between removal and shade includes situations where people describe removing dangerous trees but missing the shade, in addition to descriptions of removing trees because they provide too much shade.

The themes of love, danger, mess and nativeness can be understood as axes of tolerance. They are variables by which people decide under what conditions to foster, tolerate or remove trees living close by. They can also be understood as axes of belonging; they specify the conditions under which trees are allowed to belong. The themes are connected. We aim to tease out the range of variability, the reasons for particular attitudes and potential connections to ways of behaving.

People use the word 'love' to describe attachments to particular trees in their backyard. Keith and Gay had their house on the market when interviewed about their backyard, which was dominated by a large camphor laurel. Keith said, 'I love me tree', and for Gay, 'The tree is a

Figure 8.4: Large camphor laurel with built-in deck in Keith and Gay's outer northern suburbs backyard, Wollongong

big part of it . . . we'll be sorry to leave it when [we] sell but then we'll just have to create another one'. Their timber deck is literally built around the tree, thus embedding it in the valued times of entertaining family and friends (Figure 8.4). Maureen describes how the use of a favoured tree, also a camphor laurel, has changed with the growth of her family.

> *I love that tree . . . we now have tables and chairs and a paved area underneath it so we tend to sit out there a lot in the summer when the weather is nice . . . [it] has a ladder going up there, we used to have a tree house in there when the kids were younger. That's gone but the ladder's there so my son has built a crawling insect that's going up the ladder using I think an old shovel head and different pieces of metal . . . he'll have his mates over too, they like to hang out there as well. (Maureen, inner Wollongong)*

Camphor laurel (*Cinnamomum camphora*) is a large spreading tree that grows to 30 m. It originated in China and Japan, but has been widely planted in New South Wales since the mid-nineteenth century, and scientists now consider it invasive from Wollongong northwards (Muyt 2001: p. 233). The features that make it a successful invader include longevity, high seed production, shading out of competitors under the canopy and a massive root system from which it suckers vigorously. The seedlings of camphor laurel can take up to a year to develop strong root systems so it is relatively easy to dig these out, but control of well established plants is much more difficult. These features are recognised by our backyard participants, some of whom describe a love-hate relationship with the species. The things that make camphor laurel a successful weed also create a spectacular tree. Although many of our participants recognise it as a problematic weed, and pull out its seedlings, they also value it as a mature tree. The social life of the tree overrides its weed status in terms of belonging.

Removals of ground cover and shrubs arouse nowhere near the same degree of guilt as removing trees. There seems to be something about the size, life form and longevity of trees that leads people to ascribe more rights to them than other forms of life. Even when people see trees as messy and potentially dangerous, many do not like cutting them down. There is a sense that a well established tree cannot be a weed. Barbara describes the clearing they had to do when she and her husband came to their house as 'quite heart breaking, especially for Brian, cutting down trees [camphor laurels] that were weeds.'

A tension between nativeness and beauty, or nativeness and the desires of the backyarder, may work out either way, the *but* in each of the following statements indicating the attribute that swung the decision.

Figure 8.5: Jacqui's son mimics cutting down his favourite tree, Port Kembla, Wollongong

> *There were some beautiful trees but they were exotic trees.*

> *I do love this gardenia; it's not a native but it's a fragrant plant.*

> *I'm not happy about cutting down the trees but the fact that it was an oak tree and some other awful looking thing, um, lessened the guilt. When it comes to enjoyment of, you know, like we had to get rid of the tree to build the pool really, to make the pool worthwhile. So it lost.*

The primary reason cited for tree removal is danger. Dangerous trees are trees deemed unsafe for reasons such as disease, age, angle, and the shedding of large branches; being planted too close together, wind affected, a fire hazard or a threat to plumbing. Words like 'dangerous' and 'diseased' are used to legitimise the removal. (This is influenced also by local government tree protection regulations. In many areas the main legal ground for removing a tree is that it poses a safety hazard to people or buildings.)

> *It was huge, it was taller than the pine trees and it was quite dangerous and it was diseased so I was advised to take it out and there were also gum trees up along the back boundary, which I wanted to get rid of because I wanted to do the garden differently.*

> *That one has got the priority because it's dangerous. My son always climbs in that tree, it's his famous tree so he will be upset but it's too dangerous for him to climb in at the moment. So that one is going to go, and then this will, and we are going to put more palms down the back. We really like the palms and because we've found that they seem to grow so well. (Jacqui, Port Kembla (Figure 8.5)*

When trees are removed for reasons related to danger, size or aesthetics, they rarely appear to be replaced.

Large trees in the backyard are not always

Figure 8.6: Large trees grow on a steep slope in this outer northern suburbs backyard, Wollongong

seen as a threat to security (Figure 8.6). We heard several accounts of large trees falling during storms and high winds and, while these could have been turned into disaster stories, attitudes are generally neutral. When Alison, who has several very large eucalypts in her Hills District backyard was asked if she was concerned about the trees she answered:

Only that they might fall, but you know, if they fall they fall, don't they. I don't think they will. I think because I watch them and they swing about a bit and they all seem to be going that way rather than this way. So I'm not going to cut them down just because they might fall on the house . . . and I wouldn't cut a tree down to get a view either.

Leo's equanimity regarding trees is linked to his view that people are inextricably a part of nature: 'it is a fire situation and I realise you've got to live with it. But it doesn't worry me because if I'm here I think with the hoses and things I can control it until I get some help'. Leo speaks from experience, as for example in his account of the big storms of 1991.

There were two big trees in that gap there that came down on to the back property. They fell down in between two houses, and further down there was a very big eucalypt that went down on top of a house and went through the roof. People arrived from everywhere to help clean up. They had to rebuild half the house. (Leo, North Shore)

Danger is often encoded in the size of the trees, or more specifically size of the tree relative to the backyard. Trees can occupy that ambiguous, liminal space described by Sibley (1995) that creates anxiety. This leads to a range of reactions including the banishing of trees from the backyard, most frequently by those who understand the environment or nature itself as something 'out there'. The size of eucalypts in particular is often generalised to exclude their belonging from back-yards, an attitude encapsulated by Lance; 'I don't think gum trees have a place in suburban backyards somehow.' Similar attitudes are most common in new housing areas with small blocks of land.

> **The backyard is pretty weed free. There were two gum trees in the garden when we came here. We took them out because they were too big for a backyard like this. (Cindy, Hills District)**

> **I feel guilt because I don't adhere to them at home, but I sort of appreciate our national parks and the need for trees and things like that. But if you look around we don't have any trees in our backyard. My husband won't have a tree. I would have one, but he feels threatened by trees falling on us . . . When I was a child I got a lot of good feelings out of national parks and picnic areas and that. But to be honest, I get a better feeling in my own backyard now; you know, I can sit out on that grass and feel like I'm in a national park. I have my own space there, so I'm fine with it. (Kathy, Albion Park, Wollongong)**

A further important theme in attitudes to trees is the 'mess' they make by dropping leaves and sticks and shedding bark. Eucalypts are seen as particularly messy, probably because this process occurs throughout the year.

> **We've got gum trees everywhere; here, right here and what a mess it makes. (Bill, inner Sydney)**

Sylvia was able to enjoy the trees in other people's gardens because she did not have responsibility for cleaning up the mess.

> **Everybody else has got the gum trees, I love the gum trees but I don't like the mess, so everybody else has got them. (Sylvia, northern Wollongong)**

Maureen's attitude that 'the leaves make such a mess on the lawn but I just think it's lovely', is

a rare exception. The more common association between leaves and mess may also be negatively affecting some people's attitudes to mulch. For example, one woman commented about the fig leaf litter she was using as mulch, 'It doesn't look like mulch, it looks like a mess.'

Participants who are strongly committed to restoring native trees indigenous to their area are often highly critical and in some cases intolerant of the choices made by neighbours, and of the reasons people give to legitimise removal of native trees. Discussions of nativeness and belonging become moral judgments as they are contrasted with the desires of neighbours to grow what they want.

> **When we moved in there were quite a few young camphor laurels in the front and she [the previous owner] said to us 'look after our trees' and as soon as she left we cut them down. People don't realise what they've got, they think if it's green it's okay . . . As far as getting everyone to see the merits of native plants, indigenous plants, that's not really feasible. It's hard just to get them to cut down a weed. If they think it's pretty then they don't really care about the damage it causes to the native bush. (Miranda, North Shore)**

The moral battleground became a physical one when one participant confessed to killing the neighbour's camphor laurels where the informal boundary line between the two properties merged. Another participant described fraught relations on all except one of her neighbourly boundaries:

> **there is supposed to be protection on the trees and you know, every year someone is cutting a tree down for whatever reason. She has used the excuse that she is old and frail so . . . the council came and cut the tree down for her. The neighbours down the back have used an excuse to cut down the tree. The neighbours up over the other side don't even use any excuse, they just hope they don't get caught. (Kris, inner Wollongong)**

Birds—More than Welcome

Nearly everyone talked at some length about wild birds visiting the backyard; indeed, bird visits are the most talked about animal activity (Figure 8.7). Even people who describe themselves as non-gardeners talk about bird visitors in the backyard, naming types and the places in the backyard to find them. This points to a strong engagement with birds who, although relatively transient visitors, afford great pleasure to the keen and casual watcher alike.

> *We have a lot of birds . . . I've got three kookaburras that come. There's a couple of magpies. White sulphur crested cockatoos. Mitchell's cockatoos. Top knot pigeons which come and go. They come around for a while and then they disappear. (Leo, North Shore)*

Some people encourage birds with food and water. There are birdbaths in twenty per cent of the backyards we visited although water and food can be provided in less formal ways, such as throwing stale bread out for the birds, or leaving water in a variety of containers.

> *But we feed birds, we feed the wild birds, you can see that and they eat out of Ted's hand which is lovely. They are king parrots, they are terrific. (Jenny, North Shore)*

The question of feeding is contentious. Many people felt it wrong to feed wild birds as it encourages dependence on human beings and the spread of exotic seed into bush areas, and encourages destructive tendencies in aggressive species such as white cockatoos. For other people the pleasure factor of engaging with wild birds

Figure 8.7: Frank chats to a regular visitor in his Campbelltown backyard

outweighs any disadvantages They look forward to particular types of birds visiting at regular feed times.

Fed birds are mainly seed-eating brightly coloured parrots, and meat-eating kookaburras, magpies and currawongs. People who feed these birds rarely reflect on the appropriateness of the actions. In contrast, people who plant flowering native plants are less likely to hand feed and more knowledgeable about the less flashy nectar feeding and insectivorous birds. Some people in this group are keen enthusiasts, not just casual bird watchers. Many bird identification books were brought out during our interviews. Several dozen species were named, but some people were embarrassed that they could not name many. However, even those who profess to be 'not good on birds' value their presence highly.

People with domestic animals and people with mainly non-native gardens are just as likely to talk positively about visiting birds as keen bird enthusiasts who have planted bird attracting native plants. However the latter talk more about lesser-known birds such as insect eating species, and are more likely to identify 'balance' as an issue in their local bird communities. So, for example, while it is widely accepted that the common myna (*Acridotheres tristis*) is an introduced pest, only bird enthusiasts mention the Australian noisy miner (*Manorina melanocephala*) as being invasive. Another point of conflict is the pied currawong (*Strepera graculina*), with the rising populations and aggressive behaviour of these birds being held responsible for the demise of smaller birds. Some committed native gardeners speak of a desire to cull such birds, equating the imbalance in a native species with invasiveness. This is discussed further below.

Because it was such a shared response across the study sample, it was important to try and understand why people valued birds so highly. At the simplest level it affords them a great deal of pleasure to see wild birds come voluntarily into their backyards. It is an important part of the rhythm of people's days to be woken by birds, to look at them out the kitchen window, to sit and watch them on or from a deck.

> *I like the bird life and we are constantly having birds such as king parrots and black cockies and all that sort of thing coming over into the trees there. And it's my way of meditating really out in the backyard. (Peter, Hills District)*

> *I talk to lots of people who are like me, go out into your garden and look around and watch the birds and see what happens, you forget if you've got any stress. I think everybody needs a backyard. (Jessie, Wollongong)*

It is also a relationship with limited responsibility. Thus while people might say they do not have pets because they go away a lot, or do not want the burden of looking after them, this does not apply to birds.

On another level, visits from wild birds are considered an indicator of getting something right in the backyard, particularly by those who make close observations and who are keen to encourage smaller and rarer species. Margaret, who has watched the adjoining bushland become suburbs in the twenty years she has lived in the Campbelltown area, calls the larger birds, even when native, 'grosser' birds—a reference to their aggressive habits.

> *There's a bit of a bowl down there for the birds, so the birds do come in. Only the grosser natives now. The miners and the parrots come and use the garden now. We don't have the little birds any more. I'm a bit sad about that.*

For Tao, close to the urban centre of Campbelltown, visiting birds are the connection between a backyard and the beginnings of an ecosystem.

> *But we see a lot of birds in here. That's also the reason we went for natives, for the bird life. We realised it attracts the birds, native birds. And it attracts that whole whatever goes together with the birds, the insects and the whole thing. We try to encourage [them].*

Pets and Pests

What makes a pet? At one level it is a question of intimacy, interaction and responsibility for animals. People describe a variety of regular and interactive relationships that challenge any neat definition of a pet. These include the bird feeding discussed above, and the regular Alice Springs practice of leaving water outside the back fence for visiting kangaroos and euros.

> *I have a little pet butcher bird that comes here, and I give it a piece of meat every couple of days . . . I've got a big lizard about a metre long that comes and say hello to me now and again and then disappears. (Leo, North Shore)*

> *I was doing some hand watering yesterday . . . and a frog poked his head out of the pot to me. (Neil, northern suburbs, Wollongong)*

> *I have a family of pee wees that spend their time here on my back lawn and one or two of those have been coming for years, the same couple . . . (Vi, northern suburbs Wollongong)*

> *Why [have] a caged bird when you can sit there with a bowl of sunflower seed and you know, a pair of king parrots will come and sit on your lap and feed out of it and then they can fly away when it suits them to fly away. (Ted, North Shore)*

> *[People] think their animals have a right to wander wherever they will . . . when people talk about their ruddy pets I think that the birds are my pets so far as I'm concerned. (David, northern suburbs, Wollongong)*

On the other hand things that are technically pets may not feel like it, as when one women said of her goldfish, they 'are too little to be pets but they live here, yeah'.

The two most common and significant companion animals in people's lives are dogs and cats. That one person's pet is often another's pest is seen most vividly in the discussions over cats.

Dogs—Part of the Family

People talk about their dogs affectionately as active members of the family. For example, 'a domestic dog isn't nature really, he's just another species that you share your life with'. Another woman says of her dog, 'she is the chief gardener at the moment; she likes digging up the dead roots of the kikuyu grass'.

While occasionally positioned as disruptive in regard to digging up garden beds or dragging washing off the line, dogs are most often talked about in terms of their general good naturedness and companionship (Figure 8.8). In relation to wildlife, opinion differs. Some people are aware that their dog hunts lizards, birds, mice or the

Figure 8.8: Roz's dog looks content, but the corrugated iron along the base of the fence is an attempt at containment, Port Kembla, Wollongong

occasional domestic chook or rabbit, and feel that the dog really doesn't belong in the backyard. Others feel that the dog belongs and is no threat to wildlife, or that visiting wild animals have to look after themselves. In these interactions with wildlife, and in describing various doggy activities such as guard duty, playing ball games and digging holes, dogs are always spoken of as active in the backyard.

If both animal types are responsible for wildlife killings, it raises the question why dogs occasion less outrage than cats. Dogs are considered to be 'doing their duty' in behaving territorially in the backyard. There is a high level of interaction between dogs and the people who own them; thus dogs are described or defined as guard dogs, as protectors of home and family, as companions and as playmates. For a dog to act territorially and chase, maim or kill wildlife is therefore seen as an unfortunate overzealousness on the part of the dog and the emotion most frequently expressed is regret. There is also the assumption, sometimes articulated but more often implied, that dogs can be trained out of this 'habit' by monitoring and punishing bad behaviour. Thus the interactions described by dog owners include control and intervention on their part.

Figure 8.9, inset: Marilyn's cat stretches out asleep on the Sir Walter Buffalo lawn, Shell Cove, Wollongong

Figure 8.10, above: Thelma's cat sits atop a makeshift sheltered bird feeder. There are scattered water dishes set out for the birds, inner northern suburbs, Wollongong

Cats—Allies and Enemies

Cats are positioned differently by both owners and non-owners. Cat are held by their owners to be independent animals with whom a relationship is on a less interactive level than is the case with dogs. Cats are most frequently described in passive terms; they are asleep, sitting in the sun or simply 'being' (Figure 8.9). 'Fat' and 'old' are frequent adjectives.

> *David said it's the best thing the cat has ever had done for her, is build a deck . . . She tends to sleep, well, mainly in that flower pot.*

Construing cats as either acted on, as in 'our cats we keep in at night' or just being, as in 'our cats mainly stay in the backyard', allows owners to remove responsibility from the cat. Cats could however be boss in relation to their owner:

> *He used to talk to me and he was my boss. He told me what he wanted and I had to hop to it.*

When they do act in connection to wildlife it is not necessarily as a causal agent. For example one person told us 'Well I have a cat and I have lots of birds. I've always been lucky in that we've had lots of different kinds of birds come to our garden.' There is not an explicit connection made between being lucky, having birds and having a cat, although implicitly the cat is exonerated from any activity surrounding the visiting birds. Cat owners are obviously used to having to justify having a cat; people were quick to go into long and detailed explanations of their cat's innocence, even though we made no accusations.

Others acknowledge that their cat does kill wildlife, despite intervention strategies such as bells, collars and keeping the cat in at night. The acceptance of instinctive behaviour by owners acts to negate the cat's actions as in the examples below.

> *We love the birds, so our last cat before I must admit, she was seventeen when she died but it doesn't matter how many bells, you would still find birds, and I'd be devastated with the birds. And then I'd think well its nature and you have to put up with that.*

> *Elizabeth: The cat was very self sufficient.*
> *Ned: Caught its own dinner. (northern suburbs, Wollongong)*

However, for the majority of cat owners, their cats are too old or too well fed and are not construed as culprits because they are rarely portrayed as *doing* anything. 'The little blue wrens were nesting up there and my cats don't touch anything like that; I think they are so well fed.'

In contrast, people who do not own cats see them as agents of destruction and blame them for the loss of bird life. Cats are killers, and people without cats either decry cat owners' lack of control or dislike what they consider cats' instinctive urge to 'seek and destroy'. They report deliberate decisions not to have a cat for this reason, and regular findings of corpses:

> *I would never have a cat and I know my neighbour would never have a cat either because there are just so many birds in our gardens that to have a cat would just be the end of them.*

> *It's very distressing when you come out and this poor little ringtail possum has been mauled by a cat during the night; it breaks my heart.*

For Helen, the cats come first, but it affects what she plants in her Port Kembla garden:

> *I probably haven't got much in the way of natives, but I also have got to be careful having two cats that I don't want to attract too much around.*

Cat haters recount detailed fantasies about getting rid of their neighbours' cats. These involve hoses, traps, guns and poison, and some have been acted on. For the most part these neighbourly conflicts are more hidden than those related to trees. This may be because the connection between the tree and say a damaged building or drain is visible, fixed in space and affecting private property. Cats are mobile, hard to catch in the act, easier to deny, and the asset being defended (the wildlife) is not personal property to which someone is legally entitled.

Cat owners who are committed native gardeners are more likely than others to explicitly express the tension of having a cat, instead of sidestepping the issue like most other cat owners. Describing her cat as the queen of the household, Kris explains that

> *The thing that I really love about them is that they can be affectionate at times but they are their own creature, I was going to say person ... I'm very compromised with my cat in that respect. (Kris, inner Wollongong)*

In comparing what people say about and do to dogs and cats, there are several important summary points. First, on the question of belonging, people have much less to say about dogs. For most people, it is taken for granted that dogs belong—in suburbs, in families, in backyards. In the end, this is all that needs to be said if their behaviour is destructive towards wildlife. There is a widespread view that dogs have a right to be there. The place of cats is much more contentious.

Second, we attribute the contentiousness of cats to the popularity of birds and, to a lesser extent, other wildlife. The belonging of cats is linked to the wellbeing of birds. Thus lovers and haters of cats both refer to birds in their justifications. Many people use birds and other wildlife as their reason for not having pets at all. For haters, cats are bad *because* of what they do to birds. For lovers, cats are recognised as a problem for birds, but there are several responses. Either their own cat is exempted on the grounds of age, sloth or being well fed, or is loved despite what it does to birds.

Third, although we have no comparative historical data, we believe that the conceptual position of cats in suburban Australia is quite unstable. (Their physical position will not depend only on decisions made by humans, given high feral cat populations in some areas.) People are consciously negotiating this position, as evidenced by the fact that they have a lot to say about it. Long justifications of cat activity and inactivity in the interviews suggest this is an issue that cat owners have thought about a lot. When it comes to a point where they have to make a choice between cats and birds, increasing numbers of people are choosing birds. Perth residents, including cat owners, have expressed willingness to support stricter regulation of domestic cats (Lilith et al. 2006) However there is debate among ecologists as to the exact effect of cats on urban bird populations (Parsons, Major, and French 2006).

Nativeness and Belonging

In Wollongong, white cedar (*Melia azedarach*) is a native rainforest tree, planted when people want to encourage locally indigenous plants, and valued for its spectacular flowers and deciduous nature. The main annoyance it causes is that each autumn it is host to the white cedar moth (*Leptocneria reducta*), the black furry caterpillars of which often manage to find their way indoors. In Alice Springs, by contrast, where it was extensively planted as a shade tree, it is now a hated pest. This is mainly because it sprouts prolifically in unwanted places, an invasive status recognised in its listing as one of the ten most serious invasive garden plants available for sale in the arid Northern Territory (Groves et al. 2005). It is frequently mentioned by Alice Springs participants when asked about plants or animals that do not belong. These opposing views of white cedar provide a graphic illustration of the old gardeners' maxim that a weed is a plant in the wrong place.

In one Wollongong backyard, an area of lawn overlooked by a 10 m high white cedar had recently been planted over with native grasses and shrubs, then mulched. The prolific seeds of the white cedar were barely noticed when they were dropped on the lawn and mown over, but they were very noticeable against the mulch, particularly when it provided a perfect site for germination. By late the following summer the mulch was thick with white cedar saplings (Figure 8.11), all competing against the carefully nurtured native grasses and ground covers. So, it was not just a question of belonging or not belonging, but that the status and behaviour of a plant can change by virtue of changes in surrounding circumstances.

In fact, because of their ongoing engagement with many plants as active colonisers of backyard space, our participants are much more likely to talk about weeds in terms of their invasive qualities than their nativeness per se. This is a commonsense understanding borne out of the labour of maintaining a garden, or frustration at not having the time or inclination to do so. Thus Angus talks of weeds as plants that 'run over everything else'. For Jo, an active participant in bush regeneration projects, there is a strong distinction between good and bad exotic plants, separate to their nativeness. The bad ones, including Madeira vine (*Anredera cordifolia*) and lantana, are invasive in the bush, while those that sit quietly in the domestic space of her garden (specimen conifers, port wine magnolia, daffodils) are very welcome despite being exotic.

Lack of knowledge is an important issue with some species. For example, people can maintain ambivalence towards rats if they think they are native. Because they are rarely actually seen, and are then hard to identify, people may not be sure. Thus they might poison them, and hope that they are not native, or tolerate them, and hope that they are.

An interesting contrasting example of actively using weeds for particular purposes is provided by Dan and Sue, who live in a suburb that has experienced heavy industry for decades, where people need to check the lead levels in their vegetable gardens. Sue notes that too rigid a line between natives and exotics

doesn't actually work here because I've got impatiens there and I know is a weed where I go in the bush, but I'm actually using them for a different purpose . . . I'm trying to create habitat for animals.

Dan: *We actually have water hyacinths growing in our pond here and . . . they took a photo for an article in the paper and I think that's where it was spotted. The Noxious Weed Authority knew Sue, knew the garden . . . and saw the water hyacinths in there and paid us a visit and*

Sue: *But I did try to explain to him that water hyacinths are used in other countries to remove heavy metals . . . in China . . . they actually put them through the furnaces and get them and recoup the heavy metals.*
(Dan and Sue, Port Kembla)

Water hyacinths (*Eichhornia grassipes*) are among the world's most invasive aquatic plants.

More detailed illustrated examples are shown here by examining attitudes and practices towards two contrasting plants, lantana and pittosporum, and the networks within which they exist. A literature survey of environmental weeds in 1997 in Sydney sandstone bushland found that *Pittosporum undulatum* was the highest ranked locally native environmental weed, and that lantana was the top exotic environmental weed (Rose 1997). Lantana is the weed most frequently mentioned by our backyard participants. Pittosporum is mentioned less often and not necessarily as an environmental weed.

The Case of the Invasive Alien— Lantana

Lantana (*Lantana camara* L.), a perennial aromatic shrub usually 1 m–2 m, occasionally 6 m, tall originated in Central and South America. It has been hybridised extensively since the eighteenth and nineteenth centuries, its brightly coloured flowers making it attractive to gardeners during

Figure 8.11: Self-seeded white cedars growing in a newly mulched garden bed, outer northern suburbs, Wollongong

the period of European colonial expansion into the tropics (Cronk and Fuller 2001: 82–86). The numerous hybrid forms are now 'collectively referred to as the *Lantana camara* complex or *Lantana camara* sensu lato'. It is now invasive throughout many parts of the tropics, and Australia (Figure 8.12).

Lantana has many ecological characteristics of the successful invasive species—including being dispersed by birds, toxicity to herbivores, vegetative reproduction, a tendency to thrive on disturbance, and setting copious seed. It is mainly a weed of highly disturbed habitats rather than an invader of natural ones (Cronk and Fuller 2001: 84). These characteristics are seen in Wollongong backyards. Many original suburban subdivisions in Wollongong were of farmland that had been cleared by early European settlers, then invaded by weeds following the cessation of grazing. A number of our participants recall a backyard

Figure 8.12: *Lantana camara* flowering in a densely planted garden bed, inner Sydney

Figure 8.13: Jennifer's steep bush backyard. At the bottom dense lantana thickets enclose the backyard, outer northern suburbs, Wollongong

overgrown with lantana and other weeds when they first came to their houses, or that they knew as children. They describe the struggle first to get rid of it, then to keep it at bay.

> *So we actually borrowed a goat . . . and we used to move this goat around say 12 feet a day with a chain about 20 feet long . . . and that goat single handedly chewed through the whole of the reserve, right to the bridge, down to the highway all the way, the same distance up the other way. So he covered about a kilometre and that's where the lantana was and he single handedly demolished all that lantana. (John, northern suburbs, Wollongong)*

> *Now where that fern is, all that area was all covered in madeira vine and lantana, and so I've just gradually got rid of it all and I have to keep vigilant. The madeira vine still comes back but we've just worked on, I just work at it, you know, it's painstaking work but I suppose I seem to have the right kind of mentality . . . when something gets away you just go back into one area and clean that completely . . . (Jo, northern suburbs, Wollongong)*

> *It was pretty impenetrable with the lantana and I couldn't cope, not with work and all the rest . . . one year we had a working party and Ron came up and . . . he tried to . . . chop down all the lantana but I mean it sort of came back up . . . it wasn't until I had the extension [done and a bulldozer brought in and] he got in and really rough landscaped it and got rid of the lantana that you could actually really . . . do anything with it. (Jennifer, northern suburbs, Wollongong) (Figure 8.13)*

The epic nature of the struggles described above reminds us, further to Robbins' (2004) discussion of the social frameworks of invasion, that managing invasiveness is also an intensely social process, requiring mobilisation of human labor. While lantana is still an issue for a number of people in their backyards, the greatest struggles are described in the context of first coming to a backyard that had been neglected for various reasons. Although the contemporary forms are horticultural hybrids, lantana is still sold in some nurseries, enhancing some people's perception that it is not too problematic. For example, Bruce in Port Kembla says:

> *I've got lantana now. Lantana is classified as a weed but it's sold at the garden places . . . I think that they're controllable weeds.*

If removing invaders is not a simple process, nor does it return an ecosystem to a previous pristine state, as ecological relationships are likely to have changed. A key tension that participants encounter in relation to lantana is that its dense thickets provide valued habitat for many small native birds whose traditional habitat has been decimated by land clearing. This dilemma is particularly felt by indigenous purists such as David, who describes work over several years to remove a variety of weeds from his backyard in an attempt to revegetate with local native species. David recognised that he could not remove all his exotic plants at once because of the risk of erosion, and also because they provide him with some noise protection from the road below his block.

> *I feel pretty passionate about not having exotics. But I'm beginning to realise it's a bit more complicated than that now, that lantana isn't necessarily totally bad because it's bird habitat.*

> *We're regenerating the coastal banksia forest on our block and [these bowerbirds] go through from the block next door which has been sort of rented and has just gone to weeds and lantana and morning glory for years now, but they like the thicket I think . . . the bowerbirds seem to use the whole thing as a sort of corridor . . . ' (Jan and Elaine, northern suburbs, Wollongong)*

In spite of this observation, Jan and Elaine still note lantana as a weed on their block and pull it out when they can.

I think we've lost sight now that lantana has been here for so long that it has become the understorey and we have so many small birds, particularly the eastern whipbird which is beautiful to hear and which you'll never see because it's within that. (Neil, northern suburbs, Wollongong)

Invasive Natives— Pittosporum and Currawongs

Pittosporum [*Pittosporum undulatum* (Vent.) (sweet pittosporum, native daphne, mock orange)] is an important example because it challenges the idea that invasives are necessarily alien. Further it has the dual status of invasive and endangered species in different contexts.

It usually grows as a slender branched shrub or tree, 5 m–13 m tall, with a broad geographic range throughout southeastern Australia. Prior to European settlement it was mainly confined to wet forest and rainforest environments, but now encroaches from sheltered gully environments into adjacent vegetation communities on drier slopes.

Trudi Mullett (2001) has summarised a number of factors contributing to its spread, highlighting the social and ecological complexity of invasiveness. Five factors that she identifies are

—*Ornamental plantings.* Pittosporum was widely employed in the nineteenth century garden as a local equivalent to the English use of the Portuguese laurel. Its ornamental status is also the source of its invasiveness in places outside Australia, where it was widely planted in the network of British colonial botanic gardens. Cronk and Fuller give the examples of Jamaica and South Africa (2001: 109).

—*Increased dispersal opportunities.* These occur particularly through bird activity, for example expanded populations of the introduced blackbird and the native pied currawong in urban and suburban areas (Low 2002).

—*Changes to fire regimes.* Pittosporum is fire sensitive, and may have been kept in check by frequent, low intensity burning by Aboriginal people. Attempts at fire suppression in and around urban and suburban areas over recent decades have allowed it to expand out of topographically protected gullies.

—*Inherent plasticity and adaptability.* As with most invasives, its resilience and opportunism favour it over more specialist species.

—*Process of population expansion.* Clumps around mature trees offer perching sites for birds, and create their own micro-climates. The deep shade and litter fall create feedbacks that prevent germination or expansion of competing species.

The fundamental importance of ecological and social context in debates about invasives is illustrated most strongly by pittosporum's dual status as both invasive and endangered species in Victoria:

> *P. undulatum* invasion is listed as a 'potentially threatening process' under Schedule 3 of the Flora and Fauna Guarantee Act 1988 . . . Under the same legislation, *P. undulatum* is identified as a component of a rare plant community (Dry Rainforest (Limestone) Community) listed under Schedule 2 of the Act . . . ' (Mullett 2001: 210)

This creates significant problems for environmental managers who often respond by directing resources towards introduced species 'as these have a clearer invasive status' (Mullett 2001: 120).

Given the confusion among environmental professionals, it is unsurprising that pittosporum is not strongly established in the consciousness of our backyard participants, despite its frequent occurrence in the Sydney-Wollongong region. Many people scarcely see it in the backyard (Figure 14). Even when present, it was often not mentioned by the backyarder either in the taped interview or the informal walk around the garden, and only recorded by the interviewer in fieldnotes. This is a typical pattern where plants are self seeded; they may not be an important part of the backyard as perceived by the owner. In several cases people did not recognise pittosporum, and had to ask the interviewer what it was.

a variety of responses. A number of participants enjoy the idea of nature 'doing its own thing', and are content to just let things go, at least for a while. Others describe pulling the seedlings out, or moving them to other parts of the garden.

Few factors would enhance the likely success of an invader as much as the relative invisibility that attends pittosporum. This apparent lag time in the public consciousness of a species as a problem may have significant implications for its management, particularly by comparison with lantana which is well entrenched in people's consciousness.

In contrast to pittosporum the currawong is highly visible. It is the most hated native bird because of its aggressive behaviour, and even the most nativist gardeners will consider culling currawongs. David argues for culling on the basis both of bird behaviour, and of the fact that the context in which they are flourishing is created by humans:

> **if native species like currawongs turn out to be invasive, then we treat those in the same way as we would treat cotoneasters or camphor laurels . . . I mean human beings create environments which allow birds of particular species to dominate and they drive the others out. So I think there's a strong argument for culling in that context. (David, northern suburbs, Wollongong)**

> **Currawongs have just come back, having not had them for several years they have just come back, and I dislike them because they kill all the small birds. So whenever I see those I get the dog to go and bark at them and chase them away, and [I] hose them and generally make them very unwelcome. (Julia, Eastern Suburbs, Sydney)**

Earlier in the interview Julia had said, in relation to plants, 'well I'm a bush regenerator so it is likely that I would not like exotic species', but here she is prepared to use her exotic dog to get rid of native currawongs. Noisy miners are

Figure 8.14: Pittosporum undulatum *growing against the wall of an inner Sydney block of flats*

For Kris, the regeneration of pittosporum is part of the process of restoration in her backyard; 'There's some pittosporum coming up which is really nice seeing that my neighbour's cut down most of hers.' As an environmental professional who moved from Victoria to inner Wollongong, Kris was quite aware of pittosporum's problematic status, but for her, its belonging was allowed to overrule its behaviour.

> **One of the worst species is the Pittosporum undulatum, I know that from Victoria because that's just taken over down there, but it's actually native to this area so that's fine [laughs]. It's allowed to take over because it grows fast and it bushes out . . .**

The agency of nature, as expressed in the appearance of pittosporum and other species independent of direct human intervention, evokes in a similar category, annoying many committed native gardeners 'even though they are native'. As one explains, 'when things get out of balance that's when we consider them not to belong.'

Others considered that the native status of the currawong and the noisy miner absolve them of any recriminatory action when they flourish in a clearly 'adjusted' environment, on the basis that it is a natural situation.

> **You could argue that they have taken over the North Shore from the little birds. To that extent they're undesirable species. Our view on that is that that's been almost a natural selection process. We cannot do anything about that . . . We don't find them dreadful at all. They just happen to live here, and add value. I think the Australian mynas for example, are great . . . they keep the insects under control. They are, all the time, pruning, picking one thing and another. They're part of an adjusted environment . . . You have to accept that things happen beyond our control. (Angus, North Shore, Sydney)**

On the other hand, Angus does not accept the introduced common indian myna as natural in this adjusted environment, regularly chasing them out of his garden.

The Contingencies of Belonging

We have illustrated some of the diverse ways in which suburban backyarders structure conceptual and material boundaries around spaces and species, and also some of the diverse ways in which boundaries are crossed. The dividing line is drawn in many different places under a variety of influences: between inside and outside spaces, between domesticated environments and restored bushland, between trees and the suburbs, between native and non-native species, between exotics that sit quietly and ones that behave

badly, between neighbours who kill good trees and neighbours who kill bad trees.

Trees, cats, native plants, dogs, birds and weeds are situated in various ways, and in relation to each other. Trees are most welcome into backyards and lives when they are entwined, sometimes literally, with the rhythms of daily or family life. At other times they are sources of social conflict. People who are impassioned and vigilant about certain boundaries are most likely to have fraught connections to their neighbours. After expounding at length on what he described as his 'bloody minded' passion against his neighbours' exotic plants and cats, one committed native gardener laughed, 'You can see I'm not a very good neighbour, you won't want to live next to me now.'

Underlying these discussions of plant and animal belonging is the question of human belonging, and particularly the extent to which settler Australians consider themselves to belong, a tension voiced in the following quote.

> **I guess the other angle is that you know ultimately we're probably not meant to be here either in terms of you know, white Anglo-Saxon human beings. And then every-thing we eat, well ninety-nine per cent of the things we eat aren't native to Australia either. (Dan, Port Kembla)**

It is worth noting that most Aboriginal people do not insist that only native plants and animals belong. A 'multi-dimensional set of Aboriginal responses' that indicate considerable intellectual flexibility in dealing with changing ecological and socio-economic conditions is documented by David Trigger (2004). To borrow Trigger's words, the way different cultural groups interpret and express belonging is an open—and important—empirical question.

The question of human belonging is explored further in chapter nine.

CHAPTER NINE

Nature and Urban
Australia

Urban Australia values its relationships with plants, pets, birds, other animals, the earth and the weather. Connections are developed through daily habit and close observation, and involve all the senses. Some of these are shared across the community, some differ from person to person, and some cause conflict. These relationships both reinforce and rupture a dualistic view of humans and nature. The passion engendered in suburban backyards, and the everyday, habitual nature of these engagements, provide an under-rated human resource of considerable potential in the necessary shifts towards more sustainable cities.

We started the book examining the conventional wisdom that Australians are alienated from nature, and locked into a destructive and unsustainable relationship with it unless they can rapidly effect a significant change of culture. This means a change away from a dualistic Western land ethic that separates humans and nature—for example by thinking of nature and the city as antithetical—towards a more dynamic and integrative one that can come to terms with the particular requirements of the Australian environment. In this concluding chapter we take each element separately, and draw together the individual threads of our argument.

Alienated and Separated?

Scholarly research from diverse disciplines and perspectives has shown the fiction of thinking of humans and nature as separate, and that all our interactions are embedded in complex entanglements. Yet, the idea of nature as something separate and apart from humans is powerful and has wide vernacular appeal. The dualisms have become strongly entrenched in Western thought through a complex layering of historical processes.

The backyard is our window onto contemporary Australian interactions with nature; a place where people spend a lot of time, and where, as individuals and households, they have a relatively high degree of control over what happens. The backyard and the garden are nature-culture hybrids, so we would expect to find all manner of interesting networks and embeddedness. Yet both are also inside the conceptual space of the city, so for many people whatever nature is here cannot be seen as 'real' nature. We have both theoretical and empirical grounds for challenging that understanding.

The first thing we can do is demolish the myth that Australians are uniformly alienated from and antipathetic to the nonhuman world. Our findings show otherwise, as has other research using methods that focus on the lived experience of people in the suburbs. Outdoor domestic spaces are highly valued environments for the privacy and freedom they offer, and for the interactive relationships they facilitate with family, friends, pets, birds, other animals, sunsets and breezes. Connections are developed through habit and close observation at different times of the day, in different seasons, over different years. The most striking and shared aspect of this is the important role of birds in everyday life, and the ways people are actively remaking gardens for birds. People value backyard interactions with the natural world more highly than they value the material structures of the space. They recognise that the nonhuman world has agency, some of it out of their control and at the limits of their perception or interest.

In this hybrid space, we see processes that both reinforce and break down the dichotomy between humans and nature. The widespread valuing of native and exotic plants in combination seems to indicate comfort with the hybrid ecologies and cultures of modern Australia (Trigger and Mulcock 2005).

The thing that needs to be explained, then, is the persistence and resilience of the separationist views. Why are they so strong? What keeps them in place?

Locked In?

We found shared cultural change on the water issue, and suggested that the position of cats is unstable because birds are increasingly welcome in human living environments. We do not suggest that environmental sustainability comes about by an easy choice of a self-evident pathway. In a complex system there are many different ways to engage in good environmental practices, just as there are many ways to do damage. We specifically do not want to romanticise our backyarders as eco-angels labouring at a small scale in good faith while something much larger called 'the city' burns around them. But cultural changes towards more

Figure 9.1: Jo and her son
crossing their dying lawn.
The hose is provided to
water individual trees

sustainable practices are not an impossible dream—they are in fact occurring. The passion engendered in the backyard, and the everyday, habitual nature of these engagements, provides an under-rated human resource of considerable potential in the necessary shifts towards more sustainable cities. We regard it with cautious optimism.

The economic and social pressures of modern life do not lead inexorably in a predetermined environmental direction. To take one apparently small example, among some people there is an aspiration to low maintenance, paved surfaces (which are at times anything but low maintenance, and may require increased water consumption to be kept clean). But for many others the same pressures are met by creating habitat for visiting birds and havens for themselves, by using the backyard as a place to 'de-stress'.

While the attitudes of our study participants can be read as a defence of suburbia, this does not lend weight to arguments for undifferentiated suburban expansion without appropriate infrastructure. Individuals and households have a variety of needs, especially at different stages of the life cycle. The private space that they value does not have to be big, particularly if house design is compatible and shared public spaces are easily accessible. More innovative ways to combine private and public responsibility clearly need to be sought.

In the water issue, several factors contribute to the consensus we found on the need for change, and a mobilisation of practice that crosses various social boundaries. Some factors, such as intensive public education campaigns, are visibly influential. We have argued also that an important reason people respond to the water issue is because they can see and participate in many stages of the cycle of production. They don't see the whole infrastructure of storage and transportation on a large scale, but they do see a more localised expression of it. They see whether it rains or not, they observe plant responses to lack or abundance of rain; they channel, store and redistribute water on a domestic scale (Figure 1). They see ways in which they can make a difference, and this feeds into other environmental practices, both inside the house and out. This understanding is likely to have implications for changing consumption in areas such as transport. There are no easy recipes or neat environmental management policy solutions here. But we hope the evidence presented can contribute to the broader conversation about what exactly a sustainable human presence in Australia might entail.

Ruptured and Resilient Dualisms

Many different land ethics are given voice in this book. Some of the attitudes and practices it records have destabilised or broken down the dichotomy, while others have reinforced it. While in summary they appear very theoretical perspectives, they have practical importance because they shed light on the likely tractability of different issues to change, for better or worse. Most individual backyarders and their yards do not fall distinctly on one side or the other; in fact most of them express combinations of several elements.

RUPTURE 1: NATURE IS DYNAMIC

In contrast to widespread visual and linguistic imagery of a timeless, unchanging nature, the study shows a strong vernacular understanding that change is normal in the nonhuman world. Change is understood as variously cyclic, long term, unpredictable, directional, for better and worse, depending on circumstances. People insert

Figure 9.2: Jan and Elaine in the rainforest they have planted over the past 42 years

themselves into the process of change through observation and memory. Some want to contribute actively to change, for example in the process of designing, planning and establishing a garden and shaping it over a number of years. Others are more content to let things happen, and might conceptualise change more as unfolding before them.

RUPTURE 2: NATURE AND THE BODY

There are many people for whom an embodied, physical engagement, perceived by senses other than just the visual, is highly valued. They touch, smell, hear, taste, breathe and desire. This is seen particularly among the gardeners who engage with soil, but also among those who engage with the cycles of growth via the process of their labour (Figure 9.3). Sometimes this process starts with apparently simple and regularly repeated observation, for example of birds outside the kitchen window, or of plants and their cycles of growth across the seasons.

RUPTURE 3: BRINGING NATURE INTO THE CITY

Nature is welcomed into the city in many but not all forms. Birds are widely welcomed, but various filters apply to most other fauna and flora. In their attempts to 'bring the bush back in', committed native gardeners consciously create a place for species less noticed by others, including native grasses and other herbs, and smaller native birds disadvantaged by altered predator-prey relationships.

RUPTURE AND REINFORCEMENT: AUSTRALIAN NATURE IS HYBRID

The widespread preference for exotic garden plants—either alone or in combination with natives—and the assumed belonging of dogs are just two examples that indicate a level of comfort with and attachment to an Australian ecology that has changed radically since 1788. These attitudes horrify some native purists, but they are arguably more in line with the ecological reality that Tim Low calls 'The New Nature' in his book of that name (2002). They are also a potential resource for thinking through and living with the 'novel' and 'emerging ecosystems' that are likely to confront us in the next century (Hobbs et al. 2006). The same attitudes however can reinforce old dualisms when they see the hybrids as simply part of the cultured environments of the city, and continue to position a pure nature as existing somewhere else, 'outside', 'in the bush'.

RUPTURE AND REINFORCEMENT: NATURE IS ALIVE, NOT DEAD

There are much stronger perceptions and understandings of the organic rather than inorganic worlds. People are much more likely to think of their networks of connection, and thus responsibility, to plants and animals rather than to rocks, soil or sand. At one level this is self evident, but to the extent that rocks, soil and sand are fundamental contributors to the built, agricultural and backyard environments, it is relevant to consider what might be an appropriate ethic of care. Apart from gardeners like Vi who attributes the healing properties of the earth to the soil itself, people more often consider the inorganic to be part of the 'natural' background, not requiring comment. This is evident in the statements of landscape suppliers that most customers are not interested to know where things come from, but are driven by price. The view expressed by one participant of the rocks in her front garden, 'well there is something there; there's certainly something there, that's alive', was an unusual one.

Water occupies an interesting place along the living/dead, organic/inorganic continua. The dynamic nature of people's engagement with water suggests that it is widely understood as part of a living nature. The lively presence of water connotes life (Figure 9.4).

REINFORCEMENT 1: TIDYING NATURE UP

Most people want to put some distance between themselves and the perceived messiness of nature. This is an expression of a need for order, and anxiety created by the liminal state of disorder (Figure 9.5). The distances needed to relieve that anxiety vary and the reasons vary. At one extreme are those who conceptualise and are happy with a clear distinction between suburban environments and 'the bush'. This we found particularly in negative attitudes to trees. Trees belong, but somewhere else. Of course, this attitude is not general, but we have presented a number of examples where people say, 'these things are OK, but out in the bush, not in my backyard', or they belong, but not in the suburbs'. Another expression of this view is the highly ordered and manicured backyard (Figure 9.6).

At the other end of the spectrum is the common combination of an open space, say a patch of lawn and/or a paved area close to the house, with garden beds or more 'messy' plantings at some distance. This is the idea of the backyard as 'a clearing in the forest', another contemporary expression of which is a deck providing open space and an outlook onto an environment with varying levels of disorder. As one participant put it, 'I don't mind wildness as long as it's not too messy'. This distancing is also seen in those backyards that are themselves quite ordered, but which are adjacent to bushland or reserves in which the backyarder is active in bush regeneration activities.

Most people want a living environment that is clean, safe and tidy, and the reason nature should stay 'out there' is because of its challenge to those attributes, usually expressed in terms of dirt, danger and/or mess. Tidiness is valued for a complex set of reasons that include social respectability, a certain moral quality, and the stress occasioned by mess, the latter expressed with some weariness by the working mother who said of her backyard, as if of another child, 'I resented the mess and the constant need.'

Those who are prepared to share their space, for example, with snakes, are a clear minority, as are those, like permaculturists, who positively enjoy the perceived messiness of nature.

With a few exceptions, tidying is not the 'domination of nature' often critiqued within the Western psyche—rather an expression of a need for order within busy lives and dynamic domestic spaces. It recognises the importance of nature being able to 'do its own thing', indeed it is often able to celebrate that, provided it is not right on the doorstep. Perhaps this also helps to explain the popularity of birds. Although there were some negative comments about birds 'making a mess', birds are a part of nature that does not outstay its welcome, demand attention or create new responsibilities, in contrast say to weeds and leaves.

REINFORCEMENT 2: NATURE IS NATIVE

The view that Australian nature is defined at least in part by what is native, as seen in the practices of committed native gardeners, ruptures the dualism that contrasts urban environments with wild environments, by facilitating and enhancing biodiversity conservation in their backyards, 'bringing nature in' to the city. But it reinscribes two other boundaries, that between humans and nature, and the temporal boundary based on a declaration that nothing arriving after 1788 can be considered natural, or really belonging. This view strongly influences public environmental management programs.

The boundary between humans and nature is reinscribed in several ways. The first is what Ted Mosquin (1997) refers to as the paradox of human exemption, the extent to which one exempts oneself and other human beings from a classification of the world into natural and non-natural. The paradox applies for example when people leave themselves out of classifications of 'alien' species. That the dividing line is drawn around humans is also shown by the fact that 'alien humans' (refugees, for example) would not generally be put in the pest category by this group. 'Exotic' is used as a term of abuse, but mainly for plants and animals.

Second, although purity is articulated in ways that exclude people, or in which people are invisible, any attempt to maintain or foster the dominance of locally indigenous species in a backyard requires an enormous amount of human effort, at least as much as maintaining a weed free and luxuriant lawn. It is not labour which can be invested just once, but must continue if it is to

Figure 9.3, above: Vi composting
Figure 9.4, above right:
Water pot with bubbling fountain
Figure 9.5, below right:
Garden path

Figure 9.6: A sense of everything in its place in this North Shore backyard

succeed. This point extends to spaces far beyond the backyard, for example the intensive human effort required to manage invasive species in rural environments, including national parks. It is important that this labour is not hidden, or it will become even harder than it is at present to fight for the allocation of scarce public resources.

Third, the intensely social dimensions of this view of nature are also shown by the way attempts at species purification often exacerbate social boundaries with neighbours. In denying or ignoring the human and the social 'in here', many committed native gardeners are just as separatist

in framing distinct realms for humans and nature as those who want to banish gum trees from the suburbs.

The temporal boundary of nativeness is overlaid on that between humans and nature. It is this combination, we suggest, that makes the ideal of purity so resilient. That is, in advocating a particular set of plant choices on the grounds that only what belongs is tolerable, but absolving themselves of any requirement to belong, the committed native gardeners (not alone, but in particular) are expressing the tensions and ambivalences that accompany questions of their own belonging to the land. Further, this well educated group is also strongly influenced by scientific ecology which, as previously discussed, has traditionally maintained a strong separation of humans and nature. These points can be illustrated by two examples. In the following statements, a committed native gardener from Alice Springs is talking about the importance of locally indigenous species over more general natives, and locates the concept of nativeness in a time before human damage:

> *I mean you can talk about regional natives, but the indigenous species is actually what exists on the land before you played with the land and started to manipulate it.*

Another committed native gardener connects genetic purity, localness, environmental fitness and past times in explaining the decision to source seed only from within 200 m of her backyard.

> *If we are going to plant something, we don't want it to interfere with the genetics of what is growing down in the regional park . . . we are pretty mindful of the fact that things need to be local to keep the genetics pure; that's why I'm encouraging it, you know, local plants do better, grow better, they are adapted to their local environment more than other plants. So it makes sense to plant what would have grown here.*

As Gould argued, those plants are not better adapted, they just got there first (or second, or third). They are in fact very vulnerable to more aggressive invasives, requiring the intervention, care and commitment of this participant to survive. The human is a crucial actor in this ecosystem, but does not admit her own effort into her conceptual schema (Figure 9.7). For example, later in the interview she considers people 'not really' part of nature, unless they are indigenous. Ethical reasons for investing such effort would be stronger, and likely to garner wider support, if expressed less as maintaining what belongs

and more in terms of an acknowledged human responsibility to nurture species that grow nowhere else and may not otherwise survive here.

It is often argued in popular debate that gardener obsessions with introduced rose bushes and azaleas, for example, exemplify the failure of settler Australians to feel at home in Australian nature. Others have shown with considerable cultural depth how the process of planting is used in the process of making a home in a new country (Brook 2003, Trigger and Mulcock 2005). We read the purist end of the committed native gardener thinking as a greater expression of postcolonial anxiety than the rose gardener or the lawn enthusiast, precisely because of the purists' unease about their own human presence. (Another expression of this anxiety is the level of guilt expressed by many people who do not like native plants.) This is not to argue against the value of the intensive environmental commitments they

Figure 9.7: A native gardener points out self-seeded plants

demonstrate. It is to suggest rather that efforts to conserve and restore native biodiversity are likely to be more effective if they acknowledge the human dimensions of these activities, and if they understand as much about the social dimensions of networks as the ecological ones. The high levels of social conflict, some of it just below the surface of neighbourly relations, render some of this restoration activity highly vulnerable.

Beneath the surface, even the purists recognise that the purity to which they aspire is ruptured not only by changed ecological thresholds, but by other elements of their own lives, including houses, dogs, cats, vegetable gardens and their own presence. They know that none of their backyards can be understood as pure in the terms that the narrative demands. They contain the impure plantings of previous owners, and are juxtaposed against the backyards of neighbours with very different ideas and practices. Our participants are conscious of these tensions and deal with the paradoxes in various ways. There are tolerances, such as when a large camphor laurel is kept because it is the children's swing tree. There is acknowledgement of contradiction in relation to cats; 'I think they should be phased out of the country, but I do love them'. There is the attempt at conceptual naturalisation for one couple, who named their dog 'Poa', after the grass genus containing a number of Australian native species, in a presumably subconscious attempt to naturalise his presence in their landscape.

Or they change their practices, they 'give voice' to the hybrids. Thus restorationists leave the lantana, or at least remove it more slowly, as it provides bird habitat, and someone else distinguishes between good and bad exotics based on her observations of which ones behave themselves in the bush. A self described former 'indigenous fascist' in Alice Springs said, 'well the whole shade tree thing got me undone in the end. It's really hard to find a tree that provides deep shade ... so we planted a jacaranda ... and an African mahogany'.

REINFORCEMENT 3: NATURE IS FOR LOOKING AT

The attitude which considers the visual more important than the other senses, particularly touch, is arguably on the increase, and is another example of a distancing process. There are a number of manifestations.

The most dramatic is the stylistic presentation of nature in magazines and related media. Everywhere we look there are images of beautiful nature, both within our homes and gardens and in more distant environments. Nature in these pictures is not touchable, it doesn't smell and it doesn't leave a mess.

On a more everyday scale, the now widespread visual connections between the inside living area of the house and the outside, via extensive windows and/or glass doors, makes a very specific connection to nature. It allows us to look, but does not require us to touch or necessarily even feel or smell. We are bringing the outside in, but we want to be able to control which aspects of nature are allowed in. The influence of fashion, style and household consumerism ratchets together, to use Shove's metaphor, with the visual at the expense of other embodied connections (Figures 9.8, 9.9). Or rather, the other senses are invoked and utilised, but towards a cleansed and commodified nature. Thus we might have reference to the smell of flowers, the serene sounds and feelings provided by a water feature, the touch of natural textiles in our living spaces, but this is a nature that does not require us to get our hands dirty, nor to think about the relations of production that brought that nature to our living room.

Finding a Place for the Human

The central tension in the broader conversation of this book concerns the place of the human being. In Australia we have an extremely limited conceptual vocabulary for positive human environmental actions. Arguably, middle

Figure 9.8: A trickling water feature adds visual pleasure

Australia does not have one for itself, the only symbol of sustainable human presence being an Aboriginal one. Non-indigenous people who consider proper Australian nature to be native cannot allow themselves to belong. As discussed previously, exclusion of the human element from nature is not generally accepted by Aboriginal people, among whom a much more pragmatic and flexible acknowledgement of recombinant ecologies, including a human element, has been found. Our halting steps towards Aboriginal reconciliation are thus connected to the possibility of developing cultures of environmental sustainability.

The strong agency of humans is spoken of by participants as an inevitable ('natural') force, and a force with negative and positive consequences. Many people with backyards discuss the destructive power of humans on the environment. This is usually seen as an aggregate power, of humanity altogether, for it often goes with the apparent contradiction of the individual being powerless to change things. For some, the individual's power within the backyard is a way of coping with a perceived wider powerlessness. I can't fix the world, but I can do things better here in my own space. For others, working in the backyard is an explicit manifestation of a wider engagement and commitment.

The sense that human dominance is a positive and productive force is rare, but is seen more clearly in the agricultural engagement. For those who produce food, there is a strong sense of engaging with the earth to do good things. And to a lesser extent among passionate gardeners, who see themselves as helping to bring forth the productivity and abundance of nature.

Environmental management strategies developed on the basis of an ecological literature that is either blind to the human presence, or views it solely as a threat, are unlikely to work in a world where human activities now pervade virtually all earth processes. Alternative strategies are not self evident, but require considerable discussion. Not all the human actions surveyed in this book are environmentally positive. It is important to acknowledge however that they are occurring. It is time then to be considering ways to harness the positive potential of behaviours grounded in rationales that are not obviously 'environmental', for example ones to do with pride in private property.

Finding a place for the human requires us to contest two opposing views of the city. These are views that are applied to cities in general, and a region in our study which includes Sydney and Wollongong furnishes a particularly clear illustration.

A biodiversity conservation view is that Sydney lies in one of the most species rich bioregions in Australia. Protection strategies focus on patches, corridors and reserves, but with little sense that there are also five million

Figure 9.9: The decorator in her backyard

human beings within this bioregion. The other view is that a city is a place of economic and cultural activity in which questions of nature can be ignored or removed to another place (as 'preserved', 'protected' or 'real' nature).

While contrary in some ways, these viewpoints share a sense that the city is unnatural, and they offer no space for a beneficial human engagement with the nonhuman world.

Conservation management strategies need instead to acknowledge the presence of those five million human agents. The 'networks' under discussion can then include not just 'ecosystems' or biogeographic communities, but also the social activity and tenure patterns of human suburban life. Although it carries an imagery of reserves, fences and hands off, biodiversity conservation is labour intensive, particularly in relation to invasive species management. Effective actions are based on regular observation and understanding of species' behaviour, rather than imposition of a priori categories such as native and exotic. Many backyarders show a good ability to distinguish such behaviours because of their day to day engagement. Public environmental programs that seek simply to educate the public about scientific truths, for example in relation to appropriate plantings, need to develop a more sophisticated understanding of how local environmental knowledge is developed. Further, vigilance behaviours such as removal of invasives are just as important as nurturing behaviours in fragmented landscapes. This issue was also identified by Zagorski, Kirkpatrick and Stratford in their 2004 study of bushland edge gardens in Hobart. They found lower levels of invasive exotic species in highly manicured gardens than native ones, attributing this to less frequent weeding by native gardeners. So we might ask, how can we harness people's desire to 'tidy up nature' to control invasives in bushland patches and corridors within the city, without also giving rein to those who might make it so tidy that they destroy the species we are interested to protect?

Figure 9.10: Open fencing and gates allow easy access to the reserve at the back

(Figure 9.11) We are not pretending there are simple solutions, but rather that the variety of practices we have documented provides a resource for a more creative rethinking of people into nature.

The argument that human actors can and must be imagined as forces for environmental good as well as environmental degradation is also consistent with the new thinking demanded of ecologists and biogeographers in relation to urban ecosystems. For example,

> the maintenance of native-plant biodiversity on the [Hobart] Domain requires such counterintuitive measures as the maintenance of exotic trees and the control of native trees, demonstrating the contingencies of conservation management in fragmented vegetation that consists of a mixture of native and exotic species. (Kirkpatrick 2004: 597)

There is a considerable reservoir of environmental stewardship and good will among backyarders. More people than not are keen to do the right thing, albeit the way they express this and their motivations vary considerably. For example, restorationists are not the only ones prepared to nurture public bushland by planting and fostering locally indigenous species. People who clearly separate their domestic spaces from nearby bushland can be just as keen on native biodiversity outside the fence.

Many conservationists are nervous about articulating human activities in this way because they think it poses yet another threat to pure nature somewhere else. As we outlined at the beginning of the book, it is now abundantly clear that there is no pure nature that somehow stands apart from social processes. The city, the wilderness and the farm are all linked in complex material and conceptual networks in which humans and others are actively enmeshed. This is not to say that in all such networks the human role is the same, or that there is no way to define and condemn environmental damage. It is to say that each of those things depends on a variety of circumstances and needs to be examined empirically, rather than assumed. The city is not an essence any more than the wilderness is.

To paraphrase William Cronon, who wrote 'The Trouble with Wilderness' in 1995, the question then is not whether we are actors in any situation, but rather, how should we act? 'We need an environmental ethic that will tell us as much about using nature as about not using it' (Cronon 1995: 85). The gardening metaphor is one such ethic—or rather many, as there are many kinds of gardens and gardeners—which Australians can adopt to guide them in their environmental roles. We might compare for example the welcoming gardener, who savours the abundance of life, with the cleansing gardener, whose welcome is much more conditional, according to criteria that are themselves variable. The imagery and material reality of destruction and damage are so strong that it is hard not to be nervous in proposing the gardening metaphor as the way to help us think through environmental issues. The idea of thinking of Australia as a garden is, to many people, part of the problem, because it is an imposition of a foreign ethic onto a particular ecology.

But there are several points to make in favour of the gardening metaphor. First, evolution does not have anything in mind for Australia. There is no recipe or predetermined way for humans to live in Australia. Cities and gardens are not natural entities, but nor are they particularly unnatural. We have to work out how to have a sustainable Australian city. Second, it would be a mistake to try and define too tightly what good Australian environmental practice might be. As the backyard examples show, the best thing to do will depend on circumstances, even if the needs of the human householders were to be constant. Australia is not one thing or place or set of social or environmental circumstances, although there is some value in a national consciousness, if by this we mean a shared understanding and commitment. Third, we have sought to challenge the idea of 'environment' as a stand alone phenomenon, separate from people. We need to think of ourselves not as adapting to the environment, but as making decisions how to act in complex networks of connection.

The diversity of backyards and human-nonhuman engagements presented in this book demonstrates both resilience and change in the environmental cultures of middle Australia. Some dimensions have been shared; others have had variable expression across age, ethnic and socio-economic differences. That diversity is in itself an important resource for the hard thinking and necessarily altered practice that lies ahead of us in other dimensions of sustainability, particularly food supply and transport.

Figure 9.11: Bush regeneration activity on a North Shore nature strip contrasts with the more ordered backyard

Epilogue

These backyards did not stand still while we were studying them, and they have not stood still since we visited.

Some aspects of what we recorded have already passed into memory. Plans have been put into practice, or changed, or forgotten about. The residential mobility in Australian society is also a strong force for landscape change in the backyard. Cycles of life and death have continued among people, plants and animals.

Kris moved to another city for love. She sold the house and the backyard with spotted gums to people who cleared about a third of the understorey she had planted, and returned it to lawn, removing a number of her frog ponds. The remaining two thirds was 'neglected' in gardening terms, but this meant that many of the shrubs became well established and were providing good bird habitat, albeit with a lot of weeds such as privet and asparagus fern. The house has since been sold again.

Connections to the intensive vegetable production of post-war migrants continue to be severed. Lennie recently died after an illness lasting several months. It remains to be seen how much of the garden Connie will attempt to keep up without him, or what her involvement with the spotted gums on the reserve next door will be. Theresa's vegetable growing Italian father is now in a nursing home.

British born Pat, who loved birds and flowers, including native ones, also did not live till this book was published.

Angus's old cat died and he has noticed an increasing number of birds visiting the backyard and the bird baths he has provided, in view of continuing dry conditions. More species are present than before, with only one resident currawong.

Jacqui of Wollongong West has been using grey water rather than her beloved hose.

Keith and Gay sold their house and the new owners removed the house, the deck and the camphor laurel to create their own blank slate.

We do not know whether Rebecca got grass for her son to play on, whether Kellie's backyard was ever 'finished' or how far Evan and Sonia have progressed with their plans.

APPENDIX 1

Method

As authors we engage in many acts of translation. Our aim is to do so with ethnographic integrity; to give voice with empathy to people who express their lived experience of nature in its own terms. The process of selecting, sampling and analysing is by no means straightforward. It creates a constant tension, one to be lived with rather than resolved.

In chapter two we accepted Dovey's claim for the importance of the lived experience of residents, neglected in critiques of suburbia and many planning studies. We endeavour to understand lived experience using qualitative research methods such as oral history, in-depth interviews and ethnographic observation. Such methods allow conflicting or contradictory experiences to be explored in some depth. They complement survey data which suggest that, unlike academic and activist environmental debates, the environmental issues that contemporary urban Australia is most likely to engage with are precisely the ones closest to home.

Necessarily then, this project uses a combination of diverse methods and field sites. The team joke that the project has been based on 'gardenwork' rather than 'fieldwork' gives us pause to reflect on a tradition of geographic enquiry where the object of study has been somewhere else and someone else. For to go to the 'field' has often been to go to a remote place, often to study the Exotic Other. Yet, after crossing physical and cultural barriers, researchers engage with someone's domestic and everyday practices, as they might for example in researching 'remote' Aboriginal communities. In turning instead towards the domestic and everyday in the suburbs, we reflect the increased attention being paid towards attitudes and practices that are taken for granted, or naturalised, in Western urban settings. By the same token, being close to home physically is not a guarantee of cultural proximity. The diversity of backyards presented here took us into a number of different worlds. By undertaking large scale study within the ethnographic tradition, we aimed to provide a more systematic analysis than had hitherto been undertaken.

Sampling and Recruitment
(or How Did we Get 330 People to Say Yes?)

We studied 265 backyards, speaking to 330 backyarders, in Sydney, Wollongong and Alice Springs. Sydney was chosen as Australia's largest city, with high levels of projected population growth and severe constraints on spatial expansion and sustainability. Wollongong is a restructuring industrial city of about 300,000 people, 85 km south of Sydney on the Pacific coast. Confined to a narrow coastal plain by the Illawarra escarpment, it is experiencing urban expansion onto bushland and farmland, and urban infill in more densely occupied areas. It is an ethnically diverse community following migration, after World War II, to meet the labour force needs of its coal mining and steel making economic base. These industries are now in decline and the area is remaking itself for a post-industrial future. Alice Springs, a Central Australian desert town of 26,000 people, was chosen to provide an arid zone and small town comparison with the other two sample areas. Our sampling strategy was designed to encompass the socio-economic and ecological variability in each of these main study areas. Most of the 'gardenwork' was done between April 2002 and December 2003, a period of drought across eastern Australia.

Recruiting people to talk about their backyards was a protracted process, involving several strategies that were launched at the beginning of each new stage of interviewing in a particular suburb or area. These included media advertisements and appeals on local newspaper and radio, letterboxing, snowballing from acquaintances and participants, and targetting of community groups. While interest in the project was generally positive, a preconception of 'research scrutiny' sometimes acted as a deterrent. People were keen to talk about their backyards but not always willing to have their ideas and what they did in the backyard recorded for research. Often this had to do with a 'taken for granted' approach to the backyard: some participants felt that 'ordinariness' meant their backyards could not be of interest except to themselves, while others were self conscious about the unfinished or 'messy' state of their backyards. (It was clear that most people had tidied up before we arrived.) Time was another constraint on recruiting participants, reflected in the higher proportions of retirees and at-home parents participating. We had to work much harder to talk to the people who did not have time to talk to us.

When our initial approaches yielded few participants of non-English speaking background, we worked through the Macedonian Welfare Association in Wollongong to obtain fourteen participants of Macedonian background (in ten backyards) who were interviewed through an interpreter. In Sydney we worked through the Fairfield Migrant Resource Centre to do the same thing with sixteen Vietnamese community members. Ten of these interviews were recruited through the Vietnamese Support Group, and five through connections to the Buddhist Temple. One participant was recruited through the interpreter.

Another way of encouraging participation in the project was to give short slide presentations to specific groups. Two groups were identified to fill gaps in the project demographics. The first group were parents with young children living in new housing suburbs and the second were committed gardeners. The slide presentations were given to parents of toddlers during playgroup at community centres and to garden club members at their monthly meeting. Direct appeals to participate using visual presentations had the advantage of being able to show slides of people engaged in domestic activities in quite 'ordinary' backyards.

A final group of dedicated native plant growers was recruited through a 'request for participation' email sent to Mt Annan Botanical Gardens. The snowball effect from this general email illustrates the strength of community groups; it made its way over email channels to a diverse set of native plant growers involved as industry professionals or volunteers in conservation groups. Fifteen interviews with native plant growers resulted from this one email.

One other critical factor influencing some peoples' participation related to their need to express views on specific issues or agendas in relation to their backyards or to backyards in general. In some instances it was as simple as an expression of love for the space they had. Other people made suggestions for change to councils, developers and state and federal government. While the physical manifestation of backyards was very diverse and the particular contexts of discussion sometimes very different, people shared a belief that backyards are important.

Each backyard was visited. The participants were interviewed on site in a semi-structured way by one of a team of three researchers, including the two authors. Generally we spent one to two hours in each location, conversing with participants, mapping backyard spaces and taking samples and photographs. This 'slice of life' ethnographic method generated a diverse picture of suburban Australian backyards in the 21st century. An initial set of questions related to the activities of different members of the household, changes that had occurred over time, people's feelings about the space and what sorts of plants and animals belonged there, their attitudes and practices relating to the wider environment, and major influences. Each backyard was mapped and photographed, and checklists were completed on the demography of the household, the structures in the backyard and the biogeography. Interviews were transcribed and imported into the qualitative data analysis program, N6. Each interview was read through and indexed according to themes. We could also incorporate our own emerging ideas into the coding system. For particular themes or issues, sub-samples of the whole data set were analysed in more detail. These are explained in the relevant chapters.

Interviews were also undertaken with a variety of professionals—for example, real estate agents and landscape suppliers—and our field sites included garden shows and display home estates. There was considerable marketing and media coverage related to the home and garden during the study period. To provide a systematic examination of media coverage, a content analysis of four magazines (*Better Homes and Gardens, House and Garden, Burke's Backyard,* and *Gardening Australia*) was undertaken by Wollongong student Laurel Waddell.

We were fortunate to be able to draw on a collection of documentary evidence about backyards held in the National Museum of Australia, collected in the early 1990s. This adds historical context in a comparable degree of detail

and richness to our contemporary study. Changes over time have created physical differentiation– archaeological layers – in individual backyards and the landscapes from which new backyards are fashioned. Although our research methods take 'slices in time' through individual backyards, they also have to deal with the fact that these spaces never stand still. Memory is the means by which we here pursue the lived experience of backyards through different times. We show that most of our study participants have a strong consciousness of the dynamism and constant changes occurring in their backyards.

Pseudonyms are used for some participants.

The Participants

Two hundred interviews were with a single participant and sixty five were with two participants, mostly couples, sometimes parents and teenage children. Thus the total number of backyards and households was 265, and the total number of people interviewed was 330. Variables such as household structure, sex, age, ethnicity and socio-economic status all play a role in influencing the attitudes and behaviours discussed in the book. None of them is dominant, and they all interact with each other, but it is important to outline these characteristics as they apply to the sample as a whole.

Widely shared structural features of the 265 backyards include division into functional zones, and porous boundaries between informal living areas at the back of the house and outdoor recreation/entertaining areas. Comparative case studies of older suburbs with large backyards, newer suburbs with smaller ones, and apartments with none are used to analyse what people like and do not like about their living spaces.

Household Structure

Nearly half the backyards visited (47%) were occupied by families with children (Appendix 2.1). Thirty-five per cent were nuclear families; the other 12% were sole parent or extended

Socio-economic status	Education/ skills	Number of backyards	Percentage of backyards	Example occupations in backyard sample
upper	high	4	1	Paediatrician, barrister, broker
	low	0	0	
upper middle	high	21	8	Architect, planner, industrial chemist
	low	0	0	
middle	high	118	44	Social worker, aged care coordinator, accounts manager, programmer
	low	58	22	Miner, teachers aide', administration assistant
lower middle	high	13	5	Bush regenerator, community arts coordinator, video editor
	low	34	13	Concreter, lab technician, fast food cook, lawn contractor
low	high	3	1	Unemployed computer technician, tertiary student, retired insurance office manager
	low	14	6	Storeperson, labourer, unemployed
Total		265	100	

Table 32: Backyards by class. Socio-economic status of householder derived from ABS occupation classifications. High education/skills = post-secondary qualification. Percentage data rounded to nearest whole per cent.

families, or families comprising adult children living with parents. Of the households with children, 54% had two children, 20% one child and 19% three children. Children were not interviewed, and we depend on what their parents say about them for knowledge of their engagement with the backyard. Research directly with children would be productive. Most households owned or were buying their home (Appendix 2.2), with much smaller numbers of renters and housing commission tenants.

Age, Sex and Ethnicity

Two thirds of the participants were female. In most of the family households, we interviewed the mother, in many cases the parent who is more likely to be home based. Nevertheless many of the female participants are very busy people, juggling jobs, family and other responsibilities.

The age structure of the study sample is summarised in Appendix 2.4. Forty seven per cent of participants were aged between 36 and 55, reflecting the importance of family households in the sample. The couples were concentrated in the over 45 age group. Most participants in the study were born in Australia (224, or 68%)(Appendix 2.5), with twenty three other countries of birth represented. There were thirty-seven British-born

participants (11%), sixteen Vietnamese (5%) and fourteen Macedonians (4%). Our proportion of overseas-born participants (32%) is higher than in the total Australian population, recorded in the 2001 Census at 21.9% born overseas, but consistent with figures for Sydney (33% born overseas 2001). Britain being the main country of overseas birth is consistent with the Australia-wide pattern. We deliberately focused on the Macedonian and Vietnamese groups to study the influence of migration in depth.

Socio-economic and educational status

We grouped the sample into broad 'class' divisions that combine occupation (as classified by the Australian Bureau of Statistics) and education (where the dividing line between high and low is a post-secondary qualification) (Table 3.2). We did not collect income data for our participants, but these groupings provide a generalised proxy of relative affluence. As the *Social Atlas of Sydney* shows in its analysis of the distribution of high and low income households, areas with high household incomes also have high percentages of people with university qualifications, white collar workers and home ownership. Conversely there is a correlation between high percentages of low income households and unemployed people, one parent families with dependent children and, to some extent, people aged sixty five years or older.

The analysis of socio-economic status should be treated with caution, as there is considerable blurring of boundaries. We have generalised for each household, although occasionally two partners have quite different status from one another. Nevertheless, the broad trends are robust. There is a clear concentration within our sample in the middle-class category, reflected across all household types (Appendix 2.6). None of our upper and upper middle class households have low education/skills, but a number of lower middle and lower class households have high education/skills.

Participants in the age range 36–55 have markedly higher education and skills than the two older cohorts, particularly those aged over 65.

The Sample

Nuclear family	92
Sole parent family	14
Parent with adult children	4
Adult with aged parent	4
Total family	125
Heterosexual couple	80
Same sex couple	5
Total couple	85
Single household	52
Shared household	3
Total	265

Appendix 2.1: Household structure of study sample. Unless otherwise stated, we use the term 'family' for a household with at least one adult and one related child, and 'nuclear family' for at least two adults and one related child.

Own or buying home	240
Renting	18
Housing Commission	7
Total	265

Appendix 2.2 Housing tenure of study sample

Female	202
Male	128
Total	330

Appendix 2.3: Sex of study sample

Less than 26	11
26-35	42
36-45	78
46-55	78
56-65	49
Over 65	72
Total	330

Appendix 2.4 Age structure of study sample

Country of Birth	Number	Per cent
Australia	224	68
Britain and Ireland	36	11
Vietnam	16	5
Macedonia	14	4
Italy	6	2
New Zealand	6	2
Holland	5	2
Subtotal	307	94
Total other	23	7
Total	330	100

Appendix 2.5: Highest ranked participant countries of birth by number and percentage. Percentages exceed 100 due to rounding.

Socio-economic status	Hetero-sexual couple	Family	Single	Shared household	Same sex couple	Total
upper	1	3				4
upper middle	5	9	6			20
middle	58	86	25	2	5	176
lower middle	13	20	14	1		48
low	2	7	8			17
Total	**79**	**125**	**53**	**3**	**5**	**265**

Appendix 2.6: Number of backyards by household structure and class.

When house built	Size of backyard, excluding structures, in square metres									
	20–99		100–199		200–299		300–500		over 500	
1–2 years ago	kelly	1	shell	2	kelly	1			north	1
			kelly	4						
3–4 years ago			shell	1	shell	1				
			kelly	1						
5–6 years ago			shell	2	shell	1				
			kelly	1						
1995–1996					kelly	1				
1990–1994	north	1							north	1
1980–1989					hills	1	hills	1		
1970–1979			north	1			hills	1	north	1
							north	1	hills	1
1960–1969					north	2	north	2		
1880–1959			north	1	north	1	north	2	north	3
		2		**13**		**8**		**7**		**7**

Appendix 2.7: Case study suburbs by age of house and size of backyard. Shell = Shellcove, North = North Shore, Kelly = Kellyville, Hills = Hills District excluding Kellyville.

Magazine	Readership as percentage of population aged 14 or over, at Dec 2003	Television program associated?
Better Homes and Gardens	9.1	Yes (commercial)
House & Garden	4.3	No
Burke's Backyard	4	Yes (commercial)
Gardening Australia	2.2	Yes (ABC)

Appendix 2.8: Magazines analysed.

Circulation figures derived from Roy Morgan Readership Results for the year ending December 2004 (http://www.roymorgan.com/news/press-releases/2005/375/) Accessed April 2005.

Backyard activities	Macedonian	Vietnamese	British	First Generation	All others
Gardening, weeding, pruning	6	14	29	13	163
Sitting, thinking	2	11	23	12	123
Animal activities	3	1	1	1	23
Eating, entertaining	1	5	16	12	82
Kids'activities	14	13	3	9	72
Mowing	4	9	22	16	96

Appendix 2.9: Section of a matrix table in N6 intersecting demographic data on ethnicity with numbers of participants describing what kinds of activities they do in the backyard

Dualisms

Some environmental dualisms, and examples of the liminal spaces between them. (The liminal spaces are not suggested to line up with a particular dualism. Indeed their liminal status often derives from the fact that they transgress several dualisms.)

Nature	Liminality	Culture
Sciences	suburbs	Humanities
Country	backyards	City
Wild/savage	ferals	Tame/domestic
Protected area	some Aboriginal people	Unprotected
	environmental weeds	
Natural heritage	some migrants	Cultural heritage
Native	invasive aliens (human and non human)	Non-native (except some Aborigines)
Deep past	hunter-gatherers	Present

Notes

1   It has not been possible in this book to provide a comprehensive review of the extensive academic literature on backyards, gardens, urban nature and environmental cultures. Readers interested in this broader context are directed to the following papers:

Head, L., P. Muir and E. Hampel 2004. Australian backyard gardens and the journey of migration. *The Geographical Review* 94:326-347.

Head, L. and P. Muir 2004. Nativeness, invasiveness and nation in Australian plants. *The Geographical Review* 94:199-217.

Head, L. and P. Muir 2005. "Living with trees – Perspectives from the suburbs", in M. Calver, H. Bigler-Cole, G. Bolton, J. Dargavel, A. Gaynor, P. Horwitz, J. Mills and G. Wardell-Johnson (eds) *A Forest Concienceness. Proceedings 6th National Conference of the Australian Forest History Society Inc, 12-17 September 2004, Augusta, Western Australia.* pp. 84-95.

Head, L. and P. Muir 2006. Suburban life and the boundaries of nature: resilience and rupture in Australian backyard gardens. *Transactions, Institute of British Geographers* NS 31:505-524.

Head, L. and P. Muir 2006. Edges of connection: reconceptualising the human role in urban biogeography. *Australian Geographer* 37:87-101.

Head, L. and P. Muir 2007. Changing cultures of water in eastern Australian backyard gardens. *Social and Cultural Geography* 8(6) in press.

2   See for example debates at the 2003 State of Australian Cities Conference www.uws.edu.au/about/acadorg/caess/uf/conference .

3   "Bioregions are relatively large land areas characterised by broad, landscape-scale natural features and environmental processes that influence the functions of entire ecosystems. They capture the large-scale geophysical patterns across Australia. These patterns in the landscape are linked to fauna and flora assemblages and processes at the ecosystem scale, thus providing a useful means for simplifying and reporting on more complex patterns of biodiversity." http://www.nationalparks.nsw.gov.au/npws.nsf/Content/bioregions_explained accessed 28/6/05.

4   Pauline Hanson was a controversial Australian politician in the 1990s. She led the One Nation Party, a far right party with a staunch anti-immigration platform, and was considered to have mobilised a disaffected white working class sensibility ignored by the two main parties.

5   For more data on backyard sizes, see Appendix 2.7, where the strong relationship between age of house and size of backyard is illustrated by focussing on a comparison of three case study suburbs.

6   Backyard sizes were measured excluding garages or structures. As a number of writers have noted, decreasing size of backyard is also due to increasing proportions of the block covered by the house.

7   *The Nursery Papers*, February 2004. Available www.ngia.com.au .

8   *Cenchrus cillaris*, a native grass of southern Asia and east Africa, introduced to Australia to improve pastures.

9   *Macropus robustus*, a small species of kangaroo.

10 *The Nursery Papers* 2002 No. 10, p. 2 (available www.ngia.com.au).

11 *The Nursery Papers*, 1999 No. 5 (available www.ngia.com.au), reporting on the results of the 1996–97 census of the Australian nursery industry conducted by the Australian Bureau of Statistics.

12 Purchases reported for the six months previous to survey. *The Nursery Papers* 2001 No. 13, p. 2 (available www.ngia.com.au).

13 http://www.bom.gov.au/climate/averages/tables/cw_015590.shtml accessed March 2006.

14 All information on the Alice Springs water supply is sourced from the Northern Territory Department of Natural Resources, Environment and the Arts http://www.nt.gov.au/nreta/naturalresources/water/waterwise/alicespringswater.html accessed March 2006.

15 http://www.sydneywater.com.au/SavingWater/InYourHome/Saved_Display.cfm . As we discuss in chapter 7, 25% of domestic water in Sydney goes on gardens.

16 Average annual rainfall at Wollongong University is 1344mm and at Wollongong Post Office a few kilometres away, 1136mm. The Wollongong region has high spatial variability in rainfall due to the orographic effect of the Illawarra escarpment, but such variability alerts us even more to problems of generalising for the whole continent. The annual average for Sydney's Observatory Hill is 1217mm http://www.bom.gov.au/climate/averages/tables/cw_068188.shtml .

17 Brussels' average annual rainfall is 780mm http://www.kbinirsnb.be/cb/documents/regions/brussels/brussels.htm . Per capita water consumption in Australia is more than twice as high as in most European capitals (Kaika 2005: 135).

18 Similar trends have been observed by F. Allon and Z. Sofoulis (2006) in "Everyday Water: Cultures in Transition", *Australian Geographer* 37:45-55., and there is some independent evidence emerging that households are reducing water consumption (*Sydney Morning Herald* 11.2.06).

References

Allon, F., and Z. Sofoulis. 2006. Everyday water: Cultures in transition. *Australian Geographer* 37: 45-55.

Armstrong, H. 2004. Making the unfamiliar familiar: Research journeys towards understanding migration and place. *Landscape Research* 29: 237-260.

Armstrong, T., A. Bauman, and J. Davies. 2000. *Physical Activity Patterns of Australian Adults: Results of the 1999 National Physical Activity Survey*. Canberra: Australian Institute of Health and Welfare.

Australia, Commonwealth of. 1991. *Plant Invasions: The Incidence of Environmental Weeds in Australia*. Canberra: Australian National Parks and Wildlife Service.

Australia, Commonwealth of. 2001. *Australia State of the Environment 2001. Human Settlements*. Canberra: Australia State of the Environment Committee.

Australian Bureau of Statistics. 2002. *Sydney: A Social Atlas 2001*. Canberra: Australian Bureau of Statistics. Cat. No. 2030.1.

Australian Bureau of Statistics. 2002. *Domestic Water Use, New South Wales, October 2002*. Canberra: Australian Bureau of Statistics Cat. No. 4616.1

Australian Bureau of Statistics. 2005. *Australian Social Trends, 2005*, Canberra: Australian Bureau of Statistics Cat. No. 4102.0.

Bertram, M. 1992. Written account of backyard in Maryborough, Queensland. National Museum of Australia collection.

Bonyhady, T. 2000. *The Colonial Earth*. Melbourne: Melbourne University Press.

Boyd, R. 1952. *Australia's Home: Why Australians Built the Way they Did*, 2nd. (1978) edition. Harmondsworth: Penguin.

Boyd, R. 1963. *The Australian Ugliness*. Melbourne: Penguin.

Brett, J. 1992. *Robert Menzies' Forgotten People*. Sydney: Sun.

Brigden, V. 1992. Written account of backyard in Wooloomooloo, NSW. National Museum of Australia collection.

Brook, I. 2003. Making here like there: Place attachment, displacement and the urge to garden. *Ethics, Place and Environment* 6: 227-234.

Bunce, M. 1994. *The Countryside Ideal: Anglo-American Images of Landscape*. London and New York: Routledge.

Burke, E. 1992. Written account of backyard at Oaklands, NSW. National Museum of Australia collection.

Chen, K. 2005. "Counting bushfire-prone addresses in the greater Sydney region" in *Planning for Natural Hazards: How Can We Mitigate the Impacts?*, University of Wollongong, 2005.

Crittenden, V. 1983. "Introduction" in *Three Sydney Garden Nurseries in the 1860s*, vol. 3-7. Edited by J. Gelding. Canberra: Mulini Press.

Cronon W. 1995. The trouble with Wilderness; or, getting back to the wrong nature, in W. Cronon (ed.) *Uncommon Ground*. New York: Norton pp 69-90.

Cuffley, P. 1989. *Australian Houses of the '20s and '30s*. Melbourne: The Five Mile Press.

Davison, G. 1994. "The past and future of the Australian suburb" in *Suburban Dreaming. An Interdisciplinary Approach to Australian Cities*. Edited by L. C. Johnson, pp. 99-113. Geelong: Deakin University Press.

Dovey, K. 1994. "Dreams on display: suburban ideology in the model home," in *Beasts of Suburbia: Reinterpreting Cultures in Australian Suburbs*. Edited by S. Ferber, C. Healy, and C. McAuliffe, pp. 127-147. Melbourne: Melbourne University Press.

Everitt, M. 1992. Written account of

backyard at Oaklands, NSW. National Museum of Australia collection.

Fox, P. 2004. *Clearings. Six Colonial Gardeners and their Landscapes*. Melbourne: The Miegunyah Press.

Gandy, M. 2002. *Concrete and Clay: Reworking Nature in New York City*. Cambridge, Mass.: MIT Press.

Gaynor, A. 1999. Regulation, resistance and the residential area: the keeping of productive animals in twentieth-century Perth, Western Australia. *Urban Policy and Research* 17: 7-16.

Gaynor, A. 2001. *Harvest of the Suburbs: An Environmental History of Suburban Food Production in Perth and Melbourne, 1880-2000*. University of Western Australia.

Gelding, J. 1983. *Three Sydney Garden Nurseries in the 1860s*. Canberra: Mulini Press.

Gould, S. J. 1997. "An evolutionary perspective on strengths, fallacies, and confusions in the concept of native plants" in *Nature and Ideology: Natural Garden Design in the Twentieth Century*. Edited by J. Wolschke-Bulmahn, pp. 11-19. Washington: Dumbarton Oaks Research Library and Collection.

Groves, R. H. 2001. Can Australian native plants be weeds? *Plant Protection Quarterly* 16: 114-7.

Groves, R. H., R. Boden, and W. M. Lonsdale. 2005. *Jumping the Garden Fence: Invasive Garden Plants in Australia and their Environmental and Agricultural Impacts*. CSIRO report prepared for WWF Australia.

Halkett, I. P. B. 1976. *The Quarter-Acre Block: The Use of Suburban Gardens*. Canberra: Australian Institute of Urban Studies.

Hobbs, R. J., S. Arico, J. Aronson, J. S. Baron, P. B. Bridgewater, V. A. Cramer, P. R. Epstein, J. J. Ewel, C. A. Klink, A. E. Lugo, D. Norton, D. Ojima, D. J. Richardson, E. W. Sanderson, F. Valldares, M. Vila, R. Zamora, and M. Zobel. 2006. Novel ecosystems: theoretical and management aspects of the new ecological world order. *Global Ecology and Biogeography* 15: 1-7.

Holmes, K. 2000 "In her master's house and garden" in *A History of European Housing in Australia*. Edited by P. Troy, pp. 164-181. Cambridge: Cambridge University Press.

Hucker, W. 1993. *The Material Culture of Backyards*. Unpublished report to the National Museum of Australia.

Hugo, G. 2003. "Changing patterns of population distribution," in *The Transformation of Australia's Population 1970-2030*. Edited by S. E. Khoo and P. McDonald, pp. 185-218. Sydney: UNSW Press.

Ingold, T. 2000. *The Perception of the Environment. Essays on Livelihood, Dwelling and Skill*. London and New York: Routledge.

Johnson, L. 1997. "Feral suburbia?" in *Home/world: Space, Community and Marginality in Sydney's West*. Edited by H. Grace, G. Hage, J. Langsworth, and M. Symonds, pp. 31-65. Sydney: Pluto Press.

Johnson, L. 1999. "Powerlines: A cultural geography of domestic open space" in *Australian Cultural Geographies*. Edited by E. Stratford, pp. 87-108. Melbourne: Oxford University Press.

Jones, O., and P. Cloke. 2002. *Tree Cultures: The Place of Trees and Trees in their Place*. Oxford: Berg.

Kaika, M. 2005. *City of Flows: Modernity, Nature and the City*. New York: Routledge.

Karskens, G. 1987. "A Half World Between City and Country: 1920s Concord," in *Sydney: City of Suburbs*. Edited by M. Kelly, pp. 125-148. Sydney: New South Wales University Press.

Kirkpatrick, J. B. 2004. Vegetation change in an urban grassy woodland 1974-2000. *Australian Journal of Botany* 52: 597-608.

Lane, R. n.d. "Backyard histories: new sources for examining social and environmental change at the National Museum of Australia". Unpublished ms.

Lilith, M., M. Calver, I. Styles, and M. Garkaklis. 2006. Protecting wildlife from predation by owned domestic cats: Application of a precautionary approach to the acceptability of proposed cat regulations. *Austral Ecology* 31: 176-189.

Low, T. 2002. *The New Nature: Winners and Losers in Wild Australia*. Melbourne: Viking.

Madigan, R. and M. Munro. 1996. 'House beautiful:' Style and consumption in the home. *Sociology* 30: 1 41-57.

Malor, D. 1996. *Dream Sites: Yards and Gardens of Suburban Sydney*. PhD, University of Sydney.

McAuliffe, C. 1996. *Art and Suburbia*. Sydney: Craftsman House.

Mosquin, T. 1997. *Management Guidelines for Invasive Alien Species in Canada's National Parks*. Ottawa: Report for National Parks Branch Parks, Canada.

Mullett, T. L. 2001. Effects of the native environmental weed *Pittosporum undulatum* Vent. (sweet pittosporum) on plant biodiversity. *Plant Protection Quarterly* 16: 117-121.

Mullins, P., and C. Kynaston. 2000. "The household production of subsistence goods," in *A History of European Housing in Australia*. Edited by P. Troy, pp. 142-163. Cambridge: Cambridge University Press.

Muyt, A. 2001. *Bush Invaders of South-east Australia*. Meredith: R. G. and F. J. Richardson.

Neale, A. 2003. "Flora Australia: Native plants in the art, design and gardens of E. L. Bateman" in *Studies in Australian Garden History*. Edited by M. Bourke and C. Morris, pp. 35-53. Melbourne: Australian Garden History Society.

NSW National Parks and Wildlife Service. 2002. *Urban Wildlife Renewal: Growing Conservation in Urban Communities*. Sydney: National Parks and Wildlife Service. (http://www.nationalparks.nsw.gov.au/) National Parks and Wildlife Service. Accessed 1 December 2003.

Parsons, H., R. E. Major, and K. French. 2006. Species interactions and habitat associations of birds inhabiting urban areas of Sydney, Australia. *Austral Ecology* 31: 217-227.

Philo, C., and C. Wilbert. 2000. "Animal spaces, beastly places: an introduction" in *Animal Spaces, Beastly Places: New Geographies of Human-Animal Relations*. Edited by C. Philo and C. Wilbert, pp. 1-34. London: Routledge.

Pocock, B. 2003. *The Work/Life Collision*. Sydney: The Federation Press.

Pollan, M. 1991. *Second Nature: A Gardener's Education*. New York: Delta.

Powell, J. M. 1976. *Environmental Management in Australia, 1788-1914*. Melbourne: Oxford University Press.

Pusey, M. 2003. *The Experience of Middle Australia: The Dark Side of Economic Reform*. Cambridge: Cambridge University Press.

Robbins, P. 2004. Comparing invasive networks: cultural and political biographies of invasive species. *Geographical Review* 94: 139-156.

Robbins, P., and J. T. Sharp. 2003. Producing and consuming chemicals: the moral economy of the American lawn. *Economic Geography* 79: 425-451.

Rose, S. 1997. Influence of suburban edges on invasion of *Pittosporum undulatum* into the bushland of northern Sydney, Australia. *Australian Journal of Ecology* 22: 89-99.

Rowse, T. 1978. Heaven and a Hills Hoist: Australian Critics on Suburbia. *Meanjin* 37: 3-13.

Saunders, D. A., R. J. Hobbs, and C. R. Margules. 1991. Biological consequences of ecosystem fragmentation: A review. *Conservation Biology* 5: 18-32.

Seddon, G. 1997. *Landprints: Reflections on Place and Landscape*. Cambridge: Cambridge University Press.

Seddon, G. 2002. "Prologue," in *The Australian Garden: Designing with Australian Plants*. Edited by D. Snape, pp. 8-19. Melbourne: Bloomings Books.

Shove, E. 2003. *Comfort, Cleanliness and Convenience*. Oxford: Berg.

Sibley, D. 1995. *Geographies of Exclusion: Society and Difference in the West*. London and New York: Routledge.

Snape, D. 2002. *The Australian Garden: Designing with Australian Plants*. Melbourne: Bloomings Books.

Strang, V. 2004. *The Meaning of Water*. Oxford: Berg.

Stretton, H. 1976. *Capitalism, Socialism and the Environment*. Cambridge: Cambridge University Press.

Stretton, H. 2001. *Ideas for Australian Cities*, 3rd Edition.

Sydney Water. 2003. http://www sydneywater. com.au/everydropcounts/garden/index.cfm (accessed October 2003).

Thomas, Martin 2001. *A Multicultural Landscape: National Parks and the Macedonian Experience*. Sydney: NSW National Parks and Wildlife Service and Pluto Press.

Thomas, Mandy. 2002. *Moving Landscapes: National Parks and the Vietnamese Experience*. Sydney: NSW National Parks and Wildlife Service and Pluto Press.

Trigger, D. 2004. "Indigeneity, ferality and what belongs in the bush: nature, culture and identity in a settler society" in *Law, Plural Society and Social Cohesion in the 21st Century*. Proceedings of 14th International Congress, Commission on Folk Law and Legal Pluralism, New Brunswick, Canada.

Trigger, D. 2005. "Native vs Exotic: cultural discourses about flora, fauna and belonging in Australia" in *Sustainable Planning and Development*. Edited by A. Kungolos, C. Brebbia, and E. Beriatos, pp. 1301–1310. Southhampton: Wessex Institute of Technology Press, The Sustainable World Vol. 6.

Troy, P. 1996. *The Perils of Urban Consolidation*. Sydney: The Federation Press.

Troy, P. editor. 2000. *A History of European Housing in Australia*. Cambridge: Cambridge University Press.

Troy, P., D. Holloway, and B. Randolph. 2005. *Water Use and the Built Environment: Patterns of Water Consumption in Sydney*. Sydney: City Futures Research Centre, Research Paper No. 1, UNSW.

Zagorski, T., J.B. Kirkpatrick, and E. Stratford. 2004. Gardens and the bush: gardeners' attitudes, garden types and invasives. *Australian Geographical Studies*. 42:207-220.

Index

Y

yeoman ideal 15, 18
Yugoslavs 100

Z

Zagorski, Kirkpatrick and Stratford 166

WOLLONGONG 2007
Published by University of Wollongong Press

Copyright: L. Head, P. Muir, 2007. Not to be copied whole
or in part without authorisation (contact Halstead Press).
Produced by Halstead Press, 66 / 89 Jones Street, Ultimo,
New South Wales. Designed by Kylie Prats. Typeset by
Network Printing Studios, Kensington, New South Wales.
Printed in China by Bookbuilders.

ISBN 978 1 920831 51 6